ARCTIC PATROL

Caitlin Press Inc.
3375 Ponderosa Way
Qualicum Beach, BC V9K 2J8
www.caitlinpress.com

Text design by Libris Simas Ferraz / Onça Publishing
Cover design by Sarah Corsie
Cover image: Bringing supplies ashore from the *Beothic*; photo courtesy of the Taggart Family
Maps by Marilyn Croot
Edited by Catherine Edwards
Printed in Canada

Caitlin Press Inc. acknowledges financial support from the Government of Canada and the Canada Council for the Arts, and the Province of British Columbia through the British Columbia Arts Council and the Book Publisher's Tax Credit.

Canada Council for the Arts   Conseil des Arts du Canada   BRITISH COLUMBIA ARTS COUNCIL   Funded by the Government of Canada   Canada

Library and Archives Canada Cataloguing in Publication
Arctic patrol : Canada's fight for Arctic sovereignty / Eric Jamieson.
Jamieson, Eric, 1949- author.
Includes bibliographical references.
Canadiana 20230522505 | ISBN 9781773861333 (softcover)
LCSH: Arctic regions—International status—History—20th century. | LCSH: Canada, Northern—International status—History—20th century. | LCSH: Arctic regions—Foreign relations. | LCSH: Arctic regions—Discovery and exploration. | LCSH: Self-determination, National—Canada, Northern. | LCSH: Canada, Northern—History—20th century.
Classification: LCC FC191 .J36 2024 | DDC 971.9/02—dc23

Arctic Patrol

Canada's Fight for Arctic Sovereignty

ERIC JAMIESON

CAITLIN PRESS

*This book is dedicated to the young RCMP officers
and their Inuit assistants who, despite isolation and
adversity, persevered to protect Canada's far north.*

Contents

Introduction

I refer to this book as my pandemic book because it was largely written during the Covid contagion that swept across the country. I feel a little guilty, however, as the lockdowns/restrictions that were imposed upon all of us were not so much an imposition to me as they were a kind of relief in that they offered the solitude that a writer/researcher needs to work.

The idea for the book came to me from a colleague at the bank where I worked. It was during the bank's Christmas retirement function in December 2019 that John Taggart approached me, not for the first time, to see if I was interested in writing about his father's adventures with the RCMP in the Arctic between the years 1928 and 1930. John and I made an appointment to meet for lunch to discuss the potential project. He brought along several books on the RCMP's involvement in the Arctic as well as a stack of his father's photos. He later emailed me a digital copy of his father's diary. The diary had me intrigued, but there was not enough material there to write a book, given that John's father, Reginald Andrew Taggart, had passed away some years earlier and I was therefore unable to complete the back story. One thing that John did tell me over lunch, however, was that his father had continually drummed into his family that the reason that the RCMP were in the Arctic was to protect Canada's sovereignty there.

I then began researching Canada's early sovereignty efforts in the Arctic and came across the title to an interesting academic paper written by Professor Janice Cavell that I wanted to read. She is an adjunct research professor at Carleton University in Ottawa. Unfortunately, my alma mater, the University of British Columbia, only offers access to online academic papers to faculty and students. I emailed Professor Cavell and she willingly offered to forward me a copy of the paper, but she also offered to send me a link to a digital copy of an immense book that she had a lead hand in compiling for the Canadian government. Cavell wrote the introduction and footnotes for this voluminous collection of Arctic correspondence for the years 1874 through 1949. I quickly discovered that this was the back story I was missing.

The publication, titled *Documents on Canadian External Relations: The Arctic, 1874–1949*, was one of a series of twenty-nine volumes on Canadian external relations, but the only one on the Arctic. Stéphane Dion, PC, MP, Minister of Foreign Affairs, prefaced the 2016 edition: "The subject of this special volume, the Arctic, has an ever-growing importance for Canada as we approach our federation's 150th anniversary. This volume illuminates how and why Canada asserted its sovereignty over the Far North between 1874 and 1949, and it demonstrates how much Canadians today owe to the nation builders of the past."*

According to Professor Cavell's introduction to the publication, the collection leaned heavily on documents from the "Department of the Interior, the Royal Canadian Mounted Police, the Department of Marine and Fisheries, and other government bodies involved in sovereignty efforts, and on the private papers of mid-level civil servants and of explorers such as Joseph Bernier and Vilhjalmur Stefansson."† Cavell and her team also accessed correspondence and documents from Council (Cabinet) and the governor general's office, and crossed the puddle to access files in the National Archives of the United Kingdom. Although Professor Cavell identified that there were gaps in the correspondence for the period before World War I, where documents had simply disappeared, I found that enough material was available to paint a vivid picture of Canada's early sovereignty efforts. And, given that Libraries and Archives Canada was shuttered during the early part of the pandemic, the book offered me unfettered and immediate access to critical Arctic correspondence.

Cavell's book was also the perfect pairing to Constable Taggart's diary, especially given that during Taggart's service in the Arctic, the Canadian government was negotiating with the Norwegian government and the Norwegian explorer, Otto Sverdrup, over sovereignty of the Sverdrup Islands. The diary therefore became immensely more relevant given that Constable Taggart was the RCMP member who accompanied the legendary Inspector Joy and the equally legendary Inughuit guide, Nukappiannguaq, on the long and arduous dogsled patrol to place a Canadian footprint on the very islands that were the subject of Canada's negotiations. The legend of this 1,800-mile (2,897-kilometre) patrol has grown to mythic proportions and has iconically been referred to as "The Longest Patrol."

---

*   Stéphane Dion, PC, MP, Minister of Foreign Affairs, preface to Janice Cavell, *Documents on Canadian External Relations: The Arctic, 1874–1949* (Ottawa: Global Affairs Canada, 2016).

†   Janice Cavell, ed., introduction to *Documents on Canadian External Relations*, x.

As you read *Arctic Patrol* you will come across many Inuit (including Inughuit and Inuvialuit) names and terms. Where these names are part of a quote, I have not changed them, although on occasion I have placed the current spelling of the name in brackets behind the quoted name. I have also endeavoured to use some Inuit spellings, such as qamutiik for sled, despite the historical literature using variations of the English translation, komatik. I have also stayed with the English word igloo, instead of the Inuit word, iglu, since the former appears so frequently in historical documents. Likewise, there were variants on proper names, especially place names, used throughout this period by explorers, RCMP officers, and government bureaucrats and officials. I have left these as used in the relevant historical sources.

Another topic that requires mentioning is the treatment of animals. History has not been kind to animals, especially in the Arctic. In the south we view dogs as pets, but in the north during the period I write about, dogs were working animals, and were they to become infirm or unproductive, they were summarily dispatched even though it was at times painful for their owners. Furthermore, I was startled at the amount of game that was taken, but the seals, caribou, polar bears, white whales and various bird species, etc., were the gas that fuelled both men and dogs, and as Inspector Joy wrote, no more than was required was harvested.

The long patrol, the concurrent negotiations with Norway, and Canada's efforts to fend off various other threats to its Arctic, is a story of strategy, political and diplomatic intrigue, and of course a demonstration of the incredible determination, fortitude and courage of the RCMP officers and their Inuit companions who persevered under the most adverse conditions imaginable to protect Canada's sovereignty over its most northerly region.

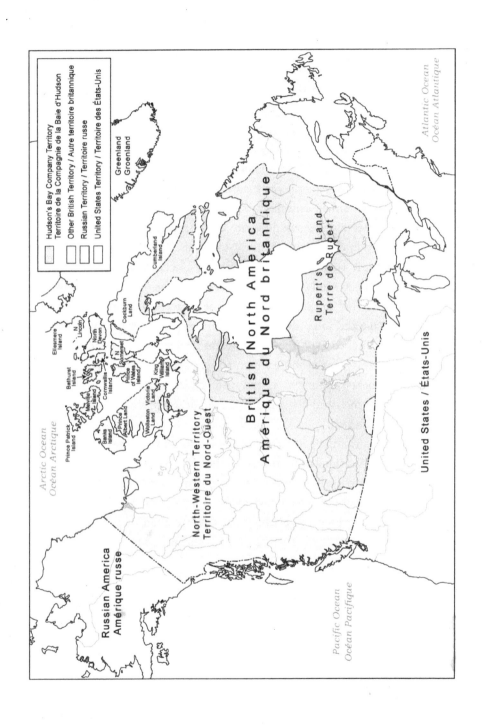

Arctic Ocean
Océan Arctique

Ellesmere
Island

N
Lincoln

North
Devon

N
Somerset

Bathurst
Island

Melville
Island

Prince
of Wales
Island

King
William
Island

Cornwallis
Island

Prince Patrick
Island

Banks
Island

Prince
Albert Land

Victoria
Land

Wollaston
Land

Cockburn
Land

Cumberland
Island

Greenland
Groenland

Atlantic Ocean
Océan Atlantique

British North America
Amérique du Nord britannique

Rupert's Land
Terre de Rupert

North-Western Territory
Territoire du Nord-Ouest

Russian America
Amérique russe

Pacific Ocean
Océan Pacifique

United States / États-Unis

Hudson's Bay Company Territory
Territoire de la Compagnie de la Baie d'Hudson

Other British Territory / Autre territoire britannique

Russian Territory / Territoire russe

United States Territory / Territoire des États-Unis

CHAPTER ONE

Vague Inheritance

The early morning was eerily silent except for the hiss of ice crystals sifting against the walls of a small igloo* perched on the wind-battered southern shore of Bathurst Island in the Eastern Canadian Arctic. It was April 3, 1929, and the trio that hunkered down within had been cautiously asleep when the sudden whine of a sled dog staked outside alerted them to possible danger. The three—Royal Canadian Mounted Police Inspector Alfred Herbert Joy, Constable Reginald Andrew Taggart, and an Inughuit† guide, Nukappiannguaq—were instantly awake. A polar bear had visited their camp early the previous morning and had been shot by Constable Taggart while it was approaching their igloo. Likely, another one was now close by. Bear meat was essential fuel for both men and dogs, but the sudden appearance of a bear so close to their camp while they were sleeping was alarming.

The three were twenty-three days into an eighty-one day, 1,800-mile (2,900-kilometre) dogsled patrol that would later be known iconically as "The Longest Patrol." The RCMP had never travelled such a distance by dogsled in the Canadian Eastern Arctic before. Inspector Joy was already a legend for his Arctic patrols by the time he received his orders and invited Constable Taggart and the northern Greenlander Nukappiannguaq to accompany him on his historic journey.

That the RCMP patrols were much more than they appeared to be was not so obvious. Enforcement was not the principal reason to conduct them, since most of the territory covered was uninhabited, barren and impossibly remote. The most pressing reason for the patrols—one that made them both highly significant nationally and internationally—was to protect Canada's sovereignty over its Arctic Archipelago, which the dogsled patrols and annual ship patrols, ice permitting, were attempting to accomplish.

As the trio continued their journey west, urging their dogs forward through biting cold, blizzard, heavily drifting snow and jagged ridges of almost

---

*   Iglu in Inuktitut.

†   The Inughuit people are from the Thule district of northern Greenland.

impenetrable fields of pressure ice, alternately running beside or riding their qamutiit* toward Melville Island, the western terminus of their journey, Canada's sovereignty in the Arctic was still being challenged. Challenges that would be drawn out over many years, and challenges that were beyond the scope of mere diplomacy, but that would require a well-publicized display of boots on the ground.

Canada's sovereignty over this remote and barren landscape had its genesis 259 years before Joy, Taggart and Nukappiannguaq began their strategic journey, when a generous charter was granted by the English king, King Charles II, to a new enterprise, "The Governor and Company of Adventurers of England trading into Hudson Bay"—now known as the Hudson's Bay Company, or simply, the HBC—on May 2, 1670. That charter granted the company a trading monopoly over an immense tract of land known as Rupert's Land,† vaguely described as "all those Seas, Streights, Bays, Rivers, Lakes, Creeks, and Sounds, in whatsoever Latitude they shall be, that lie within the entrance of the Streights commonly called Hudson's Streights, together with all the Lands, Countries and Territories, upon the Coasts and Confines of the Seas, Streights, Bays, Lakes, Rivers, Creeks and Sounds, aforesaid, which are not now actually possessed by any of our Subjects, or by the Subjects of any other Christian Prince or State."[1]

The HBC could brag that this vast tract of land, in the parlance of today's Canada, extended from the Rocky Mountains in southern Alberta, east to northern Quebec, south to below the Canada/US border and north to the southern portion of Nunavut, representing about a third of the size of Canada. However, no one really knew how large the territory was, given inconsistent estimates from the HBC, which were just as often disputed.[2] In reality, the charter granted the company no more than the Hudson Bay watershed, which was nevertheless considerable.

The company populated its empire with a myriad of trading posts on sea coasts and waterways, taking control of the area both physically and economically. It bartered western-style goods such as the iconic Hudson's Bay point

---

* A qamutiik (previously spelled komatik) is a sled pulled by a dog team. The plural for two or more sleds is qamutiit.

† Rupert's Land was named after Prince Rupert of the Rhine, a nephew of King Charles I and the first governor of the Hudson's Bay Company.

blanket—which at one point represented about 60 per cent[3] of its trade goods volume—for furs, which were shipped to Europe to feed the burgeoning fashion industry. To facilitate its trade, the HBC introduced a system of currency, or token, known as the "Made Beaver," the largest of which was equivalent to one prime adult male beaver skin in good condition.

A company of this size, however, was bound to have issues administering and supporting such a vast empire, and when its North American governor, Sir George Simpson, died at Montreal on September 7, 1860, the discipline exacted during his tenure evaporated. The company, after approximately 190 years in service, was tendered for sale. Although the Americans were interested in purchasing it, Britain exerted pressure on the company to sell to Canada. It wasn't for another decade, however, that the charter was transferred to the Dominion of Canada when the Hudson's Bay Company signed the deed of surrender on November 19, 1869. On July 15, 1870, the transfer of Rupert's Land came into effect, and simultaneously, Britain transferred to the Dominion another huge tract of land lying to the north of central Canada, the North-Western Territories. In 1870, the North-Western Territories "covered a vast area, stretching west from a disputed boundary with Labrador, across the northern portions of present-day Quebec and Ontario, through the prairies to British Columbia, and north from the 49th parallel to the Arctic Ocean."[4] A clause (section 146) in the British North America Act of 1867 had made provision for both Rupert's Land and the North-Western Territories to be folded into the confederation of Canada at some future date.

A decade later, after conferring with the Hudson's Bay Company, the British Admiralty, and the Canadian government to establish an accurate description of its Arctic assets, Great Britain transferred the Arctic Archipelago to the Dominion as well. That the Arctic still held an irresistible allure for Britain, given that it had yet to reveal all of its secrets and was the graveyard of so many stalwart English sailors, must have preyed upon the minds of those in power, but the romantic period of discovery and conquest was coming to a close. It was time to part with it: let it be Canada's problem. After a bit of wrangling between Canada and Britain over whether the transfer should be enacted by an imperial act of Parliament or by an order-in-council, at Osborne House, Isle of Wight, on July 31, 1880, Her Majesty Queen Victoria signed an order-in-council, thus transferring to the Dominion of Canada the frozen north. The transaction was published in the *Canada Gazette* on October 9, 1880.[5]

The first paragraph of the order-in-council read, in part, that

all British territories and possessions in North America and the islands adjacent to such territories and possessions, which are not already included in the Dominion of Canada, should (with the exception of the colony of Newfoundland and its dependencies) be annexed to and form part of the said Dominion.[6]

It appeared that Britain's vague description of its Arctic assets suggested that it had no idea what they were, which was somewhat true, but it turns out that being vague was part of its strategy. Muddying the works was the fact that American naval officers had explored portions of Ellesmere Island during the mid- to late nineteenth century and had even named parts of it. Members of the British Admiralty were in a quandary. If they drew a map of its northern assets excluding those parts named by Americans, then these would be lost forever since it was likely that the United States would claim them as its own, but if they left the description vague and ignored those parts, then at some future date, if the United States did not challenge it, it would simply be Canada's.

That was the recommendation of Ernest Blake, a clerk in the North American and Australian Department, Colonial Office, United Kingdom, who wrote that

the object in annexing these unexplored territories to Canada is, I apprehend, to prevent the United States from claiming them, and not from the likelihood of their proving of any value to Canada.

I doubt therefore the wisdom of attempting to define precisely, as the Admiralty Hydrographer proposes, the North East and Northern boundaries of these territories, and I shld like to see them left somewhat indefinite, as in the Address of the Canadian Parliament and in your draft Bill, with the addition perhaps of some words showing that this Country only claimed to dispose of what belonged to it by right of discovery or otherwise, and which wld be sufficient answer to the US Gov[t] if they shld at any time think it worth while to dispute the claims of Canada to some of these territories, on the ground that they had been discovered by US citizens.[7]

For Britain, defining the Arctic had not been "considered of special importance or urgency"[8] anyway, but then circumstances had precipitated a rethink. Principally, it was the actions of an American naval officer (Corps of Engineers), by the name of William Mintzer, who on February 10, 1874, penned a letter to the acting consul of the United Kingdom in Philadelphia, George Crump, requesting the right to purchase a twenty square mile (fifty-two square kilometre) tract of land "on the shore of Cumberland gulf,"[9] a strait on Baffin Island. According to Mintzer, this parcel of land, located on the south shore of Cumberland Sound, contained valuable mineral reserves. Coincidentally, Mintzer's letter was preceded by just over a month by one from a Londoner, Augustus Harvey, who later relocated to the British colony of Newfoundland. Harvey wrote to Robert Herbert, under-secretary of state for the colonies, on January 3, 1874, asking whether "the land known as Cumberland to the West of Davis Straits belongs to Great Britain and if it does, is it under the government of the Dominion of Canada.?"[10] He wanted to erect some buildings on it to support his fishing operation.

Mintzer's request more than Harvey's set off a flurry of activity to determine where this parcel of land was and whether it was a British asset or one that had already been annexed by Canada. It was undoubtedly one or the other, given that the English navigator John Davis had, in 1585, been the first European to sight Cumberland Sound. Perhaps the anxiety over the issue was expressed best by Parliamentary Under-Secretary of State for the Colonies James Lowther, who cautioned that "we must remember that if this Yankee adventurer is informed by the British FO [foreign office] that the place indicated is not a portion of HM [Her Majesty's] dominions he would no doubt think himself entitled to hoist the 'Stars and Stripes' which might produce no end of complications."[11]

A report in response to Mintzer's request was therefore commissioned by Robert Hall, naval secretary to the Admiralty, from the Royal Navy's hydrographer, Frederick Evans, and that report, dated April 20, 1874, was forwarded to the Earl of Carnarvon, secretary of state for the colonies. The report dealt specifically with the Mintzer request.

Ten days later, Carnarvon wrote in secret to the governor general, the Earl of Dufferin, forwarding Evans's report and furthermore stating that

> it seems to me desirable in reference to this and similar questions to be informed whether your government would desire that the territories adjacent to those of the Dominion on the North American Continent, which have been taken possession of in the name of this Country but not hitherto

annexed to any Colony[,] or any of them[,] should now be formally annexed to the Dominion of Canada.[12]

This was the first indication that Britain was willing to transfer the Arctic Archipelago to Canada, and perhaps it was more of a practical offer, considering that Carnarvon believed it undesirable, and possibly even inconvenient, for his government to authorize settlement in unoccupied British territory so near to Canada unless the Canadian government was prepared to administer it.

Of course, Carnarvon had no idea what the specific nature of the assets were that Britain contemplated transferring to Canada, and to that end Evans produced another report, but it added little new information. In addition, he mistakenly assumed that Carnarvon would not be interested in "those inhospitable regions chiefly visited by British Arctic Explorers."[13] His presumption excluded most of the Eastern Arctic.

Ernest Blake and another clerk, William Dealtry, in the North American and Australian Department, Colonial Office, prepared a minute, the first paragraph of which chided Evans for supposing that only those territories adjacent to Canada should be annexed to the Dominion. Their minute reviewed the history of the Hudson's Bay Company, which had been asked in 1750, 1837 and 1849 to describe the boundaries of its territory, but beyond reporting in 1837 that it stretched "all the way from the boundaries of Upper & Lower Canada away to the North Pole, as far as the land goes, and from the Labrador Coast all the way to the Pacific Ocean,"[14] the HBC's reports lacked specificity. Blake and Dealtry concluded that although the boundaries of the Dominion had been settled to the west and the south, the boundaries to the north, northeast and northwest were entirely undefined.

This was reflected in Carnarvon's next secret dispatch to Governor General Dufferin when he wrote:

From this Minute it appears that the Boundaries of the Dominion towards the North, North East and North West are at present entirely undefined and that it is impossible to say what British Territories on the North American Continent are not already annexed to Canada under the Order in Council of the 23rd of June 1870, which incorporated the whole of the Territories of the Hudson's Bay Company, as well as the North Western Territory in the Dominion.[15]

An attempt was made to define the easterly and northerly boundaries of Canada's north in April 1875, the descriptions of which were included in a memo from the president of the Privy Council, Lucius Huntington, to Governor General Dufferin. There, it was suggested, that an act of the imperial Parliament should be passed to define the boundaries to the east and north as follows:

> Bounded on the East by the Atlantic Ocean, and passing towards the North by Davis Straits, Baffin's Bay[,] Smiths Straits and Kennedy Channel, including such portions of the North West Coast of Greenland as may belong to Great Britain by right of discovery or otherwise.
>
> On the North by the utmost Northerly limits of the continent of America including the islands appertaining thereto.[16]

This description also fell short, and five years later, when Britain annexed the Arctic Archipelago to the Dominion of Canada via the order-in-council of 1880, little had changed except that on May 3, 1878, in a joint address of the House of Commons and the Senate to Queen Victoria, the western boundary at the 141st meridian had been recognized as defining the border between Canada and the American state of Alaska.[17]

The late professor of history and Arctic scholar, Gordon W. Smith, wrote in reference to the transfer from Great Britain:

> What was wrong with the [Arctic Archipelago] transfer,... was that it purported to annex to Canada, in the vaguest and most imprecise way, unnamed territories of unknown and unspecified extent, to which Great Britain's title was uncertain, and for which no boundaries were given. In this sense it was vulnerable to the charge that it was not really a transfer at all. This deficiency had a more international aspect, and if other states had become interested in establishing serious claims within the archipelago during the years immediately following the transfer, Great Britain and Canada might have found that their arrangement was by no means immune to challenge.[18]

It took fifteen years following the transfer for Canada to finally begin to take charge of its Arctic assets seriously. The long delay was the decision of Justice Minister Alexander Campbell, who believed it prudent to defer any serious development of Canada's newly found Arctic territory until an increase in the "white"[19] population warranted it.

On October 2, 1895, Mackenzie Bowell, president of the Privy Council, wrote a memo to the governor general, stating that, based on a July 26, 1895, report from Mayne Daly, minister of the interior, the "unorganized and unnamed districts of the North West Territories,"[20] for the convenience of settlers and for postal purposes, was being divided into four distinct districts: Ungava, Franklin, Mackenzie and Yukon. The Franklin District would encompass the whole of the Eastern Arctic.

Shortly after the report's release, however, it was discovered that the order had some serious deficiencies. Clifford Sifton, now minister of the Department of the Interior, recommended that the October 2, 1895, order be rescinded and a new one introduced at the next session of Parliament. The Franklin District appeared in the subsequent report of December 1897 as

> comprising Melville and Boothia Peninsulas, Baffin, North Devon, Ellesmere, Grant, North Somerset, Prince of Wales, Victoria, Wollaston, Prince Albert and Banks Lands, the Parry Islands and all those lands and islands comprised between the one hundred and forty-first meridian of longitude west of Greenwich on the west and Davis Strait, Baffin Bay, Smith Sound, Kennedy Channel and Robeson Channel on the east which are not included in any other Provisional District.[21]

This definition was little changed from that offered at the joint address of the Senate and House of Commons in 1878. It had been the opinion of Surveyor General Édouard Deville, expressed in a memo to Deputy Minister of the Interior Alexander Burgess written on February 13, 1896, that the description of the north remained imprecise. Deville had written that he

> would respectfully recommend that the District of Franklin be simply described as "comprising all those parts of Canada not included in any of the above Districts or in any Province or Provisional District of Canada" and that it be left uncoloured on the map. My reason for this recommendation is that any attempt to define with more precision the boundaries and extent of the district will thereby fix the limits of Canada and bar any claim which may subsequently be set up to jurisdiction outside of these limits.[22]

A few years later, Clifford Sifton wrote to Canada's chief astronomer, William F. King, requesting "an exhaustive report upon the title to all our Northern Islands, that is to say, to everything north of the Mainland of Canada between Greenland on the one side and the Alaska line on the other."[23] Accompanying King's report, which was "the first detailed attempt by a Canadian civil servant to survey the entire question of Canada's title to the archipelago,"[24] were maps that had been prepared by James White, chief geographer in the Department of the Interior, which showed Canada's Arctic territory extending all the way to the North Pole. Although the maps were drawn for King's report, which was an internal document, a copy found its way into the public realm. That the map was designed after the sector theory was somewhat controversial, but it was a convenient way to identify sovereign territory. The sector theory defined a territory's eastern and western boundaries by degrees of longitude forming a wedge extending all the way to the North Pole. It should be noted, however, that the sector theory was not considered a "substitute for occupation; rather, it outlined the area to which the ongoing process of Canadian occupation would ultimately extend."[25]

The map that was released to the public in 1904 became somewhat of a trial balloon to see how the international community would react. It was republished in 1925 and over the twenty-one years since the first edition was released, not a peep had been heard from any one of Canada's competing interests in the Arctic. This, under international law, was a form of acquiescence, or tacit acceptance of Canada's sovereignty over its north as well as a validation of the sector principle.

Sovereignty, however, was not just a matter of discovering and exploring new territory. These actions were but the first steps in a long and exhaustive process of claiming ownership to new land, or in Canada's case, protecting its right to land conferred upon it by Britain. William Edward Hall, an English lawyer and mountaineer who published some significant works on international law, wrote in his influential tome on the subject in 1880 that

in the early days of European exploration it was held, or at least every state maintained with respect to territories discovered by itself, that the discovery of previously unknown land conferred an absolute title to it upon the state by whom agents the discovery was made. But it has now been long settled that the bare fact of discovery is an insufficient ground of proprietary

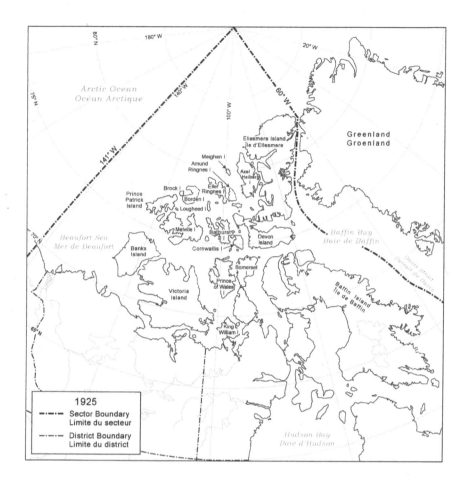

Arctic Ocean
Océan Arctique

Greenland
Groenland

Meighen I
Amund
Ringnes I

Axel
Heiberg I

Ellesmere Island
Île d'Ellesmere

Brock I
Prince
Patrick
Island

Eglinton I

Borden I

Loughed I

Melville I

Bathurst I

Cornwallis I

Devon
Island

Baffin Bay
Baie de Baffin

Beaufort Sea
Mer de Beaufort

Banks
Island

Somerset

Prince
of Wales

Victoria
Island

Baffin Island
Île de Baffin

King
William I

Davis Strait
Détroit de Davis

Hudson Bay
Baie d'Hudson

1925
—·—·— Sector Boundary
         Limite du secteur
—··—··— District Boundary
           Limite du district

right. It is only so far useful that it gives additional value to acts in themselves doubtful or inadequate. Thus when an unoccupied country is formally
annexed an inchoate title is acquired, whether it has or has not been discovered by the state annexing it; but when the formal act of taking possession is
not shortly succeeded by further acts of ownership, the claim of a discoverer
to exclude other states is looked upon with more respect than that of a mere
appropriator.[26]

And those further acts of ownership included some measure of occupation and administration. Canada had an obvious problem with respect to
occupation. The vast majority of the Arctic Archipelago was impossibly remote

and barren and except for a small population* of nomadic Inuit spread over 1.4 million square kilometres composed of about 36,500 islands, it was largely uninhabited. Canadians to the south, except for a few adventurous souls, were also uninterested in populating what many would have considered a hostile environment.

There was a way around the requirement for actual occupation, however, in what was called *effective* occupation. Lassa Oppenheim, a German law professor and renowned jurist, wrote in his book, *International Law: A Treatise*, that

> theory and practice agree nowadays upon the rule that occupation is *effected* through taking possession of, and establishing an administration over, the territory in the name of, and for the acquiring State. Occupation thus effected is *real* occupation, and, in contradistinction to *fictitious* occupation is named effective occupation. *Possession* and *administration* are two essential facts that constitute effective occupation.[27]

Effective occupation of Canada's Arctic began in earnest when problems arose that demanded attention. Just as William Mintzer's request to purchase twenty square miles (fifty-two square kilometres) in Cumberland Sound in 1874 had precipitated the transfer of the Arctic Archipelago to Canada from Britain in 1879, here was another example of a foreign influence motivating a significant change.

For decades, whalers from the United States had been whaling in Hudson Bay and British whalers had been dominant in Baffin Bay and Cumberland Sound. Typically, the whalers would arrive sometime in April and leave about October, but if unlucky could become trapped in the ice at freeze-up. Some whalers also chose to overwinter to get an early start on the following season and to take advantage of trade with the Inuit during the winter months. Winter settlements had sprung up at Cape Fullerton on the northwestern shore of Hudson Bay, and at Kekerton and Blacklead Islands in Cumberland Sound, and there were unsubstantiated rumours that some in these settlements were asserting sovereign rights.

These settlements also caused no end of problems for the resident Inuit populations. Caribou in some areas were virtually wiped out to provide meat

---

* The Canadian census reported a population of 4,000 Inuit in 1871.

for whaling crews, and muskox were slaughtered for their hides—popular in the south for carriage robes—and the Inuit were persuaded to trade these skins for European goods on exorbitant terms. In short, the Inuit had become dependent upon trade with the whalers to the detriment of themselves and the local wildlife. Liquor was also a frequent trade item, and with it came violence. Various diseases were also rampant. The situation in the Eastern Arctic was not dissimilar to what was happening to the Inuvialuit* at the hands of American whalers in the Western Arctic.

Dr. George Dawson, director of the Geological Survey of Canada, was sufficiently alarmed at what was occurring in the Eastern Arctic, principally Hudson Bay, that he pressed Louis Davies, the minister of marine and fisheries, to take action. It was eventually decided to send an expedition to Hudson Bay to investigate.

On April 23, 1897, instructions were presented to Commander William Wakeham, who was to lead the government expedition from the ss *Diana*, a versatile vessel built in Dundee, Scotland, in 1870 for the fishing and sealing industry operating out of Newfoundland. Although it was only powered by a minuscule—by today's standards—seventy horsepower marine steam engine, according to Commander Wakeham, it was fast and could handily manoeuvre around ice floes at top speed.

Whether Minister Davies had any knowledge or evidence of American whalers asserting sovereign rights in Hudson Bay or thereabouts is unknown, but after consulting with Dr. Dawson, the minister declared in the House of Commons on May 6, 1897, that the rumours were "more or less authenticated."[28] He later explained that the reason for his somewhat speculative statement was that Canada's ownership of the north was of such importance that it warranted an immediate and focussed response to avoid any future sovereignty challenges.[29]

Wakeham was principally to assess the navigability of Hudson Strait, but also to impress upon American whalers that they were operating in Canadian sovereign waters. Given the importance of this latter instruction, it was surprising that Davies's written orders to Wakeham regarding sovereignty only appeared toward the end of his instructions, almost like an afterthought.

That specific instruction, however, was none too subtle: "It will be your duty firmly and openly to declare and uphold the jurisdiction in all th[o]se

---

*   Inuit of the Western Canadian Arctic.

British territories you may visit of the Dominion of Canada, to plant the Flag as the open, notorious existence to the natives and others of our claim to jurisdiction, and our determination to maintain and uphold it."[30]

When Wakeham arrived at Kekerton Island on the evening of August 15, 1897, he found an extensive whaling settlement there. Upon speaking with the officer in charge, James Milne, a fellow from Aberdeen, Scotland, he was informed that the land was American sovereign territory—the settlement had recently been sold by an American firm, C.A. Williams Company, doing business out of New London, Connecticut, to the Scottish firm of Noble Brothers from Aberdeen.[31]

The next morning, Wakeham, following Davies's instructions, declared publicly that "in the presence of all now here assembled that I hoist the Union Jack as the open and notorious evidence that all this territory of Baffins Land— with all adjacent territories and Islands—is now as it always has been since the time of its first discovery and occupation, under the exclusive sovereignty of Great Britain. God save the Queen."[32] Baffin Island had been visited by the English seaman and privateer, Martin Frobisher, as early as mid-July 1576.

Although Wakeham was just following orders in his declaration at Kekerton, prompted also by the obvious misinformation floating about the community, generally speaking, hoisting the Union Jack and declaring sovereignty over territory already owned by the Dominion of Canada, was risky. It essentially undermined the fact that the territory was already owned by Canada. Just over three decades later, the director of the Northwest Territories and Yukon Branch, Oswald Finnie, questioned that approach when he learned of a similar incident. Why, he wondered, would Canada reassert its ownership unless it felt its claim was shaky?[33]

There were several government expeditions between 1897 and World War I, but the second expedition of 1903–04 aboard the steamship, ss *Neptune*, a 465-ton (422-tonne) combination sail and steam vessel built in 1873 for the Newfoundland sealing industry, was significant with respect to demonstrating Canadian sovereignty over its Arctic territory. The use of the *Neptune*, which was outfitted specifically for the expedition at considerable expense, was also a test of sorts, to see if it was practical to use a ship on an annual basis to inspect Canada's northern assets as well as to keep foreign whalers in check. What made that expedition special, however, was that it was the first time that members of the North-West Mounted Police (NWMP) were invited along. Finally, law and order was at hand.

Commanded by Albert Peter Low, a geologist and explorer, the publicly stated impetus of this closely guarded expedition was to explore the geology and fisheries of Hudson Bay. But the expedition had a more serious undercurrent, one expressed in a secret dispatch from the secretary of state for the colonies, Alfred Lyttelton, to the governor general, the Earl of Minto:

> I think it advisable that His Majesty's Government should be made acquainted with the objects of the expedition, which I may say have been kept very secret, and of which I have only been confidentially informed. The ostensible intention of the expedition is geological survey and enquiry into the Hudson Bay fisheries, but it has been to a great extent instigated by the apprehension of the growth of United States influence in the northern seas, as represented by American whalers and explorers, and anxiety as to possible future claims of possession by the United States. [34]

And, in an uncommon display of political co-operation, Prime Minister Laurier and the opposition leader, Robert Borden, agreed to keep the mission secret. [35] The duty to instruct the expedition would now fall to the comptroller of the NWMP, Frederick White.

White, who had immigrated to Canada from England in 1862 at the age of fifteen, worked at a number of jobs before entering government service seven years later, eventually rising to the position of private secretary to Sir John A. MacDonald in 1880, the same year that he was appointed to the position of comptroller of the NWMP. On August 5, 1903, he instructed the officer commanding "M" Division, Hudson Bay, Superintendent (Major) John Douglas Moodie, that

> the Government having decided that the time has arrived when some system of supervision and control should be established over the coast and islands in the northern part of the Dominion, a vessel has been selected and is now being equipped for the purpose of patrolling, exploring and establishing the authority of the Government of Canada in the waters and islands of Hudson's [sic] Bay and north thereof.... You will be placed at your disposal a sergeant and four constables; you will be given the additional powers of a Commissioner under the Police Act of Canada; and you will also be authorized to act for the Department of Customs. [36]

This added measure of government officialdom further emphasized that Canada was indeed serious about administering its Arctic, a significant step toward demonstrating effective occupation.

Moodie was to establish a police post in the Hudson Bay area and to begin to enforce Canadian laws. White recommended that the men, consisting of Moodie, Staff Sergeant Dee, and Constables Tremaine, Jarvis, Connelly and Donaldson, not enforce these laws in a "harsh or hurried"[37] manner, but to offer warnings to the whaling captains and the Inuit that eventually the laws in that jurisdiction would mirror those in other parts of Canada. But Moodie, who

Superintendent (Major) John Douglas Moodie. Geraldine Moodie

was astonished at the rate of muskox slaughter and the unfair trade practices of the American whalers with the Inuit, issued a proclamation that the trade in these skins was to stop immediately, despite his action being considered of questionable legality. White, however, later supported him in a letter to the president of the Privy Council, Prime Minister Sir Wilfrid Laurier, when he wrote that: "Moodie issued a proclamation forbidding the killing of musk-ox, and although he had no legal right to do so you were good enough to approve of his action, and to say that, if necessary, you would pass an Act justifying it."[38]

The instruction to Low was to take the ss *Neptune* close to an existing American whaling station for the winter and the following spring to assist Moodie to establish a permanent detachment of the NWMP, which they did at Cape Fullerton.

In the beginning, building these remote detachments proceeded somewhat by trial and error, a steep learning curve for the government and the young constables who had little experience constructing buildings, let alone so far north. There, cold, orientation to light and adequate space for about two years' worth of supplies would play important roles in design: function superseding comfort. And, since many detachments were well north of the tree line, all construction material had to be brought in by ship.

Superintendent Moodie chose Cape Fullerton not only because it was an overwintering site for Hudson Bay whalers but also reasonably close to the Hudson's Bay Company trading post at Churchill—an approximate 770-mile (1,239-kilometre) return journey—from where communiqués could be shipped overland to Winnipeg and on to Ottawa. The establishment of the Fullerton post was ideal in that the site had plenty of game nearby as well as trout and salmon* fifteen miles (twenty-four kilometres) distant. A ready supply of fresh water was also close by, at seventy-five yards (sixty-eight metres) distant from the detachment.

Moodie decided to erect the officer's quarters on a small island at Fullerton, the inlet between being easily navigable by small boats. The building, approximately fifteen by twenty-four feet (four-and-a-half by seven metres), was divided into one large room and two smaller rooms. Additional buildings, including a storehouse, a coal shed and a twelve- by sixteen-foot (four- by five-metre) lean-to kitchen with porch were also constructed. Moodie wrote that "in trying to avoid getting up unnecessarily large houses, &c., I had underestimated what would be required to hold two years' supplies of rations, fuel and light, as well as many articles required to be carried in store in a place where from one to two years elapse before anything forgotten or expended can be obtained."[39] In addition, adequate room was required for dog feed, oil and blubber.

Later, a barracks room was constructed from 2,000 board feet of lumber sold to Moodie for $50 by an American whaler from Bedford, Massachusetts, Captain George Comer. The lumber had been used as a winter deck house aboard his ship, the *Era*, that whalers often erected to protect themselves from inclement weather. The fifteen- by thirty-foot (four- by nine-metre) building was constructed by Moodie's men with the assistance of Captain Comer's carpenter, who was a house builder in the south. Moodie suggested that all future buildings should be "built in Ottawa; every piece cut and marked, ready to be put together,"[40] and that all lumber be kiln-dried and transported between decks, since any wood saturated with salt water failed to dry out. A non-commissioned officer's office was partitioned off from the main room of the detachment building, but that had to be sacrificed for a trade and quartermaster store, although even that was found to be inadequate. The floors were planked with wood and

---

*   The salmon were actually Arctic char.

the walls covered with asbestos paper and oiled canvas. Although the buildings were reasonably warm, nothing the men did could keep the frost at bay during the winter. Moodie wrote that the curtains were frozen to the floor and thick rime ice coated the skirting boards. In an effort to keep out the cold, Moodie suggested that future dwellings should be built with a double air space between the walls.

Following the construction of the Cape Fullerton post, Low was instructed to proceed north to "Kennedy Channel and Lancaster Sound, and visit as much territory as the state of the ice will permit."[41] When Moodie reported to White the following December, it was to note

Captain George Comer of the us whaling ship, *Era.* LC-B2- 6205-14

that all trading stations had been visited and that the occupants had been informed that customs duty would begin to be collected on January 1, 1904. Moodie lamented the fact that there were so many visits to make that under the present arrangements, that is, by ship, it would be impossible to spend more than two days at each station. "After much consideration," he wrote, "I have concluded that the only practical way of policing these Territories and getting in touch with the natives, is the establishment of small posts of say 1 NCO [non-commissioned officer] & 2 Constables at each principal trading or whaling (which is the same thing) station."[42]

Moodie recommended a number of possible sites, including Cape Wolstenholme on the northeast headland of Hudson Bay, which he felt could become a headquarters. Other recommended sites were a popular whaling site, Repulse Bay, located on the northwestern shore of Hudson Bay at the southern end of the Melville Peninsula, and Churchill, since that community was already populated, given that the Hudson's Bay Company had maintained a trading post there since 1717. Baker Lake and Chesterfield Inlet, all within the current whaling jurisdictions of Hudson Bay and Cumberland and Lancaster Sounds, were also suggested. Moodie believed that the establishment of a complete line of posts around Hudson Bay would facilitate communication with the outside world during the winter.

Moodie was so anxious about his suggestion that a day after writing his official report he wrote a personal missive to White, stating: "I have very little expectation that my suggestion will be carried out, but if the gov^t is desirous of taking over these Territories & enforcing the claim of the Dom: to them, I see no other means of doing it."[43] In closing, he requested White send him one of the new pattern undress caps with embroidered badge, his reasoning being that the more ornate the caps and uniforms were, the better respect one would get from the whalers.

Low also had a suggestion on how to police the whalers. All winter the expedition had been moored next to Captain Comer's ship, *Era*. Comer was less than enthusiastic about sharing space with the Canadian government because it restricted his trade with the Inuit. Low wrote that Comer would not overwinter again at Cape Fullerton as long as a government vessel was there. He suggested that the only way of policing the whalers effectively was to have a boat capable of seeking them out and following them from station to station during the whaling season. The boat, perhaps, could operate from a more central post, such as Pond Inlet on Baffin Island, where a detachment could also be established.

The presence of the *Neptune* in Hudson Bay did more than just make Comer nervous. It stirred up the American media, which resurrected the age-old argument about whether Hudson Bay was a closed or open sea, the implications of which would surely impact Canadian sovereignty over the area, the American whaling industry, and policing of the Arctic. In fact, the press speculated that American whalers would soon be expelled from the bay, suggesting perhaps that it believed Hudson Bay to be a closed sea and therefore Canadian sovereign territory. Given that the bay was bordered on three sides by Canadian territory and that the distance between Hatton Headland and Cape Chidley at the entrance to the bay was then calculated at a mere thirty miles (forty-eight kilometres)—the actual distance is about double that—Canada considered the bay to be a closed sea, making it subject to Canadian laws.

It wasn't only the media who were wondering about Canada declaring Hudson Bay a closed sea. On March 18, 1904, His Majesty's government decoded a secret telegram from the British ambassador in Washington that was paraphrased in a dispatch to Governor General Minto. The ambassador asked whether "Hudson's Bay Straits [w]as 'part of Canada,'"[44] and furthermore, that although the United States did not appear to be overly concerned about the *Neptune* being in the bay, it intimated that Canada's sovereignty declaration might "arouse popular feeling in the United States."[45] As well, the telegram stated that "there might be trouble about some of the Islands and waters to the North of Hudson's Bay Straits."[46]

Regarding the straits, Canada had the weight of history behind it should any problem arise with the United States. The charter granted to the Hudson's Bay Company by King Charles II in 1670 included Hudson Bay and Hudson Strait, among other territory, a fact which was subsequently recognized by the Treaty of Utrecht, which concluded on April 11, 1713, when Britain assumed all the rights of the French in Canada following the end of the War of the Spanish Succession. Article X of the treaty was clear: "The said Most Christian King shall restore to the Kingdom and Queen of Great Britain, to be possessed in full right forever, the Bay and Streights of Hudson, together with all lands, seas, seacoasts, rivers and places situate in the said Bay and Streights, and which belong thereunto, no tracts of land or of sea being excepted which are at present possessed by the subjects of France."

Despite the telegram not mentioning any specific island in its comment about there being trouble with some of the islands north of Hudson Strait, Ellesmere Island was one that came immediately to mind. American explorers had at various times named parts of Ellesmere Grinnell Land, "'Schley Land,' 'Arthur Land,' 'Garfield Coast,' 'Grant Land,' etc."[47] and, in *The Century Atlas of the World* (New York: Century, 1897), maps number one (world) and four (North America) conveniently coloured Ellesmere Island and Northern Greenland the same colour as the rest of the United States; the balance of the islands were coloured the same colour as Canada.[48]

Although Ellesmere Island had been explored in the mid- to late nineteenth century by Americans Kane and Hayes (1853-55 and 1860-61), Hall (1871), and Greely (1881-84), they were preceded there by the English navigators Bylot and Baffin in 1616 and by Captain James Ross in 1818. Referring again to William Edward Hall and his writings on international law, Hall wrote that in the early days of European exploration, sovereign states considered discovery alone sufficient to confer absolute title on unknown land.

Ellesmere, as well as Devon, was on the list of islands to be visited by Commander Low in the *Neptune*, which he expressed in a letter to Colonel F. Gourdeau, deputy minister of the Department of Marine and Fisheries, in July 1904, but his comment that he would erect the Canadian flag and take possession of these islands in the name of the king, exceeded his instructions.[49] Moodie, in his summary report of the expedition, appeared miffed that Low failed to inform him until mid-April that taking possession of Ellesmere Land and Devon Island was the principal reason for the expedition, perhaps because it was not. Moodie disliked Low and considered him "less than straight-forward"[50] in his dealings with him. Moodie himself was not always easy to get along with, as Captain George Comer discovered.

Comer felt sick to his stomach on the couple of occasions that he had to officially deal with Moodie, both times requiring the ministrations of the *Neptune's* doctor, Dr. Borden. The first time was when Moodie stopped Comer's trade with the Inuit and the second was when Moodie had some words with him regarding the discipline of his men. Comer advised Moodie that he had no jurisdiction aboard an American vessel and dared him to come aboard. To this Moodie replied that he certainly did have jurisdiction as long as Comer's ves-sel was in Canadian waters and it was requested of him that he intervene. But Moodie wasn't sure he was standing on firm ground; what he was intimating was perhaps even illegal. He had already shown his mettle by stopping the trade in muskox skins, despite the legality of that order being questionable. Captain Comer wrote about Moodie that "the major no doubt is a good honest man but his head is certainly swelled with his office and it is well known that seafaring men and military men never could get along well as a rule."[51] But Moodie was the type of officer the North-West Mounted Police needed on the frontier, men who were not afraid to take command and make hard decisions, as unpopular as some of them were.

Three years after Low's expedition concluded, Canada felt so sure about Hudson Bay being a closed sea that the government passed a bill, the Fisheries Amendment Act, asserting that Hudson Bay was indeed Canadian territorial water. In concert with the bill, a $50 annual licensing fee "for the privilege of whaling in Hudson Bay,"[52] was simultaneously introduced. The Foreign Office in Washington believed that the United States would protest the bill, but the Colonial Office in London was inclined to accept it.[53] When the bill arrived in England for ratification, the secretary of state for the colonies, the Earl of Elgin, commented that if the United States did not protest it before the end of the year, the bill would be permitted.

Frederick White issued a memo to Prime Minister Laurier on January 2, 1904, in reflection of the success of Low's expedition. It was time, he wrote, "that some system of supervision should be established over the extreme part of the

Dominion."[54] He recommended firstly, that the Arctic be divided into eastern and western districts. For the eastern district, he recommended that a "suitable vessel be purchased or chartered, to be continuously employed"[55] in that district; that supply depots be established and replenished by a vessel sent from Halifax; that small police detachments be established at the supply depots; and that the "Officer in charge of the police to be vested with power for the enforcement of the laws of the Dominion, and NC Officers in charge of Detachments to be given discretionary authority within reasonable limits."[56]

Not only had Moodie and Low made recommendations regarding small remote police detachments and ship patrols, but now the influential Frederick White was on board. But, despite his influence, the recommendations would not become actionable for a number of years.

CHAPTER TWO

Sovereign Expeditions

While Low and Moodie had been constructing the Cape Fullerton detachment, the conclusion of a geopolitical drama was being played out over a narrow strip of land on North America's northwest coast. This, plus the chaos of the Klondike gold rush seven years earlier, would indirectly inform the future role of the North-West Mounted Police and the direction Canada would take to protect its Western Arctic. As well, when it was all over, Canada would be more determined than ever to distance itself from the motherland. At issue was the eastern boundary of the Alaskan Panhandle, a rugged chunk of land that extends all the way down the coast from the Alaskan mainland to meet the coastline of British Columbia just north of the town of Prince Rupert. The land in question had been claimed by Vitus Bering for the Russian Empire in 1841. Russia had sold it to the United States for $7.2 million in 1867, given a declining sea otter industry and to prevent it from falling into British hands, its main Pacific rival.

When the eastern boundary was first established, it began at the southern tip of Prince of Wales Island at 54°40' north latitude, continued north to 56° north latitude, then travelled north along the mountain summits at a distance of ten leagues (approximately thirty-five miles or fifty-six kilometres) from the sea to 60° north latitude, where it intersected with the 141° west meridian, and thence north to the Arctic Ocean. As precise as this definition appears, the approximately thirty-five-mile (fifty-six-kilometre) distance from the sea created an abundance of confusion. Should the distance be calculated from wherever the sea met the land as the Americans suggested, which makes a considerable difference given the depth of the inlets, or should it begin at the western edge of the Channel Islands as the Canadians suggested?

Great Britain and Russia had signed the Treaty of St. Petersburg, also known as the Anglo-Russian Convention, in 1825, which set the southern coastal boundary of the panhandle at 54°40' north latitude, but the exact demarcation line of the eastern boundary was left to be established at some future date. The boundary problem had not been an issue then, given the small population on the coast, but it blew up after August 16, 1896, when gold was discovered on

Bonanza Creek in the Yukon. It was then that Canada sought a direct route to the Pacific coast. The head of Lynn Canal (the present-day American community of Skagway), which was the most convenient route to the Pacific, was believed by Canada to be its sovereign territory.

The NWMP was dispatched to hold the territory, control the swarms of Americans headed north to the Yukon to seek their fortunes, and to apply Canadian customs regulations on the tons of goods flowing into the country. They were soon forced away from Skagway, but held their ground on the summits of the Chilkoot and White Passes. In February 1898, NWMP Inspector Zachary Taylor Wood, great-grandson of the twelfth president of the United States, Zachary Taylor, dispatched Inspectors Belcher and Strickland to each summit respectively. There, armed with machine guns, the considerable weight of Canadian jurisprudence, a healthy degree of fortitude, and a six-month store of supplies, they established tent camps on each summit and began to build cabins to serve as customs houses. Although the boundary issue still had not been resolved, as Pierre Berton explained in his book, *Klondike*, possession is nine points of the law, and so it was soon established that the Canadian boundary began at the summit, not miles inland at the headwaters of the Yukon River as the Americans had suggested.[1]

It was at those summits that the police endeavoured to weed out the rabble of both Dyea and Skagway, whom legendary NWMP Superintendent Samuel B. Steele wrote about in his biography, *Forty Years in Canada*: "Robbery and murder were daily occurrences; many people came there with money, and next morning had not enough to get a meal, having been robbed or cheated out of their last cent."[2] The main instigator was a notorious bandit by the name of "Soapy" Smith, who, together with "his gang of about 150 ruffians, ran the town and did what they pleased."[3] Retribution for what Soapy did to others came to him in the form of a bullet to the heart on July 8, 1898, but that did little to arrest the thuggery ruling the streets. At the summits, the NWMP ensured that none of this "might was right"[4] attitude spilled over into Canada.

Although important, this was not the least of the NWMP's concerns. At the Chilkoot Pass summit, Steele wrote that "the nearest firewood was 7 miles away, and the man sent for it often returned badly frost-bitten. Belcher, collecting customs, performed military as well as police duty on the summits, had all the discomforts of a shower bath. Snow fell so thickly and constantly that everything was damp and papers became mildewed."[5] A similar environment existed at the White Pass summit, where tents had to be pitched on the ice, and firewood and logs for the cabin were no closer than twelve miles (nineteen kilometres) away. Storms raged, the temperature plummeted, and the snow accumulating around the tents and cabin threatened to suffocate the men. They performed customs duties by day and madly shovelled snow by night. Inspector Strickland, in charge, was suffering from a serious case of bronchitis, but soldiered on nevertheless. Superintendent Steele heard about him, arrived at White Pass, and despite suffering the same malady, relieved Strickland of his duty, sent him to Tagish for respite, installed Inspector Cartwright in his place, and began to work himself.

Steele was a barrel of a man, not easily intimidated or outsmarted. By the time he summited the Chilkoot and White Passes, he was a legend with more than his share of adventures under his belt. At the summit, he ruled his chaotic domain with an iron fist, enforcing the rule that no one could enter Canada without at least 1,150 pounds (522 kilograms) of food, plus their tents, bedding, tools, clothes, etc. It amounted to a ton of supplies that individuals needed to support themselves over the winter.

Steele and his men were supported in their endeavours by the Yukon Field Force, a 200-man army unit based out of Fort Selkirk on the Yukon River, a force composed of men from the Royal Canadian Rifles, the Royal Canadian Dragoons and the Royal Canadian Artillery. Members all wore the same startling uniform of scarlet coat and white helmet, an intimidating splendour guaranteed to tame the bleary and bearded rabble that they had been sent to control.[6] Steele wrote of the effect of his stringent policy:

> While there I noticed the difference in the demeanour of the people of all nationalities when they arrived under the protection of our force. There was no danger of Soapy Smith or his gang; they dared not show their faces in the Yukon. The "gun," the slang name for a revolver or pistol of any description, was put in the sack or valise, and everyone went about his business with as strong a sense of security as if he were in the most law-abiding part of the globe.[7]

Despite the chaos at the summits and the boundary uncertainty, the gold rush served as a valuable lesson for the Canadian government. Not only did it serve to protect Canadian sovereignty, but it also saved the NWMP from becoming a political casualty. Prime Minister Laurier had already made motions to disband the force and turn policing over to the provinces, but the demands of the gold rush as well as opposition from regional politicians changed his mind and therefore the fortunes of the force. The gold rush also made it ever so apparent that the Alaska boundary problem had to be resolved.

To that end, a joint High Commission with the United States was struck in 1898; both parties reached a compromise, but when its terms became public, the western states objected, and the US was forced to abandon its negotiated position. Meanwhile, the American government had begun a series of harassments, including restricting Canadian mining interests in Alaska and impeding Canadian shipping. In 1903, a treaty known as the Hay-Herbert Treaty (named for the US secretary of state, John Hay, and the British ambassador, Michael Herbert) was struck and referred the boundary matter to an international tribunal for arbitration. The tribunal comprised six members, including three Americans, two Canadians and one member from Britain, Baron Alverstone, the lord chief justice of England. In short, and to Canada's utter astonishment and outrage, Baron Alverstone took America's side, tipping the tribunal's vote in its favour. In protest, the Canadian judges refused to sign. It was later discovered that one of the reasons for Alverstone's position was that Britain was in an arms race with Germany and needed American steel to compete. Finally, however, the boundary issue was resolved, establishing the border as it is today and denying Canada a clear path to tidewater.

Although Canada was understandably angered over Britain's betrayal, the incident forced two things upon Canada that eventually were to its benefit. First, Canada now had the impetus to distance itself from Britain and take control of its own foreign policy, although that would not become a reality for more than two decades. Prime Minister Laurier stated in the House of Commons that: "The difficulty, as I conceive it to be, is that so long as Canada remains a dependency of the British Crown, the present powers we have are not sufficient for the maintenance of our rights."[8] And second, given the experience with the Americans during the gold rush, and Canada's renewed sense of nationalism in the wake of the Alaska boundary dispute loss, Canada moved to defend its northern sovereign interests, sending Superintendent Charles Constantine on an expedition to the Mackenzie delta in 1903 to check on the American whalers there whose activities had been the subject of numerous reports for well over a decade. He was to establish a detachment at Fort McPherson and then one at Herschel Island if it was required.

Constantine did find it necessary; Sergeant Francis Joseph Fitzgerald was appointed to lead the Herschel Island detachment intended to bring some semblance of order to the American whalers there, who were not only unscrupulous in their trading practices with the Inuvialuit, but were also offering them alcohol in trade. The Right Reverend William C. Bompas, Anglican bishop of Selkirk, wrote of the predicament in disgust: "From these vessels large quantities of raw Spirits are traded with the neighbouring Natives, both Esquimaux and Indian to the utter ruin of those races. Moreover, the Esquimault have now been taught to distil liquor for themselves, and they obtain sugar and molasses from the ships for this purpose."[9] Violence, a natural consequence of the introduction of spirits to a population unused to its insidiously addictive qualities, ensued—to the Inuvialuit's ultimate detriment.

It was not a petty problem and was unlikely to improve, for as many as twelve whaling ships overwintered at Herschel Island each year, bringing a total of 600–1,200 men with them, some even with their families. The small NWMP detachment there was significantly outnumbered, but the authority of the police prevailed, and order was established. A community house had been erected by the Americans to help the men pass the time when they were not whaling, and outdoors, rowdy games of hardball ensued, much to the Inuvialuit people's delight. To all intents and purposes, Herschel Island had become an American colony on Canadian soil. That the local Inuvialuit community was significantly outnumbered did not augur well for their independence or a continuance of their traditional way of life. Many of the Americans, in fact, including captains of the whaling ships, were intimate with Indigenous women, often producing children. Even Sergeant Fitzgerald had a relationship with an Inuvialuit woman with whom he had a child. The force, which at the time controlled virtually every aspect of its members' lives, refused Fitzgerald permission to marry.

Nine months following the settlement of the Alaska boundary dispute, Frederick White wrote to the president of the Privy Council, Prime Minister Laurier, to advise him that a new ship, the SS *Gauss*, renamed the CGS *Arctic*, had been purchased.[10] The *Gauss*, which had been built for polar exploration, had already seen service in both the Arctic and Antarctic and was considered perfect for its intended duty to patrol Hudson Bay and north. It also had the added advantage of being able to carry three years' worth of supplies. White proposed that it be reserved for use exclusively in the Eastern Arctic. It would replace the *Neptune*, which would then be free to return to Halifax at the end of its lease.

The *Arctic* was due to sail from Quebec in September 1904 to begin the next expedition north. At first, it was to be commanded by Captain Joseph

The CGS *Arctic*, formerly the *Gauss*, was built for polar exploration. John Davidson Craig / Department of Indian Affairs and Northern Development fonds / Library and Archives Canada / a102628-v8

Bernier, a robust French Canadian with plenty of sailing and Arctic experience, but whose ambition exceeded the administrative role that the government had envisioned for the expedition. Bernier had his heart set, as William Morrison described in his book, *Showing the Flag*, on drifting "across the Arctic Ocean in the manner of Nansen, perhaps he hoped, crossing the Pole."[11] Bernier was reassigned to the more pedestrian role of sailing master. He was also instructed to remove several years' worth of supplies from the ship since he had anticipated a five-year journey.

Superintendent Moodie would assume command, much to Bernier's humiliation and disgust. This set the stage for a difficult journey, which Bernier made very clear to the press upon his return. He was "an impossible man to work with," he spouted of Moodie, and he "wished to rule my men as he ruled his own subordinates. He even went to so far as to say that he intended the boat to be run like a barracks, with himself in command."[12]

White issued Moodie his instructions, advising him that the Department of Marine and Fisheries would commission him as commander of the expedition as well as that of a fishery department officer. He already held the commission of magistrate under the Dominion Police Act as well as the authority to act for the Customs Department. It was a confusing mix of responsibilities for one

Captain Joseph-Elzéar Bernier.

Indian & Northern Affairs / Library and Archives
Canada / PA-118126

man, one that could easily lead to misunderstandings. Moodie was to take with him RNWMP[13] Inspector E.A. Pelletier as well as ten non-commissioned officers and constables—five were already at Cape Fullerton.

White's instructions included the obvious: that Moodie was to patrol and explore Hudson Bay as well as any islands to the north, and that he was to emphasize to the captains of the whaling fleet that they were in Canadian territorial waters and would be subject to Canadian laws. "With respect to the establishment of Police Posts," White wrote,

you have already erected huts at Cape Fullerton, as being the most convenient location for controlling the natives and supervising the whaling vessels in Hudson Bay.

Your recommendation that another Post be established at Cape Wolstenholme is approved, and you are also authorized to establish a third Post in Cumberland Sound, or such other point as may be found suitable.[14]

Moodie had also recommended posts at Port Harrison, on the mid-east coast of Hudson Bay, as well as a post at either Blacklead Island or Kekerton Island, both important whaling settlements. As well, he had suggested that a post at Pond Inlet should be considered if the government was so inclined to have a detachment that far north. Moodie's primary focus as superintendent of "M" Division, Hudson Bay, though, was "until otherwise notified by the Government," to confine "the route of the *Arctic*... to Hudson's Bay, Hudson's Strait, Davis Strait, Baffin's Bay, Smith Sound, Kennedy Channel, Lancaster Sound, and other bays and channels on the west coast of Hudson's Bay, Davis Strait, or Baffin's Bay."[15]

Moodie had a year earlier stressed that a patrol steamer should be made available to enable the commanding officer to visit all the detachments on an annual basis. It would remain in Hudson Bay over the winter. "If another station was placed at Baker Lake," Moodie continued, "at the head of Chesterfield Inlet, or somewhere between Fullerton and Churchill, there would then be a line of posts around the bay, and communication could be had with the outside world during the winter, should necessity arise."[16] Moodie considered the Baker Lake and Port Harrison posts as being intermediate in importance, while the Repulse Bay, Fullerton and Wolstenholme posts were more important, given that their locations were more advantageous for monitoring ship traffic.

Although White's instruction to Moodie to patrol and explore Hudson Bay and environs by ship sounded straightforward, Moodie had enough ship-patrol experience with the *Neptune* that he was now more convinced than ever that it was both prohibitively expensive and inefficient. For nine months of the year a ship would be locked in the ice, and as commanding officer, he had been informed that he must stay with the ship, frustrating any attempt at police patrols. He again wrote to White, reasserting his position: "I would again bring my former recommendations regarding these to your notice. To patrol this country and have any sort of knowledge of what is happening during the winter, it is absolutely necessary to have posts at different places where men and dogs can rest and obtain supplies."[17] After breakup, he suggested, the annual supply ships could do the work of a steamer by visiting various posts and serving notice on the whalers, or a smaller vessel could be maintained at one of the posts for this purpose.

Of course, the ship and police patrols, although serving many functions, were there for a much greater purpose: for Canada to be seen by the world to be administering its northern assets. Assets that were still not clearly defined twenty-five years after their transfer from Britain. Dr. Henri-Marc Ami, an assistant paleontologist with the Geological Survey of Canada, wrote to the minister of justice on March 1, 1905, with a draft recommendation "concerning the ownership and rights to the Arctic Archipelago."[18] He believed, to everyone's obvious knowledge and agreement, that the description of Canada's Arctic in the order-in-council of 1880 "appears to be wanting"[19] and had suggested many months earlier that the Imperial Parliament should issue a proclamation asserting its rights to the Arctic. Dr. Ami had reason to be concerned, besides the obvious sovereignty issues. Two years earlier he had written to Prime Minister Laurier to advise him that "the resources of our northern possessions are great. Millions of tons of coal occur there, Asbestos, copper, iron, jade, & various other useful and rare metals also."[20] It was too valuable a list of resources to squander or ignore.

Prime Minister Laurier believed that such a proclamation was premature and suggested that Canada was on the right track by establishing a police post in Hudson Bay and maintaining ship patrols. He wrote: "Next year, I propose that we should send a cruiser to patrol the waters and plant our flag at every point. When we have covered the whole ground and have men stationed everywhere, then I think we can have such a proclamation as is suggested by Dr. Ami."[21] It was becoming clear that the path to sovereignty would bear heavily on the shoulders of the RNWMP and later the RCMP, although the prime minister's proposal to "have men stationed everywhere" was impractical and would never come to fruition.

The *Arctic's* first year was a bit of a wash. After leaving Quebec on September 17, 1904, the ship barely had enough time to make it to Cape Fullerton before becoming frozen in for the winter. One thing that the *Arctic's* first excursion confirmed, though, was that it was badly underpowered, managing only four or five knots, sometimes against as great a tide. The *Arctic* would need re-powering.

In January 1905, to quell some of the confusion arising from the multiple responsibilities assigned to Moodie, it had been decided between Frederick White and François Gourdeau, deputy minister of the Ministry of Marine and Fisheries, that the police would stick to the shore and the ministry, the water. Following completion of the *Arctic's* current assignment, Superintendent Moodie plus two officers and eleven men were to be set ashore on the west side of Hudson Bay and from there establish connections by land to Fort Churchill and Lake Winnipeg. Most of the *Arctic's* plans that year, however, went awry. The ship was experiencing problems with its windlass so Bernier insisted on returning south early. Moodie established a detachment at Churchill, where the Hudson's Bay Company already had a trading post, but never did tour the archipelago or set up a detachment at Wolstenholme.

Captain Bernier's next expedition north, which departed on July 28, 1906, was an exoneration of sorts; he was promoted to commander of the expedition. Despite his eagerness to depart, his journey had an inauspicious start. Planning for an early departure, the *Arctic* had anchored away from its berth in the harbour of Quebec City. During the night, in spite of its visible running lights, the ship was struck by another vessel, which carried away its bowsprit as well as causing some other damage. Coincidentally, the offending vessel, the *Elina*, was Norwegian, a nationality that would figure prominently in challenges to Canada's sovereignty as well as in the history of its north. For even as Bernier was preparing to get underway, another Norwegian, the explorer Roald Amundsen, was just completing his three-year sail/drift/motor through the Northwest Passage (east to west) with six crew aboard the seventy-foot (twenty-one-metre) square-sterned sloop, *Gjoa*, arriving at Nome, Alaska, on August 31, 1906.

It would be another thirty-six years before Sergeant Larsen of the RCMP would guide the police schooner *St. Roch* through the Northwest Passage on a west to east trajectory, although both were bested by Robert McClure, an Irishman who, on his second expedition (1850) searching for the lost Sir John Franklin, entered the Arctic from the west and despite abandoning his ship, the HMS *Investigator*, in the pack ice at Mercy Bay on Banks Island's north coast, continued his journey east by sledge. He eventually met up with another Franklin search party under the command of Sir Edward Belcher, who facilitated McClure's return to England. McClure and his crew thus became the first to complete the transit of the Northwest Passage as well as the circumnavigation of the two Americas.

Although repair to the *Arctic* delayed its departure by four days and caused its superstitious crew to wonder what was in store for them, the ship sailed safely with all hands. Gourdeau had issued his first set of instructions on June 23, but provided a more detailed set a month later, the new directives advising Bernier to take "formal possession of all lands and islands on your way,"[22] not just any new islands he discovered. Bernier was instructed to visit Pond Inlet on the northeast coast of Baffin Island to "serve notices on the whalers there."[23] In his capacity as fisheries officer, he was also instructed to implement the recently amended Fisheries Act by collecting the $50 annual licensing fee from the whalers—before proceeding west of Erebus Bay through Barrow Strait. He was then instructed to overwinter at Erebus Bay or Melville Island so that during the winter he could take possession of Banks Land (Banks Island) and Prince Albert Land (Victoria Island), leaving all the necessary records in a cairn in case his ship met with misfortune.

With respect to his instruction "to formally annex all new lands at which you may call, leaving proclamations in cairns at all points,"[24] Bernier later wrote that he took possession of all of the Parry group of islands,[25] a High Arctic cluster of islands which form part of a larger cluster now known as the Queen Elizabeth Islands. As well, he planted flags on a number of other islands along the route.

Meanwhile, to the south, the provinces of Alberta and Saskatchewan had been created a year earlier, leaving the Northwest Territories responsible for a reduced, but still vast, tract of land composed of three geographical regions: the Arctic Mainland, the Mackenzie Valley and the Arctic Archipelago, the latter encompassed by the recently created Franklin District. Frederick White had been named the first commissioner of the Northwest Territories in 1905, a position he would hold until his death in 1918. One of White's first major initiatives with respect to the Arctic was to address the wholesale slaughter of muskox in Hudson Bay, a species that would later figure prominently in protecting Canadian sovereignty over the third largest island in its Arctic Archipelago, Ellesmere Island, smaller only than Baffin Island and Victoria Island.

In response to copies of correspondence forwarded to White by the prime minister regarding the killing of muskox in the Hudson Bay area, White wrote to advise him that the situation was under control. He stated that two problems had been addressed in the bay; the first was convincing the American whalers that they were operating in Canadian sovereign waters, and the second was dealing with "the subsidizing by American whaling boats of natives, to indiscriminately kill musk-ox, and bring the skins to American ships to be disposed of by barter."[26] He reported that "this we succeeded in checking, and to-day there is not an American whaling ship in Hudson Bay. All accomplished quietly without International friction."[27]

White also had to explain to the commissioner of the Hudson's Bay Company, Clarence C. Chipman, that stopping the slaughter of muskox for their skins was in the best interest of the Canadian fur trade. The vacuum created by the departure of the American whalers, however, did not serve the Inuit well. They had become reliant upon the bartered goods this arrangement offered, a trade that the RNWMP later had to resume to a limited degree to stave off their starvation. That practice was stopped, however, when Canadian fur traders complained that the police were taking away their business, and the Hudson's Bay Company stated its intention to open a trading post at Chesterfield Inlet to accommodate the trade in that region of Hudson Bay.[28]

Upon Bernier's return, he reported to the new minister of the Department of Marine and Fisheries in Ottawa, Louis-Philippe Brodeur, who was pleased that Bernier had named a "scythe-shaped peninsula at the western tip of Baffin Island"[29] after him. Brodeur instructed Bernier to continue his work "formally securing the northland for Canada."[30] Bernier's ego stroked, he returned to Quebec to begin refitting the *Arctic* for his next voyage north.

Bernier's next voyage, in 1908, departed without the drama of the previous expedition, although he was honoured to receive a multiple gun salute ordered by the visiting Prince of Wales—later to become King George V—aboard his ship, HMS *Indomitable*, on the morning of his departure. The prince, in a brief meeting with Bernier the day before, had been impressed with his exploits. This time Bernier would supplement the larder with several live animals: pigs for slaughter and cows to supply fresh milk for the men, although the latter experiment failed when the cows consumed too much fodder to practically bring along on an extended voyage. They, too, went into the stew pot.

Bernier also brought along two teams of sled dogs. He had found that no one in the Arctic would part with their teams. Sled dogs were the main mode of transport for the Inuit, a vital necessity that often made the difference between life or death. Sled dogs would also become invaluable to the RNWMP and its successor, the RCMP, in facilitating their extended winter patrols. (Much later, out of necessity, Inspector Joy and Constable Taggart, as did most RCMP officers, became proficient at managing their dogs, repairing their qamutiit and driving their teams.) Unfortunately, both of Bernier's teams, which had been cooped up for months aboard ship, only being let out under strict supervision, breached their enclosure one day and raced away into the face of a howling blizzard, never to be seen or heard from again.

George Desbarats, the acting deputy minister of Marine and Fisheries, issued Bernier his instructions on July 18, 1908, again informing him to use his good judgment in the conduct of his duties, but also to proceed as far west as possible. Was this tacit approval to sail through the Northwest Passage? It certainly seemed so, especially when reading Bernier's response to Desbarats two days later where he comments that if McClure Strait is clear then he will proceed through the Northwest Passage and advance toward Herschel Island for the winter. He certainly wasn't speaking out of turn, for four months earlier Minister Brodeur had commented that the expedition was considering having Bernier navigate through the Northwest Passage, and just after that, the prime minister suggested that the Bering Sea was Bernier's destination.[31]

It appears odd then, that given the opportunity, and essentially the permission, to proceed through the passage, Bernier chose to honour his written instructions to the letter. Instructions that told him to travel as far west as possible, but made no mention of the Northwest Passage. And if ever there was a year to go through the passage, that was it; the next year, it would be choked with ice.

T.C. Fairley and Charles E. Israel, in their book, *The True North—The Story of Captain Joseph Bernier*, described what happened. One morning in mid-August 1908, Bernier came up to the bridge to find his first officer, George Braithwaite, in a state. When questioned, Braithwaite pointed to their position just south of Prince Patrick Island, one of the most westerly islands in the archipelago. Overnight they had travelled much farther west than both had anticipated. What was astonishing, however, was that there was no ice ahead. The passage was clear, and had Bernier been so motivated, he could have navigated through the passage in one season, an astonishing feat that would have eclipsed Amundsen's hold on the prize, which took him three years to achieve. Duty bound, Bernier ordered Braithwaite to put about. For the second time, Bernier felt personally defeated: first the pole, now this. Later, when talking to a friend, he commented that: "I felt my eyes getting moist, and I could have wept."[32]

Bernier's first port of call was Etah, Greenland, where he was to deliver a consignment of goods to an American, Dr. Frederick Cook. Commander Robert Peary had also been ensconced at Etah, and the day before Bernier arrived, he had set off for his final attempt on the North Pole. Dr. Cook, who had been Peary's surgeon on a previous expedition, and who was also a competitor in the race to reach the pole, claimed to have reached it on April 21, 1908, a full year ahead of Peary's April 6, 1909, summit. Cook addressed his delayed announcement by stating that it was because poor weather had forced him and his two Inuit companions to overwinter at Cape Hardy on Devon Island. His news reached the outside world a week ahead of Peary's, but eventually a Naval Affairs Subcommittee of the US House of Representatives sided with Peary, paving the way for a bill that passed the House and the Senate before being signed by President William Howard Taft—although not before the word "discovery" was excised from the document.* Bernier, who had conveyed Dr. Cook's pole summit announcement south,[33] heard the news that Peary was first to reach the North Pole just as he arrived back in Ottawa.

It was during this expedition that Bernier controversially erected a plaque on Parry's Rock at Winter Harbour on Melville Island on July 1, 1909, declaring that the whole of the Arctic Archipelago belonged to Canada. Some in Ottawa

---

*   A librarian, Robert Bryce, who has never set foot in the Arctic, penned an 1,133-page tome based on twenty years of research. In it, he opined that neither Cook nor Peary had reached the pole and that it was only in April 1993 that a Richard Weber and a Dr. Mikhail Malakov achieved that feat in the same way that Cook and Peary had travelled. Robert M. Bryce, *Cook and Peary: The Polar Controversy, Resolved* (Mechanicsburg, PA: Stackpole, 1997). The controversy, however, is still alive.

Captain Bernier and the crew of the *Arctic* at Winter Harbour. Library and Archives Canada / C-001198

shuddered at the implications of such a brash declaration, but Prime Minister Laurier, although distancing himself from Bernier's grandiose proclamation, was not as upset as he would have been had not the American, Peary, earlier declared his North Pole achievement.[34] When Peary offered President Taft the pole, his comment was: "I do not know what I could do with it."[35]

Bernier's declaration, in the traditional way that Canada had been meeting its sovereign requirements through effective occupation, was premature, given that not every island had even been visited and explored by Canada, or for that matter, by Great Britain. Bernier, however, according to Alan MacEachern, history professor at the University of Western Ontario, was inadvertently "introducing to international practice the emergent concept that northern nations owned all the territory from their east and west boundaries all the way to the North Pole—a concept that became known as the sector principle."[36] Bernier's declaration at Parry's Rock, however, was not the first introduction of this novel concept by a Canadian.

Most considered it far safer to approach Canada's sovereignty on a basis of "quiet penetration"[37] via ship and police patrols rather than overt attestations of ownership. That no one publicly squawked about Bernier's declaration was a testament to Canada's sovereignty efforts so far, and the fact that the US ambassador in London, Whitelaw Reid, announced in a speech a few months later that "Canada was free to occupy the archipelago,"[38] added support to that.

Bernier's last expedition north under the employ of the Canadian government was more routine than not, except for one major exception. As with previous expeditions, he was advised to use his good judgment in the performance of his duties. He was also instructed by the deputy minister of Marine and Fisheries, Alexander Johnston, to extend his journey as far west as possible. That instruction had been included on the previous expedition as well, but Bernier was now clearly being instructed to go through the Northwest Passage if it was passable, to either Victoria or Vancouver. Johnston wrote: "The advisability of attempting to make the northwest passage is, however, left to your judgement after ascertaining the ice conditions on the spot."[39] Unfortunately, the ice conditions were not favourable that year, and Bernier was once again forced to turn back.

Bernier's 1910 expedition north with the Canadian government would be his last for more than a decade, but what he had proven with his four expeditions was that much could be accomplished by ship patrol. He had not only claimed a significant amount of territory for Canada, but he had assisted the RNWMP, and would later assist the RCMP, with the establishment of their remote detachments.

Although Canada was slowly taking control of its north, it still had not explored every nook and cranny of its archipelago, but a sea change occurred following the end of Captain Bernier's fourth expedition. There were a couple of reasons for this. Not only was Prime Minister Laurier's Liberal party defeated by Robert Borden's Conservatives in the fall election of 1911—it is believed that the loss of Canada's position to the United States over the Alaska boundary dispute soured Canadians toward the Liberals and tainted public opinion about the central issue of the election, free trade with the United States—but the whaling industry was in sharp decline. There were fewer Americans causing havoc in both the Eastern and Western Arctic. As well, Captain Bernier's involvement had been at the privilege of Prime Minister Laurier. Prime Minister Borden had other ideas, in which Bernier did not feature. But Prime Minister Borden catered to his own brand of Bernier, and that was in the form of the ambitious and somewhat problematic Vilhjalmur Stefansson.

Canadian-born and a Harvard professor to boot, Stefansson would resume where Bernier left off, but would lead an entirely different kind of expedition. He would also leave a trail of controversy and tragedy, and years later, international tension—all of which was antithetical in degree to even Bernier's slightly tarnished path. And, in response to his final expedition's tragic conclusion, Stefansson would casually dismiss it as not being his responsibility.

Stefansson had already made two exploratory trips to the Arctic—the Anglo-American Expedition, 1906–1907, and the Stefansson–Anderson Expedition, 1908–1912—before he finally caught the serious attention of the Canadian government in 1913. His first expedition had explored the region to the east and west of the Mackenzie delta. That exped-ition, which lasted seventeen months, was sponsored jointly by both the University of Toronto and Harvard University. His second expedition began in May 1908 and ended fifty-five months later in November 1912.

Vilhjalmur Stefansson, Arctic explorer and ethnologist. Rudolph Martin Anderson / Library and Archives Canada / e002712839

It was sponsored primarily by the American Museum of Natural History but also received a small grant from the Geological Survey of Canada. Stefansson's record of discovery, research and collection in a variety of disciplines on this expedition was astonishing. In his own report, some "20,000 specimens in eth-nology, archaeology, geology, zoology and botany"[40] were collected. He noted that he had added a 500-mile (800-kilometre) river—Horton River—to the map of Canada; discovered populated areas where there were not known to be people—in some instances, people who had never seen white people before; discovered valuable deposits of copper, mica and coal; altered the tree line on Canadian maps; and discovered mountains, harbours and lakes.

Stefansson's second expedition received a favourable endorsement from the head of the Geological Survey of Canada, Reginald Walter Brock, who had been following Stefansson's official reports from the field for four years. Brock applauded the fact that the expedition was conducted very cheaply—in fact, in fifty-five months only $10,000 had been spent—and to his credit, Stefansson took no remuneration. Although Bernier was as competent as Stefansson with respect to territory visited and claimed for Canada, the depth of Stefansson's cultural and scientific research was beyond the reach, interest and ability of the hardy sailor-cum-Arctic explorer.

Stefansson leaned on his impressive résumé when he approached the Canadian government to assist with financing his third expedition to the Arctic. He had already secured commitments from the American Museum of Natural History and the National Geographic Society to the tune of $45,000, but the five-year expedition was forecast to cost between $75,000 and $85,000. Stefansson wrote to Prime Minister Borden on February 4, 1913, enclosing a planned objective and itinerary, the main objective being to discover new lands west of the Parry Islands. He would proceed north from Herschel Island in an endeavour to discover a "lost continent" he believed existed beneath the polar ice cap in an area previously unexplored. In an interview with the *Seattle Star*, Stefansson stated that "personally, I believe the continent is there, and that we will find it. The idea is not new.... The tides prove it."[41]

As with his previous expeditions, Stefansson planned to populate his crew with a roster of scientists, and his expedition would entail a northern and southern party. Stefansson would lead the northern party in his quest for new land, while Rudolf Martin Anderson, an American explorer, zoologist and conservationist, would lead the southern party. Anderson would conduct the majority of his scientific research around Coronation Gulf. Stefansson requested $25,000 from the Canadian government, his reasoning being that the majority of his explorations would be in Canadian territory and that the Canadian government might want to "claim any lands that may be discovered."[42]

A cabinet subcommittee was struck on February 7, 1913, after Stefansson had been interviewed by Prime Minister Borden on the 4th. Perhaps alarmed by his comment that Canada *might* wish to claim any new land that he discovered, the subcommittee members felt it advisable that the Canadian government finance the whole expedition rather than risk any new land falling into American hands—given that the bulk of Stefansson's funding thus far was coming from American institutions.[43] Prime Minister Borden wrote a memo to the governor general, Prince Arthur, Duke of Connaught and Strathearn (Queen Victoria's seventh child), repeating the advice of his ministers. He reasoned that "the expedition will conduct its explorations in waters and on lands under Canadian jurisdiction or included in the northern zone contiguous to the Canadian territory. It is therefore considered advisable that the expedition should be under the general direction of the Canadian Government and should sail under the Canadian flag."[44] Canada did absorb the cost of the expedition, disappointing the American Museum of Natural History.

Borden seems to have missed the fact that Stefansson's memo stated that he was to explore to the west of the Parry Islands when his own memo to the governor general stated that Stefansson planned to "equip a whaling vessel and take a party in via Behring [sic] Strait to Herschel Island, and from there proceed north and east to explore the vast northern seas, which are comparatively unknown to science."[45] If Stefansson's area of exploration lay west of the 141st meridian west, then any new land discovered would be outside of Canadian sovereign territory.

Stefansson's real intention was only revealed months later. He planned to proceed north along the 141st meridian west, presumably while searching for his "lost continent," until his ship became locked in the ice. He would then drift around the polar basin and, somewhere close to the North Pole, would temporarily depart the ship and make a dash to the pole by ski and dogsled. Returning to the ship, he would remain with it as it drifted into the North Atlantic somewhere between Greenland and Norway. This plan, however, was only revealed to John Douglas Hazen, the minister of Marine and Fisheries and the Naval Service, on June 1, 1913. Prime Minister Borden was notified soon after.[46]

Although Stefansson's plan to sled to the pole appeared to be seamless in theory, what he revealed in an article in the American publication, *Geographical Review*, seven years later, suggested a different reality. Unknown currents, open leads and heavy pressure ridges were standard fare. And what Stefansson discovered was that his dogsled dash to the pole was spoiled by the southerly drift of the pack ice, which frustrated any progress he made to the north.[47] If he had been a keen student of history, which I am sure he was, he would have known that prior to experiencing it. William Edward Parry had written about it in 1827, where in a three-day march, he and his men covered only twelve miles (nineteen kilometres) through a gauntlet of impossibly high pressure ridges, rotten ice and suddenly opening leads, only to discover their position changed by a meagre five miles (eight kilometres).[48] Fridtjof Nansen, in his *Fram* expedition (1893–1896), experienced it as well, to the point that he questioned whether the pole was attainable at all.

When Borden's memo to the governor general reached Downing Street the next month, there was obvious concern that Stefansson's exploration would include land "contiguous to the Canadian territory."[49] Under-Secretary of State for the Colonies Hartmann Wolfgang Just was concerned that Canada's Arctic borders still had not been defined and that both Great Britain and Canada were clinging to the vague description in the order-in-council of July 31, 1880, which had transferred the Arctic Archipelago to Canada. As well, colonial governments did not have the authority to annex new territory without the permission of the Crown. The Foreign Office was inclined to provide such authority, but in the meantime advised that nothing should be publicized. Two months later, Secretary of State for the Colonies Lewis Vernon Harcourt provided the authority necessary for the Dominion government to annex new territory, should it be discovered. Borden had written in his memo that Stefansson would be instructed to observe, fix the position of and to plant the British flag on any new or "partly unknown" lands, and to his relief, that was now officially ratified. Borden concluded his memo with the comment that his ministers had recommended a sum of $80,000 be paid to Stefansson in two tranches, although less than a decade later the true cost of what would turn out to be a calamitous expedition would exceed half a million dollars.[50]

Borden had also advised in his memo that a member of Stefansson's party would be designated a customs and fisheries officer with all the relevant authority to collect customs and fisheries dues. Stefansson appointed his topographer, Kenneth Chipman, to the position, but Chipman was reluctant, knowing that the RNWMP at Herschel Island would have the situation under control. Besides, Chipman believed that "Stefansson was trying indirectly to assert a status superior to that of the police."[51] He was indeed correct in his assessment of Stefansson's relationship with the police. During Stefansson's first expedition north he had arrived at Herschel Island in the summer of 1906 with few supplies. It had been an unusually harsh winter and the supplies he expected had not yet arrived. He was therefore dependent upon the RNWMP detachment on Herschel Island to keep him adequately supplied. The police were understandably concerned. Here was a greenhorn from the south, arriving with few supplies, and telling the constables that he expected to live like the Inuvialuit. They warned him of the privations he could expect and even informed him that they would no longer support him. At that point, he lost all respect for the force.

That respect did not improve with his second expedition. Then, he became annoyed that the police would not endorse what they considered to be his crazy schemes, and there was still the issue of food. Staff Sargeant Fitzgerald, the head of the detachment, expected anyone coming into the north would have at least a year's supply of goods to support themselves. This had been Superintendent Steele's rule at the summits of Chilkoot and White Passes during the gold rush, and it made perfect sense. Fitzgerald wrote in his diary that "such men as Stefansson claim that they can live on the country. They can[,] by someone else supplying the food. All these people are a drain on our supplies[.] I[t] is impossible to refuse a white man if he is short of food."[52] Unfortunately, Fitzgerald's dim assessment of Stefansson would get even darker in the weeks and months to come.

One did not have to look closely to observe that Stefansson's latest expedition was in trouble even before it left the Victoria dock. Stefansson, however, anxious to depart and still glowing in the aftermath of his interview with the press, chose to ignore it. The root of the trouble began with the *Karluk*, a twenty-nine-year-old 128-foot (39-metre) American brigantine with a 150 horsepower auxiliary coal-fired steam engine that had been built for the fishing industry, but converted to a whaler in 1892. The 247 NRT (net registered ton) vessel had been considered unsafe, even for carrying freight, by a naval expert with the Hudson's Bay Company, let alone being anywhere near the polar ice pack. But Stefansson had purchased the vessel for a paltry $10,000 and considered it satisfactory for his needs. That the *Karluk* was to be his flagship vessel did not augur well for the future of the expedition, and despite a refit undertaken at His Majesty's Canadian Dockyard at Esquimalt on southern Vancouver Island, the vessel was still not ready by the time its robust thirty-seven-year-old captain, Robert "Bob" Abram Bartlett, arrived to assume command. Bartlett, who habitually peppered his conversations with an assortment of salty pejoratives, was already an experienced Arctic hand, and was understandably appalled at the deplorable shape of the ship and even communicated same to the deputy minister of the Ministry of the Naval Service on the evening before their departure. He wrote that he did not hold up much hope of the ship even surviving the voyage north.

Stefansson, however, was under a crippling deadline. He had been informed by one of his original backers, the National Geographic Society, that if the expedition did not depart by either May or June, the society would take back control of the expedition. Stefansson did not want to lose the generous backing of the Canadian government, nor did the government want to lose its grip on an expedition that might just discover new land for Canada. So, thirteen days shy of the deadline, the *Karluk* departed Esquimalt at 7:30 on the muggy evening of June 17, 1913, her ensign snapping smartly before a moderate westerly breeze. Captain Bartlett was still fuming. The ship was not yet ready to face the Arctic. And, as if to confirm his opinion, the steering gave way six days later and then the engine quit, an engine that its chief engineer, John Munroe, described as "a coffee pot of an engine... never intended to run more than two days at a time."[53]

The ship put in to Nome, Alaska, for engine and steering repairs on July 8 to the delight of its passengers and crew, who had already begun to celebrate the long northern days. There they met up with the expedition's other two vessels, the *Alaska* and the *Mary Sachs*, both purchased to handle the growing needs of the expedition. The *Alaska* would become the research vessel of the southern party. Another celebration of sorts occurred on July 27 when the *Karluk* crossed the Arctic Circle. The next morning, however, the wind and waves sent most of the scientists stumbling to their bunks. The wind from the northwest was punishing, and the ship began to buck wildly and to take on water. Stefansson also retreated to his cabin for a time. Four days later, the *Karluk* arrived at the edge of the permanent ice pack, and stalled there, unable to penetrate it. The next day, however, the ship made some progress and pushed into the pack, becoming icebound a few hours later. The expedition's destination, Herschel Island, was still out of reach. The *Karluk* would remain immobile for a few days before being miraculously freed on August 6. The elation of the crew was short-lived, however, and after a number of further aborted attempts to close in on their destination, by late August the ship was held fast at the mercy of the pack ice and its uncontrollable drift to the west.

Stefansson was not a man to bide his time, and his anxiety to get on with his expedition got the better of him, blinding him to his responsibility as leader of the expedition, while the already fragile *Karluk* and its passengers and crew drifted helplessly toward a tragedy that some have compared as second only to the loss of Franklin and his men. On the evening of September 20, 1913, Stefansson left the ship with a few of his men, half believing that he was only going hunting for ten days to reprovision the ship, but in the back of his mind likely knowing that he was leaving the *Karluk* for good. Captain Bartlett and his passengers and crew would have to fend for themselves. Bartlett guessed that Stefansson would never return.

Stefansson and his party were halfway to the mainland when a storm forced them to seek shelter on an island. The next morning when they woke to clear skies, the ice had gone out and with it the *Karluk*. Held fast in the pack ice, the ship was nowhere to be seen. Over the next few months the *Karluk* drifted in a westerly direction almost clear across the Chukchi Sea. Anxiety built among the passengers and crew as the ice rafted up around the ship and snow drift settled heavily onto its deck. Strange noises echoed through the frigid air as the pack ice shimmied and shifted, grinding up against the *Karluk's* dangerously fragile hull. The men slept in their clothes, not wanting to be caught off guard, ready at a moment's notice to abandon ship.

On January 10, 1914, a noise like a cannon shot signalled the end. Captain Bartlett rushed down to the engine room where the ice pressure had opened a ten-foot (three-metre) gash in the hull. There was no way that the pumps could manage the breach. At about 3:15 p.m. the following day, Captain Bartlett dropped the needle onto Chopin's *Funeral March* on the ship's Victrola as a fitting tribute to the ship before stepping off to the shipwreck camp that he and the passengers and crew had assembled only hours before. The survivors watched with a mixture of dread and disbelief as the ship disappeared quickly through the narrow hole in the ice, the Victrola playing resolutely on, and then finally there was only the cracking reports of the yardarms snapping off as the ship settled heavily into its icy grave.

No one died in the sinking, but eight men died during the march to safety, four who disappeared entirely in their search for land, and four others who it is believed may have been overcome by carbon monoxide poisoning in their tent on Herald Island. Their remains were discovered ten years later. Another three died while marooned on Wrangel Island; one, it is believed, by murder: a summary execution for stealing food. The survivors on Wrangel Island waited six months for rescue, and that was only due to the heroic efforts of Captain Bartlett and his Inuit companion, Kataktovik, who walked 200 miles (320 kilometres) across the shifting sea ice to Siberia and then east to Emma Harbor (now Komsomolskaya Bay) to find help. In a little bit of grim irony, in May 1914, Bartlett was picked up by Captain Pedersen in the *Herman* and taken to Alaska. Pedersen, a whaling captain, was the same man who had found and recommended the *Karluk* to Stefansson.

The whole *Karluk* fiasco was a tragedy that could have been avoided, a tragedy that was evidently foreseen. An American member of the research contingent, Frederick Maurer, overheard Stefansson speaking to one of the passengers before his final departure, noting that he said he feared the loss of the ship. In the eyes of his critics, Stefansson was suspected of callously abandoning the ship, knowing that it was in peril, and it was his blame of Captain Bartlett after hearing of the *Karluk*'s loss and the deaths of so many men that confirmed their suspicions.

The sinking of the *Karluk* meant the loss of the majority of Stefansson's supplies which he had been relying upon for his northern drift. In a panic, he began buying up all the available stores from local agents, and when he fell short, he produced a letter from the comptroller of the RNWMP, A.A. McLean, requiring the Herschel Island detachment to accommodate him as needed. Inspector J.W. Phillips, commander of "N" Division at Athabaska, was incensed. He believed that Stefansson did not care about the fate of the *Karluk* and was more concerned about his forthcoming book, *My Life with the Eskimo*, which had been published after the expedition departed Victoria, than the fate of the twenty-two survivors under his leadership.

Much to Phillip's disgust, Stefansson raided the Herschel Island police storehouse, squandering precious supplies and passing a significant portion on to the local Indigenous population whom Stefansson believed were in need. Chipman, who had an obvious grudge against Stefansson, wrote in his diary: "It is strange but no one seems to have a good word for him; seldom have I seen a man for whom there are fewer good words than in the case for vs along this coast. It may be partially due to the climate or the men here but most of it must be due to vs himself."[54] John Cox, Chipman's assistant, in a letter to Anderson's wife, wrote that Stefansson has "an unfortunate knack of getting in the wrong everywhere he goes."[55] Amundsen called him "the greatest humbug alive," but others viewed him as a "genius" and a "prophet of the North."

Despite purchasing another ship and adequate stores for his drift across the Arctic Basin, Stefansson never did fulfill that dream, but he did spend the next few years drifting on ice floes, outlining the edge of Canada's continental shelf as well as discovering the last few pieces of the Canadian Arctic sovereignty puzzle: Lougheed,[56] Borden,[57] Mackenzie King, Meighen and Brock Islands. This was not his final chapter, however, and he would again surface a few years later in an effort to secure Wrangel Island for Canada, an event that created a great deal of international confusion and tension, and unfortunately, additional tragedy.

CHAPTER THREE

Administering the Eastern Arctic

The decade (1920–1930) following the end of World War I saw the Canadian government fend off multiple challenges to its sovereignty in the Arctic, precipitating a significant increase in government activity to protect its interests there. Beginning in 1922, ship patrols were conducted annually, and the RNWMP, which by February 1, 1920, had been transitioned into the Royal Canadian Mounted Police (RCMP), had stepped up its activity as well. It was not only busy establishing and staffing remote depots, but it was also conducting the long and arduous dogsled patrols to the outer fringes of the Arctic Archipelago that the force had become renowned for. And Inspector Joy, Constable Taggart and Nukappiannguaq's legendary patrol to Melville Island was the ultimate demonstration of the fortitude and determination that the Canadian government required to meet its sovereign requirements.

Stefansson was still in the picture, up to his old tricks, this time in a bid for Canada to claim Wrangel Island in the North Chukchi Sea. The Danes, in the form of Knud Rasmussen, a Greenland-Danish explorer and anthropologist, began to cause Ottawa some concern when he wrote that "it is well known that the territory of the polar esquimaux falls within the region designated as 'no-man's land' and there is no authority in the district"[1]—which the government interpreted to be Ellesmere Island. Rasmussen was in the throes of organizing his Fifth Thule Expedition (1921–1924), which was designed to "attack the great primary problem of the origin of the Eskimo race."[2] Stefansson would stir the pot further with his opinion of what Rasmussen was really up to and his advice that Rasmussen's expedition was already underway. And as if that was not enough, the Norwegian explorer, Otto Sverdrup, together with the Norwegian government, was challenging Canada over ownership of the Sverdrup Islands. Sverdrup had been the first European to visit these islands, while wintering aboard his ship, *Fram*, between 1898 and 1902.

And then there was the American explorer, Dr. Donald MacMillan, who in 1925 launched an expedition to the Eastern Arctic in concert with the National Geographic Society, and unbelievably, the US Naval Air Force—complete with aircraft—which sent shivers down the backs of the doyens in Ottawa. Just prior to his departure, MacMillan had declared to the press that the reason for his expedition was a "quest for new land."[3] A polished researcher and lecturer, who had made Arctic research his life's work, he already had a number of Arctic expeditions under his belt by the time he undertook this latest journey.

Perhaps the encouragement for MacMillan's expedition was the publication of a map in the United States that was introduced in the House of Commons by the MP for West Calgary, Joseph Shaw. This American map showed "all the lands north of Melville Island... as being a country that does not belong to anybody, and which is consequently open for discovery by any nation whose expedition may happen to locate there."[4] Stefansson had referred to this map in a letter to the prime minister on March 11, 1922, in which he cautioned:

> If the Canadian Government needs evidence that the other nations are awakening to the value of the northern lands, I would call your attention to the map just issued by the Intelligence Division of the United States Army, which shows in colors that the northern boundary of Canada is at Lancaster Sound and Barrow Strait, and that the islands to the north of that do not belong to Canada.[5]

There was a new inquiry as well. This one came from a German geologist, Dr. Hans K.E. Krüger. He planned to cross Ellesmere Island with three European companions and an entourage of Inuit, and to spend five years exploring the geology of the islands west of Axel Heiberg Island. He was asking permission to proceed, but his plan to live off the land had Oswald Finnie, director of the Northwest Territories and Yukon Branch of the Department of the Interior, wondering if there would be any muskox left at the conclusion of his expedition. Krüger was sent information on game regulations, and in his reply to Oscar Skelton, undersecretary of state for external affairs, he assured him that he would abide by the regulations as well as raise no flag on any territory explored. His expedition was to be entirely scientific and because he would be living and hunting mostly on the ice, he would shoot little upland game.

These brazen challenges—in some instances, almost attacks—made one think that the Canadian government was still reluctant to publicly recognize sovereignty over its Arctic assets, but it was more than likely that it did not want to alert the world, especially Norway, Denmark and America, to its tenuous

Otto Neumann Sverdrup, Captain of the *Fram*. Fridtjof Nansen

grip over these lands. Better to conduct its northern business with stealth and secrecy. It was Dr. Donald MacMillan's audacity, however, that spurred Canada into greater action. On June 10, 1925, Minister of Mines Charles Stewart rose in the House of Commons and proclaimed that "Canada claims the territory outlined between the degrees of longitude 60 and 141."[6]

Although this was the first time that Canada's "sector lines were endorsed by a minister in Parliament,"[7] the sector theory had been around for decades. It was mentioned as early as 1878 in a joint hearing of the House of Commons and the Senate, by an order-in-council with an accompanying map in 1897 (this map did not show the sector lines going to the North Pole), by James White's map in 1904 (this map did show sector lines extending all the way to the North Pole), and by Senator Pascal Poirier's famous speech in chambers in 1907, where he moved: "That it be resolved that the Senate is of the opinion that the time has come for Canada to make a formal declaration of possession of the lands and islands situated in the north of the Dominion, and extending to the north pole."[8] Although his motion was "adjourned" by Senator Cartwright as being premature, the idea was still very much in play. That same year, in his expedition report, Captain Bernier declared: "We took possession of North Lincoln and Cone Island, and all the adjacent islands as far as 90 degrees north,"[9] and he again made a sector declaration at Parry Rock on Melville Island two years later, the validity of his proclamations lying with the fact that he was an agent of the Canadian government at the time.

Hand in hand with the sector theory lies the doctrine of contiguity, or geographical proximity, as in the Arctic islands being contiguous to the Canadian mainland. A US Department of State lawyer, David Hunter Miller, explained it as follows:

Dr. Donald MacMillan; Arctic explorer, researcher and lecturer. United States Library of Congress

Very naturally Canada thinks of the islands now on the map north of her mainland as contiguous territory, natural geographical extensions of the country. Discovered to a great extent (not wholly) by British explorers, separated from the more southern area and from each other by comparatively narrow straits, though largely unoccupied in any sense, these lands seem to the Canadians a geographical entity and clearly parts of one domain, her own. To project this sentiment still further north; perhaps across a considerable extent of Arctic sea or ice, is less logical but seems equally natural.[10]

By itself, however, contiguity was not a determination of sovereignty; but combined with effective occupation, it was one more tool in the toolbox.

Stefansson had barely completed his last government-sponsored expedition when he floated his next proposal by telegram from Dawson City, Yukon, requesting that he extend his latest expedition by a further eighteen months. He received a rather piqued reply from George Desbarats, deputy minister of Naval Services, informing him that the department was both "disappointed and astonished"[11] that he was planning another foray north without first submitting

the reports from his latest expedition. It turned out that Stefansson
had heard from the survivors of the
Karluk disaster that they had occa-
sionally seen land north of Wrangel
Island. Stefansson became excited
by the possibility that this was his
"lost continent," and he was determined to investigate what was later
revealed to be nothing but a mirage.
In the course of his adventure, he
also planned to take possession of
Wrangel Island in the name of the
Dominion of Canada.

Knud Rasmussen; Greenland-Danish explorer
and anthropologist. Fred Goldberg Collection

Wrangel Island, located in
the North Chukchi Sea, 110 miles
(177 kilometres) due north of Siberia,
is a 2,900 square-mile (7,500 square-
kilometre), semi-mountainous land
mass that was allegedly first seen by the Cossack Sergeant Stepan Andreyev
in 1764. In 1849, Henry Kellett, captain of the Royal Navy corvette, HMS *Herald*,
landed on a nearby island, which he named Herald Island and took possession
of in the name of Great Britain. He looked to the west and saw another, much
larger island that he named Plover Land. He did not land on or investigate the
latter island, assuming that it was the same one that the Chukchi people had
reported to Baron von Wrangel,[12] the distinguished Baltic German explorer of
the Imperial Russian Navy who between 1822 and 1824 had explored the same
northern latitudes. Kellet suspected that there was an even larger land mass to
the west and north of Herald Island and Plover Land. That alleged chunk of
land later appeared on British admiralty charts outlined with dots and labelled
Kellett Land, but its location was "closer to the position of what would later be
known as Wrangel Island."[13]

Next to visit the area was the German whaler, Eduard Dallmann, who in
1866 actually stepped ashore in an unofficial capacity, and a year after that
an American, Thomas Long, captain of the whaler *Nile*, came as close as fifteen miles (twenty-four kilometres) to it. Long named the island Wrangell
Island after the baron. The first official landing was conducted on August 12,

1881, by Calvin Hooper, captain of the American revenue cutter USRC *Corwin*. He raised the American flag, left evidence of his landing, named the island, "New Columbia," and claimed it for the United States. Later the same year, an American lieutenant, Robert Berry, in search of the ill-fated ship USS *Jeannette** of the US Arctic Expedition, anchored his ship, the USS *Rodgers*, in what is now known as Rodger's Harbor, for several days. He completed a rudimentary survey of the island, but beyond that America did nothing more to secure its sovereign interest. In the days of yore, this would have been an adequate determination of sovereignty, but times had changed and under international law, occupation (effective occupation) and administration had now become a requirement to claim new land. So, in 1911, when a Russian hydrographic survey expedition aboard the Russian icebreakers *Taymyr* and *Vaygach* landed on the island, which was within spitting distance of the motherland, and erected a navigational beacon on its southwest coast, it was somewhat of a foregone conclusion that Russia would eventually claim it as its own.

Three years later, the marooned survivors of the *Karluk* eked out a meagre existence on the island between February and September of 1914 while awaiting rescue. Despite the privations they suffered there, the party acknowledged Dominion Day on July 1, erecting a flag in celebration. Years later, this simple act, which was later acknowledged to have no meaning other than the recognition of a special day, had considerably more significance to Stefansson who considered it an act of Canadian sovereignty. Although the czarist government officially claimed the island for the Russian empire two years later, it only conducted its claim through diplomatic channels, so Russian sovereignty over the island was virtually unknown to the public, including Stefansson.

Therefore, not knowing that Russia had made a claim, Stefansson still believed, conveniently, that of all the nations that had seen the island, Captain Kellett's was the one that had the most credence even though he had only sighted it and never actually set foot on it, explored it or surveyed it. Stefansson wrote to Loring Christie, legal advisor to the Department of External Affairs, on September 25, 1920, noting that "no country has made any formal claim to

---

*   The USS *Jeanette*, a prisoner of the pack ice for two years, drifted helplessly until it was eventually released, but became trapped again and was crushed and sank on June 13, 1881, 300 nautical miles (556 kilometres) north of the Siberian coast. All thirty-three crew members escaped, but eight died while sailing in a small cutter toward the coast and a further twelve after reaching land. Eventually, wreckage from the *Jeanette* was found as far away as Greenland and the Svalbard Archipelago.

Wrangel Island. The right of discovery is with Great Britain, dating from 1849–1850."[14] Stefansson must have suspected that for Canada to claim the island was a long shot, given its distance from the Canadian Arctic and its close proximity to Russia, but it was the ideal bait to entice the Canadian government to fund another expedition north so that he could resume the search for his "lost continent."

A few months earlier, Stefansson had managed to excite Prime Minister Borden with the idea that Wrangel Island would be a valuable and strategic asset to add to Canada's already enormous Arctic holdings, but Borden's hands were tied when his government fell to Arthur Meighen's Progressive Conservative party on July 10, 1920. Not one to give up, Stefansson approached the new government regarding the importance of Wrangel Island and again received a welcome ear. The danger here was later expressed by Joseph Pope, undersecretary of state for External Affairs, in a memo to the prime minister. He wrote that sovereignty over Wrangel Island "could only result in weakening our legitimate claims to the Arctic islands contiguous to our own territory, for if we can go so far afield as Wrangel to take possession of islands, unconnected to Canada, what is there to prevent the United States or any other power, laying claim to islands far from their shores but adjacent to our own?"[15] Canada's claim to its Arctic possessions was still far too fragile to risk an international challenge of that sort.

Stefansson, of course, was having none of that. He believed that Canada "must enjoy freedom of movement in the Arctic."[16] While holding that belief, he cautioned Prime Minister Meighen's Advisory Technical Board that the Dane Knud Rasmussen, who was also perhaps planning to enjoy the same freedom, was organizing a five-year semi-commercial venture to establish trading stations in the Canadian Arctic Archipelago, as well as populate strategic areas with "Danish Eskimos,"[17] who would likely kill vast numbers of muskox. In addition to the obvious sovereign threat, the Canadian government feared for the integrity of the muskox herds, which on Ellesmere Island had been systematically decimated over the years by the Greenland Inughuit for their hides, which were prized for clothing and bedding. It just so happened that the Inuit name for Ellesmere was *Umingmak Nuna*, meaning "Land of Muskox." The Inughuit were not entirely to blame; Dr. Donald MacMillan shared some of it. MacMillan had led the ill-fated Crocker Land Expedition (1913–1917), whose purpose was to follow up on Robert Peary's supposed sighting of an island in the Polar Basin, which he had named Crocker Land after the youngest son of his expedition's financier, Charles Crocker. MacMillan had camped at Etah in northern Greenland, and for the next four years, after the expedition had become stranded, relied on Ellesmere muskox for sustenance. It was all for naught, however, when Peary's Crocker Land appeared to be nothing but a figment of his imagination.

Evidence that this hunting practice continued was offered by the American whaler Captain George Comer, who appeared before a Royal Commission in Ottawa on January 24, 1920, where he offered that he had been to Knud Rasmussen's trading post at Thule in Greenland and had seen 150 dried muskox skins[18] that had been obtained from Ellesmere Island. Robert Peary, during the decade in which he sought the North Pole, had rewarded those Greenland Inughuit who assisted him with guns, ammunition and other western goods, which significantly enhanced the ease with which they secured these animals. Muskox were protected under the Northwest Game Act, which was amended on September 20, 1917, from an earlier iteration to prohibit hunting of muskox except

by Indians, Eskimos or half-breeds who are *bone fide* inhabitants of the Northwest Territories but only when they are in actual need of the meat of such musk-ox to prevent starvation. No person shall at any time trade or traffic in musk-ox, or any part thereof, and the possession of the skins of such musk-ox by any other person than the said Indians, Eskimos or half-breeds shall constitute an offence.[19]

Unfortunately, enforcement was sorely lacking; few, if any, paid it heed, but without the watchful eye of the RCMP, it would have been almost impossible to enforce these amendments.

James Harkin, commissioner of Dominion Parks, who also happened to administer the Northwest Game Act, attended a special meeting of the Advisory Technical Board, composed of the heads of various branches within the Department of the Interior, on October 1, 1920. There, Stefansson was giving a lecture. Harkin asked pointedly if it was worthwhile for Canada to

establish her sovereignty over these northern islands? We have, ordinarily, regarded them as belonging to Canada without any question. I had no doubt in my mind when our dispute with the Danes came up with regard to the Musk-Ox that the land was ours.... The whole issue seems to me:

Are the northern islands worth while, or not? That is the first issue: do we want them, or do we not? Apparently if we want them we have to do something to establish our title; that is, that we have some rights by discovery, although those are shared by the Norwegians and by the Americans. In so far as Ellesmere Land is concerned, prior discovery was British; subsequent discoveries of various portions of Ellesmere Land were carried out by the Norwegians and by the Americans. None of us have occupied Ellesmere Land; we have no population; only a muskox population, but that is all.[20]

Canada's claim to the Eastern Arctic had suddenly become urgent, precipitating a heightened state of alarm over the perceived Danish threat. Loring Christie wrote in secret to the prime minister, warning him that a Canadian government Arctic expedition should "be despatched as soon as possible to complete the mapping of lands already known and to discover any lands not now known."[21] He was particularly concerned about what he had heard about plans by Rasmussen to settle Ellesmere Island, and the fact that these plans were already in motion. He believed that the Canadian Arctic north of Lancaster Sound was at risk and Ellesmere Island particularly so, given its proximity to Greenland. He recommended Stefansson as the natural choice to lead the expedition. He also wrote that it would be to Canada's advantage to "quietly" establish a settlement on Wrangel Island by a "Canadian development company" such as the Hudson's Bay Company, as a basis for a future sovereignty claim.

Harkin released a "Strictly Confidential" memo that in part recommended that the RCMP accelerate the establishment of far-northern depots. He wrote that

insofar as the islands further north are concerned there should be a special expedition. It is considered important that a Mounted Police station should be established on Bylot Island; another on north Devon Island; one on the south end of Ellesmere Land; one on Ellesmere Island in the vicinity of Cape Sabine and probably an additional one towards the north end of Ellesmere Island. If this series of police stations is established it will effectively close up what might be called the front door of the Arctic Archipelago.[22]

Harkin also recognized the Norwegian challenge to Canada's sovereignty over the Sverdrup Islands, but suggested that it was not urgent enough to act, given that the Norwegians had "not established or validated their claims."[23]

Deputy Minister of the Interior William Cory wrote to Col. A. Bowen Perry, commissioner of the RCMP, informing him that council had approved the suggestion to establish depots on Bylot and North Devon Islands, as well as two or three on Ellesmere Island. He encouraged haste in the matter and circumspection with respect to selection of the appropriate men to staff these posts. It would take a special breed of men to handle the extreme cold, the darkness, the loneliness and isolation. The late Brian Sawyer, whose last position was as chief of the Calgary police force, and who had served with the RCMP in the Arctic as a young man, when writing to an acquaintance, retired Judge Thomas Smith, who also served with the RCMP in the Arctic as a young man, said it best when he called men such as himself and Smith a "vanishing breed—Mounted Policemen who served in the old north in almost complete isolation."[24]

Meanwhile, Stefansson continued to push his agenda regarding Wrangel Island and finally received a welcome letter from Prime Minister Meighen on February 19, 1921, stating that the government "proposed to assert the right of Canada to Wrangel Island, based upon the discoveries and explorations of your expedition."[25] But, nine days later, Loring Christie, "on further reflection,"[26] cautioned the prime minister in a secret memo that this would be "very unwise." In addition to the reasons already expressed by others, he feared that such a move might raise the ire of either Japan or Russia.

Simultaneously, the Canadian government was making inquiries through Britain to try to confirm Stefansson's claim that Knud Rasmussen was set on a course to establish trading stations in the archipelago and populate them with Greenland Inughuit. A discreet inquiry from Earl Curzon of Kedleston, the secretary of state for foreign affairs in London, to H. Grevenkop Casternskiold, Denmark's minister in the United Kingdom, on March 9, 1921, precipitated an urgent response from the minister that his government had already taken steps that made it unnecessary for the Greenland Inughuit (Cape York people) to travel to Ellesmere to secure muskox. The Danish government had secured a supply of reindeer hides to send to the Cape York population to replace the muskox hides that they had been taking from Ellesmere Island. He also stated that Rasmussen was headed to London to explain in person. Further assurance was later offered by the secretary of state for the colonies, Winston Churchill, who advised in a decoded "Secret. Urgent" memo to the governor general, that "such a step would be directly against policy of friendship which Danish Cabinet has declared towards the British Empire."[27] A day later, a "Clear the Line. Urgent" memo from Churchill explained that he had been assured that Rasmussen's expedition into Canadian territory was strictly scientific in nature.

During the subsequent interview with Rasmussen, at no time did he challenge Canada's sovereignty over its Arctic. It was suddenly clear that Rasmussen's proposed colonization of Canadian territory, and Stefansson's advice that the expedition was already underway, was a fabrication[28] initiated by Stefansson to promote his own agenda. Months before, Édouard Deville, the surveyor general, who had seen through Stefansson's subterfuge, wrote to William Cory, deputy minister of the interior, noting that

> From the information to which I have had access, I am satisfied that the alleged intention of Knud Rasmussen or of the Danish Government to occupy Ellesmere Island or to establish a trading post on it has never existed, otherwise in Mr. Stefanson's [sic] imagination. The wild schemes suggested for the immediate occupation of the island can only result, if they become known, in bringing ridicule over the Department.[29]

So perhaps it came as no surprise to Stefansson when on March 1, Prime Minister Meighen rescinded his letter of February 19 with one sentence written by his private secretary, Charles Armstrong: "The Prime Minister asks that pending further advice you make no use of his letter of February 19 about Wrangel Island."[30] Within a few months it was confirmed that the Danes were not a threat after all. The government's trust in Stefansson had waned, so it became necessary to consider alternatives. Sir Ernest Shackleton happened to be in Canada at the time to raise funds for an exploratory trip to the Beaufort Sea. If the government engaged his services for a patrol north, then that would mean that the *Arctic* could stay home that year, at a considerable cost savings to the government. And offering a grant to Shackleton would cost less than a funded expedition for Stefansson, since the bulk of Shackleton's funds would be raised privately. Shackleton would also be in a position to transport material, stores and personnel north to establish an RCMP detachment on Ellesmere Island.

Turning Stefansson down, though, had its risks, and doubly so were Canada to engage the services of a rival explorer, for Stefansson considered the Beaufort Sea to be his own private domain. He was well aware of Canada's weaknesses regarding its sovereignty in the Arctic and there was a fear that he would alert either the United States or Denmark to them.[31] One positive effect of Stefansson's deception, however, was that it motivated Canada to step up its activity in the Arctic, and the RCMP became the chief arbiter of that.

Despite Stefansson's disappointment over the prime minister's letter, he had a couple of months earlier decided to pursue his ambition over Wrangel Island through private channels, but continue to solicit the government for funding. With that in mind he engaged four individuals—three Americans, and one Canadian student, Allan Crawford—to colonize the island. Young Crawford was a University of Toronto science student and his father a professor there. Stefansson had specified in a letter to the university president, Sir Robert Falconer, that he would: "prefer to get men just out of college."[32]

The four were supported by Ada Blackjack, a young Inupiat woman from Alaska, who was to cook for them and to make the appropriate polar clothing. Stefansson appointed the Canadian, Crawford, to lead the expedition to prepare for the potential that the Canadian government would eventually accept a sovereign claim, and ordered him to erect the British ensign "in the name of King and Empire"[33] as an act of Canadian sovereignty under the auspices of his last Canadian government-sponsored Arctic expedition (1913–1918). That Crawford did so in front of the American sailors who had shepherded him and his team to the island raised the ire of the American press in New York, which speculated that the state department had been planning a sovereign challenge of its own.

Confusing matters, Prime Minister Meighen's Conservative government was replaced by Mackenzie King's Liberals on December 29, 1921, and just before the New York press spilled the beans on Crawford's brazen sovereign act on Wrangel, Stefansson wrote to the prime minister to press his case again over the island. Being a newly minted prime minister, King was unsure of his position and thus relied on the experience of his ministers. He, plus the minister and deputy minister of the Department of the Interior, Charles Stewart and William Cory respectively, as well as the director of the Northwest Territories Branch, Oswald Finnie, met with Stefansson, who requested that a long-term lease be provided on Wrangel Island to either himself or his company to facilitate his plan to domesticate and raise reindeer there. Stefansson believed that Crawford's raising of the Canadian flag on Wrangel was enough of a sovereign declaration to solidify Canada's claim to the island, and in return, the Canadian government could at least provide him with a lease to further his business interests there. But while the government was mulling over its response, the discourse took a shocking turn.

During a debate in the House of Commons on May 12, 1922, Arthur Meighen, now leader of the opposition, pressed the government over Wrangel Island: "Well, have we Wrangel Island?"[34], he asked. George Graham, the minister of Militia and Defence, responded: "Yes, as I understand it, and we plan to retain it."[35] Finance Minister William Fielding quickly followed this with: "We had it in December, and we have not let it go."[36] A few minutes later, the prime minister himself stated that: "I might say that at the present time the Canadian flag is flying on Wrangel Island, and there are Canadians on the island, members of a previous expedition of Stefansson's.... The government certainly maintains the position that Wrangel Island is part of the property of this country."[37]

Now that Canada's position on Wrangel Island had become public knowledge, the government was stuck with it, like it or not. None of the reasons advanced by Pope or Christie for not pursuing Wrangel had changed, but the narrative had. And now the whole government was coming down against the claim. Not only did the departments of External Affairs and the Interior express their concerns, but so too did the departments of Trade and Commerce, the Air Board and the Naval Service Department. There was no end of advice against the claim if one was willing to heed it. Stefansson, on the other hand, was ecstatic about his sudden change in fortune.

Russia, however, which had caught wind of Canada's—and by extension, Stefansson's—claim, was considerably exercised by it, enough to write a polite but pointed memo to the secretary of state for foreign affairs, the Earl Curzon of Kedleston. The memo stated that Russia had a valid claim to Wrangel Island and requested advice as to whether Canada's action was carried out at the behest of the British government. Whether or not it could be proven that Russia had the most valid claim, the issue was now beginning to foment to the level of an international incident. Prime Minister Mackenzie King then informed Stefansson on March 27, 1923, that Canada would not be pursuing a claim on the island, but Stefansson, not willing to let the matter rest, asked to speak to Parliament on the issue. It was resolved in a private meeting with the prime minister that Canada would pay Stefansson's way to England to present his case to the British government. It would be a year after Stefansson's visit to London in the summer of 1923 that the imperial government would respond. Based on that response, a telegram was sent to the secretary of state for the colonies by Governor General Byng on July 18, 1924, stating that "your despatch of 18th June Confidential. Minutes [sic] of the Council approved 17th July to the effect that the view taken by the Imperial Authorities as to the undesirability of laying claim to Wrangel Island is shared by the Canadian Government."[38] The issue was finally closed and Canada would not be challenging either the United States or Russia over any potential claims made by them.[39]

Stefansson, however, then tried to interest the United States in a claim, but to no avail. His team of four private citizens, which had been on the island for a year and a half, needed to be extracted. It all came to a nasty end when Stefansson sent a relief team of twelve Inuit and one American, Charles Wells, to replace his team of four. The ship, *Donaldson*, returned to Nome, Alaska, with only Ada Blackjack on board. The other four were dead; three lost—including Crawford—while trying to cross the ice to the Siberian mainland and the remaining member from scurvy. Russia later had to rescue the American and the team of Inuit, then numbering thirteen after a baby had been born on the island.

While the government had been dealing with Stefansson and the Wrangel Island affair, it had also been quietly planning to build a series of strategic RCMP posts in the Eastern Arctic. The first suggestion had been Bylot Island located off the north coast of Baffin Island overlooking Lancaster Sound in the Parry Channel. The government was now in a rush to establish a post there, because the Dane, Rasmussen, was expected to visit the island later in the year. The first European to sight it had been the English explorer Robert Bylot in 1616, and it had been claimed for Canada by Captain Joseph Bernier in 1906. It was also considered to be the ideal location for the RCMP to monitor, as Harkin had noted, the "front door" of the Arctic Archipelago. Access to Bylot Island that year, however, was an issue and therefore the Hudson's Bay Company was asked to assist. An RCMP officer would accompany the HBC supply ship, the ss *Baychimo*, but it was imperative that the ship and officer be in place on Bylot Island before mid-August 1921, when Rasmussen was expected to arrive. The officer would then make sure that Rasmussen "was compelled to pay duty and otherwise conform to Canadian law,"[40] thus demonstrating to him that the Canadian Arctic was far from being a "no man's land."

The Hudson's Bay Company had prior obligations that year and could not reach Bylot Island until sometime in September; too late to meet Rasmussen. It happened, however, that the Danish government had just assured Britain that Rasmussen's intentions were entirely innocent, which was a relief to all. The Bylot excursion and detachment were therefore shelved for that year. Attention then turned to Pond Inlet situated just south of Bylot Island, which had also been on the list of detachments to be established in the far north.

CHAPTER FOUR

Justice in the Arctic

On July 6, 1921, Staff Sergeant Alfred Herbert Joy was instructed by Commissioner Aylesworth Bowen Perry to take charge of the new detachment at Pond Inlet, which at that time was Canada's most northerly post. Perry wrote that: "You have been appointed a Justice of the Peace in the North West Territories in which Baffin Land is situated, a Coroner, a Special Officer of the Customs, [and] Postmaster of a Post Office located at Pond Inlet."[1] Perry acknowledged in his annual report that Joy had "been vested with considerable powers."[2]

There was a small problem with Joy's detachment, however; it was not scheduled to be built for another year. It was essential that officers sent to isolated locations have a rudimentary knowledge of how to construct and repair a building. Joy was expected to assemble the post's buildings from prefabricated sections whenever they could be delivered to the site. Meanwhile, he was instructed to lodge at the Hudson's Bay Company post, which also had not yet been constructed. He was cautioned that he was to show no favouritism toward the HBC, but to treat it the same as any other trading company. In addition to the list of duties were further instructions to investigate the alleged murder of the trader, Robert Janes.

Joy had come a long way by the time he arrived at Pond Inlet to investigate the killing of Janes. Born on June 26, 1887, in the tiny hamlet of Maulden, England, eight miles (thirteen kilometres) south of Bedford, he left school at the tender age of twelve to work as a farm labourer. He later immigrated to Canada with his parents and lived with them on a ranch north of Calgary. It is there that he mastered the skill of riding and breaking horses. He enlisted in the Royal North-West Mounted Police on June 19, 1909, just a week shy of his twenty-second birthday, and cut his teeth in the Western Arctic, where he quickly learned how to survive in the far north. Joy loved the life of a frontier police officer and had a gift for inspiring others as well as an aptitude for leading by example.[3] If ever there was a Mountie's Mountie, it was Joy, but he was far from being a Dudley Do-Right, the hapless cartoon character. Joy was as friendly as his cartoon parody, but that's where the similarities ended; he was stalwart, full of drive and purpose, responsible, slow to burn, and had other

Sergeant Joy aboard the CGS *Arctic* in 1924.

F.D. Henderson/DIAND/LAC

attributes that made him liked and admired by all. He was also a man who could get the job done.

His superiors took notice, and he ascended the RNWMP/RCMP ranks quickly, being promoted to corporal in 1912, sergeant four years later and staff sergeant five years after that. It was evident that Joy was already becoming something of a legend for his dogsled patrols and his leadership abilities, so his assignment to lead the Pond Inlet detachment was viewed as a reward for a job well done. It was also a not-so-subtle hint that he was being groomed for a much more promising future, one that in a little more than a decade would be tragically snatched away from him.

Following receipt of his orders, Joy shipped out on the Hudson's Bay Company's supply ship, *Baychimo*, together with the manager of the new Hudson's Bay Company post, Wilfred Campbell Parsons; his clerk, Gaston Herodier; and an interpreter from Labrador, James Tooktosin. Also on board were two Anglican missionaries, Messrs. Atkinson and Lackey, who were headed to Lake Harbour on Baffin Island's south coast. In the hold of the ship was the material to construct the HBC post buildings, which would be located about half a mile (one kilometre) east of the Salmon River, where the police detachment was also to be built. Joy would assist the HBC employees with the construction of their trading post.

Early on the morning of July 27, the ship glided cautiously through thick pack ice past Cape Chidley and the Button Islands, located at the entrance to Ungava Bay, and eased into Port Burwell harbour at 4:00 a.m. Port Burwell is located on Killniq Island at the mouth of Hudson Strait, and for decades prior to this, had been a convenient reference and stopping-off point for ships either entering or leaving Hudson Bay. In 1884, a Dominion of Canada meteorological station was established at the port, and four years later a Newfoundland-based mercantile and trading company set up shop there as well. The Moravian missionaries settled there in 1904, and in the summer of 1920, the RCMP established a post there commanded by Sergeant J.E.F. Wright. Until the detachment buildings were constructed, however, Wright and his constable bunked at the mission. The detachment was essentially a customs office intended to monitor ship traffic and collect duties from foreign vessels sailing in and out of Hudson Bay, but it also had other duties, not the least of which was a responsibility to enforce the Migratory Bird Act.

The *Baychimo* had other stops to make before it reached Pond Inlet, so a reluctant Joy, anxious to proceed with his own agenda, disembarked at Port Burwell to await its return, which was estimated to be in about a month. He lodged at the RCMP detachment, and while there, participated in a boat patrol of about forty islands with Sergeant Wright, returning just in time to meet the *Arctic*, which had returned early.

This was not Joy's first patrol in Hudson Bay. Earlier he had participated in an investigation of two murders committed on the Belcher Islands located just northeast of the entrance to James Bay. Accompanying Inspector J.W. Phillips by canoe, sailboat and motor launch, they arrived on the islands to find its inhabitants in an abject state of poverty. There was very little game there, so adequate clothing and bedding was in short supply; many slept with their dogs for warmth. And the inhabitants' kayaks were so flimsy that they could only be used when the sea was calm, which was seldom. The inspector reported that "their real condition is inconceivable to one who has not seen [it]."[4] Given the community's impoverished state and the importance of the suspects to the survival of their families, Inspector Phillips recommended that they not be charged at that time.

Joy was deposited at Pond Inlet on August 29, but it would be some months before he would begin to investigate the alleged murder of the trader Janes, who had been Captain Bernier's second officer on his 1910 expedition. Janes would become news a decade later with his demise allegedly at the hands of three Inuit: Nuqallaq, Ululijarnaat and Aatitaaq. Janes was a self-employed trader at the time and had expressed obvious contempt for the Inuit, exploiting them for his own gain, and frightening many of them with threats of violence, as well as threatening to kill their dogs. He had also become jealous of Nuqallaq, whom he thought desired his wife, Kalluk. Nuqallaq, fearful for his life and the lives of other community members, together with Ululijarnaat and Aatitaaq, neutralized the threat, as was the Inuit custom, on the evening of

March 15, 1920. It was now up to Joy to thoroughly investigate Janes's death, and if the evidence implicated the three, to bring them to trial.

On December 7, Joy departed for Cape Crauford, where he had been told that Janes had been buried, arriving there on December 21. The intent was to locate Janes's body, which Joy did within a few days with the aid of the Inuit; he then transported it to Pond Inlet for an autopsy. Joy was touched that the Inuit had buried Janes's fully clothed body in a wooden box covered with canvas, an act that he described as "an admirable and christian-like act."[5] Janes's frozen body was then transported to Pond Inlet where it was laid out in the HBC warehouse in a motor launch. Joy performed a rudimentary autopsy that determined that Janes had been shot twice; he then conducted an inquest under his authority as coroner. Joy selected three of the four white men in the area to act as a jury for the inquest, one of whom was sworn in as a special constable to enable Joy to fulfill his other role as coroner. Given Joy's multitude of government-assigned roles, some of which he could not perform as a police officer, it was essential that he be able to appoint others to act in various capacities despite those individuals still receiving direction from him.

Over the course of the approximately three-week inquest, eight Inuit were deposed. The result of their testimony was the conclusion that the three suspects had committed the crime. Joy then issued a "Warrant to Apprehend" using his authority as Justice of the Peace (Joy assumed the role of two JPS),[*] and following that, in his role as an RCMP officer, he set out to apprehend the three suspects and locate any witnesses to the killing. It was an arduous task, since the suspects and witnesses were scattered all over Baffin Island, and it took several months to bring everyone to Pond Inlet for the trial. Once the suspects had been brought to Pond Inlet, they were confined to house arrest while awaiting trial.

The resulting "show trial" in 1923, complete with lawyers and a judge delivered to Pond Inlet by the *Arctic*, would do more than convict men brought to justice by Staff Sergeant Joy; it would also demonstrate, not only to the Inuit, but to the world, that Canada could indeed administer justice even in the remotest corner of its realm. This was the first criminal trial to be held in the Eastern Arctic and the first time that the customs and traditions of the Inuit were tested against the weight of hundreds of years of western jurisprudence.

---

* Justices of the Peace usually have no legal training, so English law required that two lay justices preside over each case. But in the Janes case, Joy was acting on his own.

It was not a fair contest, and even Joy admitted in his report that the three men had little understanding of the position they were in or the proceedings that would pass judgment over them.

A jury was assembled from members of the *Arctic*'s crew, which found Nuqallaq guilty of manslaughter, Ululijarnaat guilty of manslaughter, with clemency, and Aatitaaq not guilty due to lack of evidence. It was Nuqallaq who had pulled the trigger. He was sentenced to ten years at Stony Mountain Penitentiary near Winnipeg, while Ululijarnaat was sentenced to two years of hard labour in the guard room of the Pond Inlet RCMP detachment—although the hard labour consisted of hunting, and guiding the RCMP officers on their various patrols. He was also permitted to provide for his family. The stipendiary magistrate from Montreal, L.A. Rivet, King's Counsel, "explained to the prisoners the enormity of their crime and impressed upon them and upon the other natives present that he considered the sentences very lenient and that any further occurrences of a similar kind would be dealt with much more severely."[6] That advice would tragically reveal itself almost simultaneously at a murder trial in the Western Arctic presided over by a different judge with a different jury and a totally different mindset.

Within a year and a half, Nuqallaq had contracted tuberculosis at the Stony Mountain Penitentiary and was compassionately returned home where it was believed that the cold Arctic air would arrest the progression of his disease. There he was greeted by his young wife, Anna Ataguttiaq. Following Nuqallaq's incarceration, she had had a relationship with one of the Pond Inlet RCMP officers, Constable Ernie Friel, with whom she had borne a son, Samuel, and although she had given the child to her parents to raise, she was worried that Nuqallaq would not accept him. Nuqallaq had no issue with the child, however, and quickly returned to his traditional way of life. According to Peter Freuchen, a Danish explorer, anthropologist and journalist, Nuqallaq's father considered him to be a success despite his incarceration, due to his conversion to Christianity, and Freuchen wrote that some even considered him to be a hero.[7] The contagion, however, that he had contracted in the south was far too advanced and a fatally weakened Nuqallaq would succumb four months later.[8]

Prior to Nuqallaq's return to Pond Inlet, however, and the year following Joy's arrival there, Inspector Charles E. Wilcox was assigned to command the Eastern Arctic detachments. Captain Joseph Bernier was again back in the government employ, this time as captain, not commander. That duty would fall to Dr. John D. Craig, a Canadian engineer who had served on the International

Boundary Commission, whose purpose had been to "accurately define and mark the boundary"[9] between Canada and the United States. Bernier was captaining his old ship, the CGS *Arctic*, after Shackleton had departed for London, claiming that his ship, *Quest*, was too small to transport the material and stores required to construct the RCMP post on Ellesmere Island as well as carrying his own supplies. Although Shackleton offered to make a special trip to establish the post, thus delaying his own exploration until 1922, it was too late. Prime Minister Meighen sent him a telegram informing him that he would not receive any government funding.

Bernier transported Inspector Wilcox north, together with a contingent of nine other RCMP officers. Three of the officers—Corporal F. McInnes, Constable H.P. Friel and Constable W.B. McGregor—were scheduled to report to Joy at Pond Inlet. The original intent of Wilcox's sojourn north was to establish three additional detachments: the buildings for Joy at Pond Inlet, a detachment on Ellesmere Island as close to Etah in Greenland as possible, and finally, one at Dundas Harbour on Devon Island. Because there was only enough room in the *Arctic* for the material and stores for two detachments that year, and since the Pond Inlet detachment was in dire need of its buildings, the Dundas Harbour post would have to wait.

Wilcox directed Captain Bernier to visit Pond Inlet first to drop off its building materials and stores, but as the *Arctic* nudged into the pack ice at the entrance to the inlet, it was obvious that further progress would be impossible. Wilcox then instructed Bernier to forego offloading the materials until the ship's return journey. But since Wilcox still wanted to speak with Joy, a party was sent over the ice to summon him to the *Arctic*.

Following their meeting, the ship motored west, but heavy ice conditions prevented it from landing at the desired location of Fram Fiord on the south coast of Ellesmere Island, despite two attempts. The site was a known location, because Otto Sverdrup had visited there for four days on August 24, 1899, before settling into his winter quarters at Harbour Fiord, a short distance to the west. Fram Fiord would have been an idyllic location for the RCMP detachment. Sverdrup recalled: "We anchored in a little bay a couple of miles inside the fjord, on the west side. Straight back from our place of anchorage stretched a large valley, wide and smiling and sloping gently upwards with grass and moss-grown sides.... Wherever we went we trod on grass or sank into a soft carpet of moss, and this convinced us that there must be plenty of animal life about."[10]

Evidence of tent rings from earlier inhabitants and an abundance of antlers and skulls suggested it was once rife with game, but Sverdrup saw none.

The detachment would have to find another location quickly, since winter conditions were already setting in. An alternative site opposite Smith Island in Jones Sound was identified and named Craig Harbour after the commander of the expedition. Although it was not the preferred site, the location would have to do. Smith Island, despite being located several miles offshore, protected the harbour from moving pack ice, and the close proximity to Jones Sound increased ship accessibility.

The offloading began, including a back-breaking 125 tons (113 tonnes) of bagged coal. The officers worked frantically for eight days to ferry the building material and stores to shore by small boat while the ship's carpenter erected the detachment buildings. Captain Bernier bade farewell to Wilcox and his men in a blinding snowstorm on August 28. The Craig Harbour detachment roster included Inspector Wilcox, Corporal Jakeman and Constables Fairman, Fielder, Anstead, Must and Lee, as well as an Inuit family who had arrived on board a few nights earlier. Lee described this family: "Wandering aft to the sail locker, we found that our numbers had increased during the night and that now we had on board Kakto, his wife, Oo-lar-loo, and their four children: Amer-oilee, a winsome girl of fourteen; Pangy-pa-gukto, a fine little fellow of eight; Bunny, only seeing her fifth summer; and Kownoon, just peeping out of her mother's hood."[11] Tragically, the following year, two of the children, Bunny and Kownoon, would be taken by tuberculosis within days of each other.

Constable Lee recounted the service for Bunny:

It was a scene I shall never forget. The wild, wind-swept, barren valley; the ice-dotted sea far below, and the glacier covered coast of North Devon, far across the sound, shining in the warm light of the midnight sun. We stood beside the grave, bareheaded, while Kakto, his long black hair waving in the wind, slowly and in broken tones, repeated the few prayers he knew. Oo-lar-loo, overcome with grief, sank moaning at his feet. The other children, too young to understand what it all meant, looked on with awed and frightened faces. We were nearly frozen by the time Kakto finished and hastily shoveled back the earth to regain our circulation.[12]

Sadly, this was repeated a few days later with the burial of Kownoon.

The detachment was to be the inspector's headquarters, although he would come to realize that the Dundas Harbour location would have been better. Inspector Wilcox reported that

the sun was last seen on October 25 and did not again appear until February 13, a period of 109 days of darkness and intense cold. Severe blizzards were frequent and during January the wind blew for 21 days without a break, at times with the violence of a gale; a comprehensive idea of the winds of this region can be gained from the fact that during the period of 304 days the wind blew strongly for 221 days, frequently compelling the men to remain indoors for days at a time. The coldest temperature recorded was 51 degrees below zero in March, during which month the temperature averaged 35 degrees below, the coldest month of the year.[13]

Patrols were difficult given the lack of dogs and the fact that the post was surrounded by hills 2,000 feet (609 metres) high. The men had to conduct their patrols on foot, which limited them to about 75 miles (120 kilometres). Despite the hardships, Wilcox reported that the men were happy.

On the *Arctic*'s return voyage, the Dundas Harbour site was reconnoitred by Dr. Craig, who reported that "the harbour is well protected from all winds and, so far as can be judged, open for a comparatively long period, while there is room and shelter for buildings and a good anchorage close at hand."[14] The *Arctic* arrived at Pond Inlet on September 1, but ice prevented the post's building and stores from being unloaded until the 6th. The *Arctic* departed the next day. The men would have to construct the detachment building without the aid of the *Arctic*'s crew.

Heaped upon the beach were the pre-fabricated components of the detachment building, twenty-five tons (twenty-three tonnes) of coal, and innumerable barrels containing food, clothing and the equipment required to operate the post. Just to the west were the white- and green-trimmed buildings of the Hudson's Bay Company trading post, which had been constructed the previous year. Completing this idyllic picture on the rocky shores of Pond Inlet, the Canadian red ensign snapped smartly before an onshore breeze as Joy and his three inexperienced charges set about establishing their post.

The following summer Inspector Wilcox established another detachment on Baffin Island to bookend the Pond Inlet detachment in the north. Cumberland Sound, on south Baffin Island, had always been an important whaling site and lately had become an important trading site as well. The new detachment would be located specifically at Pangnirtung Fiord on the north coast of the sound. Wilcox and his contingent landed there on September 11, 1923, and had the buildings erected by the time the *Arctic* departed on the 22nd. Wilcox, who planned to overwinter at the new post, described it thus: "The site decided upon is well protected from the winds, and a convenient spot on the southeast shore of the above-mentioned fiord.... This place is supposed to be an excellent hunting ground for caribou."[15]

Wilcox and his men barely had time to settle in when they were pressed into service to answer a couple of "errands of mercy"[16] calls: the first to bring food to a starving community and the second to alleviate the distress of an Inuit woman with tuberculosis. Augmenting these responsibilities, dogsled patrols were becoming a matter of routine, not only to keep the peace, inspect the well-being of the Inuit and assess the conditions of local game, but also to fulfill Canada's mission to stake its sovereign claim. Patrols of more than 500 miles (800 kilometres) over two months or so were not uncommon.

In the Western Arctic, new posts were also being established: at Fort Providence, located just north of where the Mackenzie River emerged from Great Slave Lake; Fort Rae, located on the northern arm of Great Slave Lake; and Fort Good Hope, located at the confluence of the Mackenzie and Bear Rivers. Cortlandt Starnes, who had only recently taken over the position of RCMP commissioner from Aylesworth Bowen Perry, wrote in his annual report that "the policy of opening these new posts was decided upon after consultation with the Department of Indian Affairs, the Commissioner of the Northwest Territories, missionaries and other interests concerned. Their principal purpose is to control the native population."[17]

The Western Arctic had not been without its share of crime, and murders there were especially troubling—especially given the small population—but what happened at Kent Peninsula in 1921 went beyond the pale. This case was perhaps the straw that broke the proverbial camel's back, because it was the third case of multiple murders to be investigated by the police within a decade.

The first case, in 1913, involved the murders of two explorers. The victims were an American Arctic veteran, Harry V. Radford, who had been in the Arctic since 1909, and his young companion, a Canadian from Ottawa, T. George Street. They were murdered, probably in June 1912, at the hands of the Bathurst Inlet Inuit, one of whom the hot-tempered Radford had struck when he refused to guide him. H.H. Hall, a Hudson's Bay Company manager at Chesterfield

Inlet on Hudson Bay, interviewed an Inuk by the name of Akulack who had previously guided Radford and Street and knew about the murders. Hall wrote to G.R. Ray, the officer in charge of the Churchill detachment, describing the event:

> Mr. Radford was about to make a start, in fact, the man supposed to go ahead had started when the other backed out and would not go, and Mr. Radford, to enforce obedience, struck him with the handle of a whip, a fight ensued and Mr. Radford was speared in the back by another native. Mr. Street made a run for the sleigh but was murdered before he had time to put up any kind of a fight.[18]

Superintendent F.J.A. Demers, Hudson Bay District, Churchill, wrote to Commissioner Perry, stating that

> it will be necessary to send a special patrol, strong enough to make all necessary arrests, which will be numerous, if these reports are correct. These natives will most probably resist arrest, and it is impossible to depend on local help. This patrol would have to stay in this country at least a year, if not two.[19]

Inspector W.J. Beyts, in charge of three men, was appointed to conduct the patrol, but Perry's instruction to him was far from the "strength" that Demers had suggested. Prime Minister Borden had been consulted and the result was something much less. Perry, in his commission report, wrote that "Inspector Beyts' instructions are to establish friendly relations with the tribe, secure their confidence and carefully inquire into all the circumstances."[20] The patrol encountered significant delays and difficulties, and it was not the two years that Demers had predicted, but six—and even then, the accused were never brought to account. The government eventually "accepted the fact that the Inuit, in killing these men, were simply following their own law and tradition."[21] The families of the accused were located, however, and the police took advantage of that to tutor them on the rule of law.

The second case of murder was somewhat similar to the first. It involved two Oblate priests, Fathers Rouvière and Le Roux, who were murdered in late 1913 near Bloody Falls on the Coppermine River. Le Roux had threatened one of their guides, and both priests were killed by Sinnisiak and Uluksuk. A police patrol was dispatched, and two years and four months later, the pair were apprehended. It would not be until 1917, however, that they would see the inside of a southern court. Two trials were held, the first on August 17, 1917, in Edmonton before Chief Justice Harvey. That trial, of Sinnisiak alone, was for the murder of Father Rouvière. He was declared not guilty by the jury. Both the Oblates and the RNWMP were astounded at this finding, but the reigning sentiment was that the priests "who disturbed the primitive innocence of Inuit had got what they deserved."[22]

The second trial, with the same judge but a different jury, was held in Calgary on August 20, 1917. Both men were tried there for the murder of Father Le Roux. Four days later the jury found both men guilty, with "the jury adding 'the strongest possible recommendation for mercy that a jury can make.'"[23] Following the verdict, the chief justice and prisoners departed for Edmonton, where on August 27, Harvey imposed a sentence of death upon the men. The sentence was to be carried out on October 15, but on September 4 a telegram was received by the officer commanding "G" Division in Edmonton, stating that "His Excellency the Governor General has been pleased to order that sentence of death passed upon Eskimo prisoners Sinnisiak and Uluksuk by Chief Justice Harvey, such sentence to be executed on the fifteenth day of October nineteen seventeen, to be commuted to life imprisonment."[24] The prisoners were ordered to be transported to the RNWMP detachment at Fort Resolution at the mouth of the Slave River, Great Slave Lake, where they would be confined for life, but since this was impracticable, they were assigned to duties around the post. Two years later, when the Tree River detachment opened on the edge of Coronation Gulf, they were sent there to work as dog team drivers, and two years after that, they were permitted to return to their communities. Far from their semi-incarceration being a hardship on them, when they returned to their communities laden with supplies from the detachment, they were considered to be wealthy men.

The third trial, held in summer 1923, dealt with the murder of several individuals by two Inuit men on the Kent Peninsula east of the Tree River detachment, as well as the murder of a constable and an HBC trader at the detachment. This trial had significantly harsher consequences for the accused. The problem began with a man by the name of Hanak, of whom Constable Doak, the non-commissioned officer in charge of the detachment, reported that his main object in life was to secure an extra wife or two for himself. In order to do this he would have to kill some of the married men, and he had threatened to do this. He had also threatened to kill Pugnana and Tatamigana, as they were too friendly with his wife.[25]

The Tree River detachment had been established in 1919 "as a demonstration of sovereignty and the government's determination to enforce the law in the Coppermine-Coronation Gulf region,"[26] and now all of that was about to be realized.

Hanak, who now had two accomplices, Ikpahohaok and his son, Ikialgina, made good on his threat and shot another man, Anagvik, with whom he had no quarrel, but only wounded him. An alarmed Tatamigana then killed Hanak, and Pugnana shot and killed Ikialgina. Pugnana then killed Hanak's wife, who was also named Pugnana, and came to the aid of Tatamigana in killing Ikpahohaok. Pugnana then went to Hanak's tent and strangled his four-year-old daughter, Okalitama, which, according to Constable Doak's report was then "considered to be an act of kindness by the people."[27] After disposing of the bodies in a local lake, Tatamigana and Pugnana went caribou hunting, at which time Pugnana requested Tatamigana's help in killing more people who were against him. Further alarmed, Tatamigana enlisted the help of Alikomiak to kill Pugnana, which he did.

The killing, however, did not end there. Constable Doak and his prisoners arrived at the Tree River detachment, where Alikomiak was put on light duty around the post, which also served as the HBC trading post, while Tatamigana was escorted to a local seal camp by another member of the Tree River detachment, Constable Woolams. Alikomiak, who was not restrained, there being no jail at the detachment, procured a rifle and shot Constable Doak in the upper leg while he slept. Doak did not die right away, and Alikomiak, who claimed that he only wanted to wound Doak as a provocation for him to use his pistol on him, remained with him for two hours until he bled out. Then, seeing the HBC trader Otto Binder coming toward the post, he shot him through the window, killing him as well.

The resulting trial, conducted almost simultaneously to the Janes trial at Pond Inlet, again with imported lawyers and judge, had a decidedly different outcome. It found Alikomiak guilty of killing Constable Doak, Otto Binder and Pugnana, and sentenced him to death. Tatamigana was found guilty of killing Pugnana and Hanak, and was also sentenced to death. Both were hanged on a portable gallows erected in the RCMP transport shed (bone house—a leftover from the whaling industry) because it had a ceiling high enough to accommodate the structure. Both Alikomiak and Tatamigana reportedly went to their deaths with no trouble. Only Tatamigana made a statement and that was to say that "he liked the Police here."[28]

It soon became apparent that the trial and executions were decidedly problematic for several reasons. In fact, it appeared to have been a foregone conclusion that Alikomiak and Tatamigana would be found guilty and executed even before the trial began. An ominous sign was that the portable gallows was transported to Herschel Island together with the judge and lawyers. Although this could be considered somewhat strategic given that were the pair to be found guilty and sentenced to hang, then if the gallows were not readily available the executions would have had to be delayed a year until a ship could deliver it, but it was also an indication of the mindset of those directing the proceedings. In the first two murder cases, leniency was the received wisdom, so what had changed with this trial? It was obvious that the government was now determined to set an example, both by the location of the trial in the Western Arctic and by the harsh sentences it imposed.

Another troublesome sign was that given the gravity of the crimes and the number of victims, the trial was mercilessly short at only four days. But even more telling was the opinion of the inexperienced defence attorney, Thomas L. Cory, who commented before being appointed to defend the pair, that "as kindness has failed in the past I strongly recommend that the law should take its course and those Eskimos found guilty of murder should be hanged in a place where the natives will see and recognize the outcome of taking another life."[29]

That these were the first, and only, executions of Inuit to be conducted in the Arctic attracted a good deal of attention in the south, and there were plenty of cries for clemency given that the Inuit had little understanding of Canadian law. There was no doubt that the trial and executions were designed to convey a message to the Inuit that murder would no longer be tolerated, but the government had an ulterior motive as well, and that was to demonstrate to the world in the strongest of possible terms that Canada was taking charge of all aspects of the administration of its Arctic.

CHAPTER FIVE

Securing the Arctic

February 22, 1924, was like no other winter day at the Craig Harbour detachment. A howling blizzard raged outside, the thermometer plummeting to a glacial –55°F (–48°C), while a stinging wind ripped and moaned about the detachment walls, scouring everything in its path. The men were hunkered down inside, drying clothes, chatting and planning excursions. Corporal Michelson and Constable Anstead were making dinner and the smell of their cooking permeated every corner of the little shack. Michelson and Constable Lee were planning to travel to Grise Fiord the next day, weather permitting, to pick up a load of muskox meat that had been cached there some time previously, and Lee was engaged in making a small stove to take along on their trip. It was 3:00 o'clock in the afternoon and the shack was cozy from the little Bose Cone coal-fired heater in the bedroom.

Suddenly, a new smell permeated the shack. Constable Anstead smelled it first—SMOKE. They all rushed to the sleeping area and saw that the heat from the stovepipe had ignited the burlap insulation in the ceiling and the wood framing around it was already ablaze. Rushing for the Pyrene fire extinguishers, the men quickly realized that they were useless: they were frozen solid.

Constable Lee climbed into the attic with a bucket of water and crawled toward the fire, the acrid stink of the smoke choking and blinding him. As he threw the water toward the flames, he quickly realized that it was too late. The fire was already licking the tarpaper roof. Constable Anstead grabbed a fur coat and rushed outside into the driving wind and piercing cold, stumbling toward the blubber shed to get an axe to chop a hole in the roof that would permit them to drop ice onto the fire. He roused the Inuit and they rushed over to help. Anstead chopped a hole in the roof, but it was to no avail. The sudden realization that the building was doomed immediately switched their priorities. Forming a human chain, they passed bedding, guns and ammunition out the door, tossing whatever else they could find through the heat-shattered windows. The Inuit gathered everything they could find and ferried it by sled to the blubber shed, but the wind caught some items before they could reach them. They would later find things scattered over the ice, some as far as two miles (three kilometres) from the detachment.

It was a terrifying night. Lee recounted in his memoir that "the gale increased in fury. It was the worst storm of our experience on Ellesmere and only by bending double could we force our way across to the blubber-shed."[1] The men were safe, for now. The RCMP officers as well as the Inuit had suffered frostbite, but it was a small price to pay for their lives. It was also a relief that the blubber shed and nearby storehouse had been spared. But the night was not yet over, and more trouble awaited them.

Their stove had been lost in the fire. Although they had a replacement in the blubber shed that had been left at the detachment sometime previously by mistake, they could not find the fittings for it. These were buried outside in several feet of snow. They finally discovered the cracked and bent fittings from the old stove in the remains of the detachment, and although they fit the replacement stove, that night the repair almost cost them their lives. Lee, who was lying on a work bench reading while the others slept, noticed that his candle flame was dimming. As well, he had a pounding headache. Feeling dizzy, he got up to investigate and suddenly felt ill. Stumbling toward the door, he fell through it with a crash. Anstead and Michelson heard his fall and got up to assist him. They were dragging him back into the shed when Michelson also felt faint "and sank down onto the floor in a stupor."[2] Anstead, feeling like he too was about to collapse, rushed outside. In a few minutes the deadly coal gas (carbon monoxide), which had leaked from the cracked fittings, dissipated from the shed. It had been a close call.

In the morning, nothing remained of the detachment building but the smouldering remains of the porch, which had been constructed from stacks of full coal sacks. Fires in any of the remote Arctic detachments in the winter could very easily become a death sentence; dryness, persistent wind and the lack of water offered the perfect conditions for a conflagration to succeed, and the officers' sudden and unexpected exposure to the hostile environment could easily lead to their demise. (The Dundas Harbour detachment would have a small taste of that a few years later.)

Although operating from the blubber shed was inconvenient, the ever-resilient trio managed to carry on and even conduct their patrols with their six dogs. Patrolling west up Jones Sound, they travelled as far as 100 miles (160 kilometres) from the detachment. In August, a new detachment building was delivered and the post resupplied so that the following winter patrols could proceed in earnest. Commissioner Starnes reported that "many patrols were made during the winter of 1924–25, and particularly to Fram Fiord, Grise Fiord, Havn Fiord and Starnes Fiord. The total distance travelled was approximately 7,000 miles."[3]

It was also intended that the permanent detachment at Craig Harbour be moved 200 miles (322 kilometres) north to the vicinity of Cape Sabine located on Pim Island in Smith Sound on the east coast of Ellesmere Island. Ice, however, often made access to the cape difficult, and when it was finally reached by the annual ship patrol in 1924, it was found to be unsuitable for a detachment. The plan to move Craig Harbour was abandoned.

The conditions at Pim Island, however, had not stopped First Lieutenant Adolphus Greely, in charge of an American government-sponsored polar expedition in 1881, from establishing a base there. He was directed to establish a far-north meteorological observation station, collect astronomical and magnetic data and to keep an eye out for the USS *Jeannette*, lost two years earlier. Under horrific circumstances, the Greely expedition lost most of its men to starvation and cold (one unfortunate soul was found with no hands and feet, and with a spoon strapped to his right wrist[4]). When rescued, there were obvious signs of cannibalism although Greely later discounted that, advising that the men may have used human flesh as bait for catching "sea lice." Approximately two decades later, between 1899 and 1901, the German-born Robert Stein, who was employed as a clerk with the United States Geological Survey, established Fort Magnesia on Pim Island and proceeded to study the Cape York Inughuit.

Therefore, despite Pim Island having been used twice as expedition bases, the *Arctic* bypassed its rocky features to drop the building material and supplies on the Ellesmere shore side of Rice Strait, which separates the two islands. The small building erected by Corporal Michelson, Constable Dersch and the crew of the *Arctic* would act as temporary quarters when visiting the area and to cache supplies. This detachment was known as the Kane Basin sub-post, since it was located on the southern edge of Kane Basin, named for the young American explorer, Dr. Elisha Kent Kane, who in 1850 had been a member of the Grinnell-sponsored Franklin rescue expedition.

The Kane Basin sub-post was an important addition to Canada's far-north strategy. It was not only vital for Canada to be seen to be administering its Arctic sovereign territory—especially the vulnerable Ellesmere Island—but also to protect the muskox herds from foreign poaching. Immediately across Smith

Sound was the settlement of Etah, Greenland, which at one time was known as the most northerly settlement in the world. It was an important staging ground for many North Pole and other exploratory expeditions, and it was a natural departure point for Greenland Inughuit travelling to Ellesmere to hunt. It was important for Canada to monitor this transit hub and the RCMP would soon build a permanent detachment to facilitate that on the Bache Peninsula, approximately thirty-eight miles (sixty-one kilometres) north of the sub-post.

Meanwhile, the RCMP continued to conduct its arduous and lengthy dogsled patrols with the assistance of its Inuit companions, despite often impossible conditions. Corporal Michelson discovered that when he set out from Craig Harbour to patrol to the new sub-post at Kane Basin only to be rebuffed by weather. His next attempt a couple of weeks later, however, was successful, and together with seven Inuit, they travelled to the sub-post as well as Alexandra Fiord among other locations for a total of 486 miles (753 kilometres).

At Pond Inlet, Staff Sergeant Joy was busy patrolling now that the Janes murder trial was concluded. Although the various northern detachments were visited by the government ship every year, Joy wanted to explore the feasibility of communicating with the Craig Harbour detachment during the winter. It was Joy's intention to cross Lancaster Sound, traverse the Devon Island ice cap, which had never been done before, and then navigate across Jones Sound to Craig Harbour. He reported: "I left the detachment at noon on March 5, [1925] with Eskimo Oo-roo-re-ung-nak (Ululijarnaaq) and a team of fourteen dogs, together with Constable Friel and Eskimo Kachoo (Qattaaq) and a second team of ten dogs to assist us for a few days in carrying dog feed, to see if it were possible in an ordinary season to communicate with the Ellesmere Island detachment."[5]

The going was smooth at first, but three days into the journey they were beset by driving winds and heavy snow. Where Navy Board Inlet entered Lancaster Sound, they encountered an Inuit camp consisting of three igloos. There Joy was informed that the ice on the sound was very rough; the Inuit reported that they had never seen it so bad. Joy wrote: "We travelled through rough ice and deep, soft snow, with a continual heavy snow falling the next days, and made very slow progress."[6] On the evening of March 10, the party camped near another group of Inuit on Admiralty Inlet, and looking out across the sound, their gaze was met by large stretches of open water and moving ice. Five days later, Constable Friel and Kachoo turned back for Pond Inlet. The Inuit advised Joy not to cross the sound in one komitik alone because it was not safe, so he enlisted the help of a local Inuk, Ahteetah (Aatitaaq), who was busy but would overtake them in a day or two.

Poor conditions continued to beset the party so it was not until March 24 that they set out across the sound, killing two bears that first afternoon, which their fifty ravenous dogs devoured in less than five minutes. By midnight of the next day, they had reached the middle of the sound in line with the centre of Prince Regent Inlet behind them. The Inuit had informed Joy that the crossing of Lancaster Sound usually took about a day and a half, but with impassable fields of pressure ice and numerous open leads, it was going to take much longer, if it could be accomplished at all. Joy described the conditions:

> We were confronted by a perpendicular wall of ice 30 to 40 feet high, separated from the drifting ice by several yards of open water, or alternately by a heaving grinding mass of broken ice. We eventually succeeded in getting Ahteetah's outfit on firm ice just as darkness came on. By this time the ice was piled up all around our komitik 20 feet high, so that it was impossible to move. The noise made by the grinding ice was deafening, and the pressure was increased during the night by a gale from the southwest.[7]

The conditions were impossible that year, so on April 7, Joy and Oo-roo-re-ung-nak broke camp and made their way back to the Inuit camp on Admiralty Inlet preparatory to starting their return journey to Pond Inlet the next day. On the outbound journey, Joy had found these people in a desperate state, short of both meat and oil, a condition which time had only served to deteriorate. They informed Joy that they had been in this state all winter, and had wanted to make a journey to Pond Inlet, but could never get enough meat stored to make a start. The men had been out hunting with no success, and the dogs were close to starvation.

At the conclusion of their journey, Joy reported that they had travelled a total of 650 miles (1,000 kilometres) over forty-seven days, which prompted Commissioner Starnes, who had read Joy's patrol report, to state in his annual summary that "these detachments represent much travelling often in circumstances which entail hardship."[8] He further reported that "the task of preserving order and protecting the natives in the Far North grows with the years. At present we have twenty detachments which conduct their operations under arctic or sub-arctic conditions."[9]

These detachments were divided between four subdistricts for administrative purposes: Ellesmere Island, Hudson Bay, Arctic and the Mackenzie River. The Ellesmere subdistrict encompassed Ellesmere Island, Baffin Island, Devon Island and Killiniq Island. This subdistrict included the Craig Harbour detachment and the Kane Basin sub-post on Ellesmere, the detachments at Pangnirtung (headquarters) and Pond Inlet on Baffin, the newly created detachment at Dundas Harbour on Devon Island, and the Port Burwell detachment in northern Quebec, which was administered directly from Ottawa. The Hudson Bay

Dundas Harbour detachment. Photo courtesy of the Taggart Family

subdistrict included detachments at Chesterfield Inlet in northern Hudson Bay, and Port Nelson, Manitoba (131 miles [210 kilometres] south of Churchill), while the Arctic subdistrict included detachments at Aklavik, Herschel Island, Baillie Island and Tree River. The Mackenzie subdistrict, which was more of a Subarctic district than an Arctic district, included another nine detachments.

With this level of presence in the Arctic, enhanced by dogsled patrols and annual ship patrols, Canada was in a strong position to defend itself against any sovereign challenges, but undermining that assurance were troublesome threats on the horizon. Also somewhat disturbing was Commissioner Starnes's reluctance to commit more men to the Eastern Arctic islands north of Lancaster Sound, believing that the government focus should be on increasing the number of detachments on Baffin Island to control the trading there. The commissioner appeared to be more concerned about law and order than sovereignty, but law and order was still an effective method of demonstrating sovereignty.

In the other camp were Oswald Finnie and Dr. John Craig. Both believed that Canada needed to have a stronger presence in the northern islands to monitor foreign exploration and to keep any other potential threats at bay.[10]

Finnie was not shy about expressing his opinion on the matter, which he did in a memo to James Harkin, commissioner of parks:

> I think we are all agreed that the proper course to insure sovereignty over the various islands in the arctic is to have a Government boat patrol those waters each year and to have Government officials stationed, permanently, on the larger islands. This was the scheme suggested last year but which, unfortunately, was abandoned early in the spring.
>
> Just as soon as the Minister returns this matter will be revived, and if it is possible, the steamer "Arctic" equipped and furnished with the necessary supplies and men to take possession.[11]

It appeared that there was no time to lose, and again the RCMP was tasked with the responsibility of representing those "government officials" in the far north.

Long overdue—by two years—was the establishment of the post at Dundas Harbour on Devon Island. Robert Bylot and William Baffin had been the first Europeans to sight the island in 1616. A little over 200 years later, Edward Parry named it North Devon Island after Devon in England—although the bucolic sweetness of the rolling hills and dales of Devon must have appeared in startling contrast to the bleak and frozen wasteland before him. On August 14, 1852, Captain Sir Edward Belcher of the HMS *Assistance*, while conducting the last of the extensive Admiralty expeditions to discover the fate of Sir John Franklin, took possession of what is known as the Grinnell Peninsula on Devon Island's extreme northwest coast. The Grinnell expedition two years earlier had named the peninsula after its benefactor, an American businessman, Henry Grinnell, who had financed one of the American searches for Franklin. Toward the end of the nineteenth century the name of the island was shortened to Devon, and in 1904, during Canada's second official government expedition to the Eastern Arctic, Commander Low of the SS *Neptune* took possession of it in the name of the Dominion of Canada.

Whoever has lived temporarily on this, now the largest uninhabited island in the world, in size an impressive 55,247 square kilometres, has bemoaned its terrific winds, glacial cold and extreme topography. The latter was one of its drawbacks until 1997 when the American National Aeronautics and Space Administration (NASA), through its Haughton Crater Mars project, recognized that the terrain of parts of Devon, a vast polar desert, closely mirrored that of the planet Mars, thus making it a terrific playground for scientists to test rovers and such, but hardly an advertisement for any prospective residents. The NASA website reports that "this harsh climate mimics the environmental conditions on Mars and other planets. Devon Island's barren terrain, freezing temperatures, isolation and remoteness offer scientists and personnel unique research opportunities."[12]

In 1924, though, Devon Island was still just a large piece of the Canadian Arctic puzzle, sandwiched between Baffin Island to its south and Ellesmere Island to its north. Baffin was well known because it was a popular overwintering site for whalers and traders, and Ellesmere was well known because it needed protecting from foreign territorial claims and muskox poaching, but little was known of Devon Island other than that it would make a convenient and strategic headquarters for the RCMP both to conduct its winter dogsled patrols and to monitor ship traffic in Lancaster Sound—considered the gateway to the Northwest Passage.

The location of the detachment at Dundas Harbour on Devon's southeast shore had been scouted by Dr. John Craig on his return journey from depositing the men and equipment at Craig Harbour in the summer of 1922. Initially, the detachment was to be called the Bernier Detachment, but it eventually became known as Dundas Harbour. The Inuit referred to Devon Island as *Tallurutit*, meaning "a women's chin with tattoos on it," because the north-south oriented fiords on the south coast mimicked the straight-line pattern of these chin tattoos. Dundas Harbour was considered ideal because there was a good site for the detachment buildings, but most importantly, the harbour remained ice free longer than other sites, which would nicely accommodate the annual supply ship. As well, archaeological evidence suggested that there had at one time been plenty of game on the island.

Almost two years to the day since Dr. Craig's reconnoitre, the *Arctic* dropped anchor in the harbour on August 17, 1924. Within a few days, the detachment building and a storehouse were erected from prefabricated components. The storehouse was located a quarter of a mile (400 metres) away from the detachment, likely to prevent any human interaction with bears and as a precaution against fire destroying both buildings. Constable E. Anstead was assigned to lead the detachment, which would only later become the temporary headquarters of the Eastern Arctic detachments following a change of command. He was assisted by two other constables, G.T. Makinson and V. Maisonneuve; tragically, the latter would never leave the island. For the first year, the men would be on their own since no Inuit special constables or their families had been hired to assist them.

During the first year, the three reported that they saw no one as well as very little game, contrary to the archaeological evidence. They stayed close to the post, citing the inhospitable nature of the island's interior and the danger posed by pressure ice in the sound for their reluctance to venture too far from the detachment. They thus made only two patrols that year, both to Croker Bay for a total of 250 miles (400 kilometres). Another reason for the short patrols was a lack of fur clothing as well as the assistance of Inuit hunters to help stock the larder.

During the second year (1925), Constable Anstead described the weather as being "very poor, being dull and misty with lots of rain and snow, which continued throughout August."[13] The men thought the supply ship would not be coming that year and were worried, given that they had only two tons (1.8 tonnes) of coal left, barely enough to last the winter. It was so cold that even before summer had passed they found it necessary to install the storm windows on the detachment building in an effort to keep warm. The previous October, Finnie had written to Commissioner Starnes about his plans for the following year. These included chartering a ship in England to travel to Wales to obtain 600 to 700 tons (544 to 635 tonnes) of coal that would be stored at Dundas Harbour and would resupply all of the Eastern Arctic detachments so that the annual supply ship would not be so burdened on its outbound journey from Quebec. This had yet to occur.

When the supply ship eventually arrived at Dundas Harbour, it was a relief, not only because the officers would be warm during the following winter, but also because the ship represented their only link to the outside world. The annual supply ship was not only vital to the physical well-being of the officers, but also to their mental health. The complete isolation and other related privations that the men endured would break the most hardy if they were not prepared for it, thus the RCMP's rigorous circumspection with respect to anyone assigned to or requesting far-north service. As well, there was no two-way radio at the detachment, so letters from home and world news were anticipated highlights, as were conversations with the Arctic's crew. The ship also relocated an Inuit family from Craig Harbour to the detachment to assist the young constables with making and mending their winter clothing, with hunting, and conducting their extensive dogsled patrols.

The year 1925 was pivotal for challenges to Canadian sovereignty in the Eastern Arctic. In March 1925, the Norwegian government, represented by Acting Consul General S. Steckmest, made a polite inquiry to the secretary of state for external affairs regarding the Sverdrup Islands. His communiqué stated that a recent Canadian report had mentioned the Sverdrup Islands, which had been visited and mapped by a Norwegian, Otto Sverdrup, between 1899 and 1902 while wintering aboard his ship, *Fram*. Sverdrup had named three major islands after his benefactors, members of the beer-brewing Ringnes family, Ellef Ringnes and Amund Ringnes, and after the brewery's financial director, Axel Heiberg. The report that they referred to happened to be Dr. Craig's log of his 1922 government expedition. The communiqué stated that "the Norwegian Government have instructed me to apply to the usual kind assistance of the Canadian Department of External Affairs at Ottawa in order to be informed as to whether the Canadian Government contend that said islands belong to the Dominion of Canada, and, if so, on what basis such claim of sovereignty is founded."[14] He further stated that the reason he was asking was for the "orientation of my Government."[15]

Two weeks later, Captain Bernier, who together with James White, then a technical advisor with the Department of Justice, were asked for their opinions about the Norwegian inquiry by Finnie, who had been forwarded the Norwegian correspondence by William Cory, the deputy minister of the interior.[16] Bernier wrote that Otto Sverdrup had visited the eponymous group of islands but had failed to claim them for Norway. Sverdrup's own account of his expedition recorded several instances where the Norwegian flag had been raised, but none were considered to be possession ceremonies.[17] However, in his account of his expedition, he wrote: "An approximate area of one hundred thousand square miles had been explored and, in the name of the Norwegian King, taken possession of."[18]

Bernier also noted that during his 1906-1907 expedition, on August 12, 1907, he had instructed his second officer to "land a record and official document at King Edward Point, about four miles south of Craig Harbour, thereby taking possession of the following: Lincoln Land, Grennell Land, Grant Land, Ellesmere Land, Axel Eiberg Island, Amund Ringnes Island, Allef Ringnes Island, North Cornwall, Finlay Island, Graham Land, Table Island, also all adjacent islands to Ellesmere Island."[19] Bernier then mentioned that Stefansson had taken possession of the Sverdrup Islands, but it was later revealed that he had only visited Ellef Ringnes, Amund Ringnes and King Christian Islands, never actually raising the flag or conducting a ceremony to take possession of them in the name of the Dominion of Canada.[20]

White also wrote to Finnie, his extensive memo noting that he had

> omitted all reference to any acts of taking possession of Ringnes Islands by Stefansson, because I regard such acts as being in derogation of Canada's title as set forth in my memo. To raise the Canadian flag subsequent to discovery by Sverdrup was a tacit admission that our title was defective; whereas, I have endeavoured to state a claim to the effect that these islands, though undiscovered, were our possessions both by contiguity and as forming part of the Canadian archipelago.[21]

He further stated that "the Canadian Government has established posts on Ellesmere, Devon and Baffin islands in the eastern portion of the archipelago and at other points in the western portion of the area, those posts being so placed as to dominate the whole of the archipelago, thus furnishing all the control required to maintain its title."[22]

White was buoyed by the fact that

> Norway, during a period of one-quarter of a century has neither planted "settlements or military posts" nor has she kept her claim alive "by local acts showing an intention of continual claim."
>
> Again, Norway has not made a "public assertion of ownership" nor has she carried out "further exploration" nor has she made "temporary lodgements in the country" whereas Canada has made definite claims of ownership without protest or opposition.[23]

White also noted that Axel Heiberg Island was only six geographical miles (ten kilometres) from Ellesmere Island, which had been taken possession of seventy-five years earlier by a British naval expedition. Amund Ringnes and Ellef Ringnes Islands were eight and twenty-five miles (thirteen and forty kilometres) respectively from Cornwall Island, which had been claimed by Britain in 1853, and King Christian Island was only twenty-five miles (forty kilometres) from Finlay Island, which had also been claimed by Britain in 1853. White also informed Finnie that "with the exception of Heiberg, Ringnes, Meighen,

Borden, Brock and some smaller islands, all the known insular areas in the Canadian Arctic Archipelago were discovered and formally taken possession by British commissioned navigators from a century to three-quarters of a century ago and such acts of possession were formally announced to the world in British Government blue-books."[24]

Despite their lack of effective occupation of the Sverdrup Islands, the Norwegians had accomplished what they set out to do with their simple but polite request for information. They probably knew that their seemingly innocent appeal, however insubstantial, would stir the passions of a Canadian government still insecure about its northern claims. Were the Norwegians seriously considering a run at the Sverdrup Islands or was this a clever ploy to leverage for something else? The story would unfold over the next few years with the real goal of the Norwegian government eventually being revealed.

While Canada was in the midst of dealing with the Norwegian inquiry, an old menace popped up. Dr. Donald MacMillan was returning to his old stomping grounds. That he appeared not only to be oblivious to Canadian laws—having broken Canada's game laws during his 1923 expedition—but also posed a threat to Canadian sovereignty, was alarming. He was not to be trusted. His brash statements to the press generated a headline in the *Montreal Gazette* on April 11, 1925, that proclaimed: "MacMillan Will Endeavour to Find Arctic Continent." And two months later, the *New York Times* reflected his bombast with the following piece:

> While the activities of MacMillan are to be multifarious, the discovery of land north of Alaska which could be claimed as American territory would stand out as his greatest achievement.... Perhaps the new land could never be used, not even for an aeronautical station between the North American continent and Japan, but geographers would be no less elated than the plain American. The North Pole is ours (if we want it) by virtue of Peary's planting the national colours. Why shouldn't the land that has been indicated by peculiar ice formations seen in the polar sea, by significant tidal variations, and by the sight of birds nests and eggs in the drift that comes from somewhere in the unchartered [uncharted] space, be found and claimed by Americans?[25]

This mythical continent was not a new idea: first Peary, then Stefansson, and now MacMillan.

MacMillan's use of the press was effective, while Canada's attitude toward the same reflected its unease with any public discussion of its sovereign rights in the Arctic, and therefore it had refused to budge from one of outright caution. Its semi-secretive policy with respect to its northern plans and activity had served it well in the past, but then Finnie wrote to Roy A. Gibson, acting commissioner of the Northwest Territories, stating that "we read so much in the American and Canadian press of the MacMillan, the Amundsen and other foreign expeditions that the world at large will begin to think that Canada possesses no part whatever of the Arctic archipelago."[26] Earlier, Gibson had advised Finnie that Charles Stewart, the minister of the interior, was of the opinion that an order-in-council should be passed declaring publicly that "Canada claims the northern islands as Canadian or British Possessions."[27] Canada's tight-lipped attitude was about to change. Initially, Gibson objected to the free flow of information, but eventually relented. It was still hard to let go, however, for any press releases would still be controlled and vetted by the Northwest Territories and Yukon Branch of the Department of the Interior.

Some events, of course, were just too important for Canada to remain silent about. That MacMillan was being accompanied by a United States naval aviation unit, which lent a "quasi-official status"[28] to the expedition, was one. And leading that unit was none other than the indomitable Lieutenant-Commander Richard E. Byrd, a man well versed in risk and adventure. His participation and knowledge of the expedition was brought into sharp focus by John Wilson, assistant director, Royal Canadian Air Force. Wilson had paid Byrd a visit in Washington, DC—they had become acquainted during World War I in Sydney, Nova Scotia—where Byrd mentioned that it was the navy that had instigated the request to partner with MacMillan, not the other way around. Wilson wrote in his report that "Captain MacMillan, for his own reasons, has persistently refused to recognize the jurisdiction of the Canadian authorities in the North. The US Naval Air Service, unfortunately, have looked to him [MacMillan] for most of their advice and it is evident that he has not been quite frank with them as to the situation existing in the North."[29] MacMillan was probably unaware that William Cory had also met with Byrd and had been assured by him that "no expedition would go forward without the approval of the Canadian Government."[30] Byrd was obviously speaking for himself and not for MacMillan, who was keeping any talk of permits under wraps.

MacMillan's initial plan was to travel to the Kane Basin and use Ellesmere Island as a base before flying to Axel Heiberg Island. From there he would explore, by air, any new land to the west, which he would presumably claim for the United States. Given MacMillan's plans, Dr. Craig was becoming anxious that Canada still did not have a permanent presence at Cape Sabine or any presence at Bache Peninsula, both of which were in the vicinity of MacMillan's anticipated expedition route. He was also concerned that Commissioner Starnes continued to believe that Canada had no need for a detachment that far north, but Craig was of the opinion that more pressure should be made to bear on the authorities to promote a post at either location and that an agreement with the RCMP should be sought to that effect.

Inspector Wilcox was in full agreement because he, too, believed that such a post was vital. It was becoming all the more so given that MacMillan had yet to apply for any permits or licences to enter Canadian territory. Ditto that for Hans Krüger, although that was understandable given that his expedition had been temporarily delayed due to problems with his sponsor. Finnie read in the *Montreal Gazette* that MacMillan had sought permits from the Danish government to explore Viking settlements in Greenland. Why then hadn't he applied for Canadian permits, he wondered? Finnie fired off a memo to Gibson, using language that spoke of his frustration: "It should be further pointed out that this permission should be secured before Canadian territory is invaded."[31] He suggested that the secretary of state for foreign affairs should send memos to the secretaries of state for the US and Berlin.

Meanwhile, Knud Rasmussen was rattling Finnie's cage, demanding to know why the Canadian government was permitting MacMillan to enter the Canadian Arctic when his stated aim was to discover new land, while he had only been permitted to enter after agreeing, in writing, that he would not trample on Canadian sovereign rights in the north. Although Rasmussen and MacMillan's actions were concerning, the Norwegian inquiry, despite Finnie characterizing it as "mild," still needed addressing: Why did Canada feel that it had ownership of Axel Heiberg Island, among other questions, Norway was asking? One thing the inquiry did was to spur the interest of Oscar Skelton, much to Finnie's relief[32]—someone else to share the load with. After conferring with Minister of the Interior Charles Stewart, Finnie suggested the formation of a special committee, to be called the Northern Advisory Board, to bring several minds to focus on the complicated and international nature of the issues facing Canada in the north. The board's first meeting, held on April 23, 1925, was to discuss the American interloper, MacMillan.

James White, who was one of the board members, was asked to speak to the issue. He believed that were MacMillan to discover new land west of Axel Heiberg Island, Canada would "have considerable trouble in establishing title thereto."[33] He was of the opinion that the right of possession would not lapse as quickly in "inaccessible territory" such as the Arctic as it would in a temperate zone, and that there was no definite period after which the right would lapse. "The effect of measures of control, of contiguity and of settlement must be given very much greater weight that would normally be attached to similar measures in more temperate and habitable regions,"[34] he wrote. That spelled trouble for Canada were new land to be discovered.

White was also queried about how much territory one RCMP post could protect, his response being that one post per island would be sufficient. White returned to his office to prepare a written account of the issue. His memo ran to fourteen pages, a verbosity he was well known for. But it was a memo that "secured White's position as one of Finnie's most valued advisors and, as it turned out, provided the framework for Canada's new Arctic policy."[35]

Attached were two maps, the first showing "British, American and Norwegian discoveries in the archipelago plus the planned route of and flights by the MacMillan expedition."[36] MacMillan's route and flights were based on a National Geographic map that had been published in the *Washington Post* on May 12, 1925. The second map, showing "Explorations in Northern Canada," was the same map that had been prepared in 1904 by a much younger White. It showed the exploration routes of various explorers as well as Canada's Arctic Archipelago neatly sandwiched between eastern and western meridians that ran all the way to the North Pole: an artful display of the sector theory. White now enhanced the map by adding Stefansson's explorations and discoveries and stated rather clearly in his memo that "there can only be one discovery of an island."[37] He noted that Ellesmere Island had first been visited by the British over three centuries earlier.

On May 13, 1925, the Northern Advisory Board met for the second time. Over the three weeks since its inaugural meeting, its membership had swelled considerably, suggesting the importance and urgency of the MacMillan issue. A subcommittee had prepared a draft memo—based on one that White had earlier sent to Skelton[38]—that Skelton reworked before forwarding it on to the

British ambassador in Washington, who was to make representations to Frank B. Kellogg, the American secretary of state.

Kellogg responded close to a month later with facts about MacMillan's expedition: that he would fly from Etah in Greenland over Ellesmere Island to land on Axel Heiberg Island—he referred to it as Axel Heiberg Land—where he would establish another base. From there he would fly to the west and north—looking for what, Kellogg did not elaborate. That he referred to the expedition as "scientific" in nature was encouraging, but that he requested detailed information about RCMP posts in the area was somewhat worrisome; it appeared that he was endeavouring to suss out Canada's validity to its sovereign rights in the area. He wrote:

> In order that full information may be available for use in studying these questions, I shall be grateful if you will inform me what constitutes a post of the Royal Canadian Mounted Police mentioned in the second paragraph of your note and the establishment thereof; where such posts have been established; how frequently they are visited; and whether they are permanently occupied, and, if so, by whom.[39]

Henry G. Chilton, the British chargé d'affaires in the United States, responded with a frank and accurate assessment of the RCMP's role and distribution of its posts in the Eastern Arctic, but he received no useful reply. Kellogg's response was only to say that "the questions raised by your Note No. 627, of June 15, 1925, and by the Note under acknowledgement, are receiving the careful consideration of this government and a reply thereto will be forwarded when the necessary study of this matter has been completed."[40] The United States was keeping its opinions to itself, but a draft response written three months later, but never finalized nor sent, revealed that it agreed with Canada claiming the archipelago, but did not think that under the recognized rules of international law it had demonstrated effective occupation over many of the islands.[41] Irving Nelson Linnell, attached to the Division of Western European Affairs, Department of State, however, offered his opinion that "a note to the British Embassy on this subject would probably begin a controversy which might be avoided by refraining from sending any note until that mission raises the question again."[42]

Three months earlier, it had been made very clear what Canada's position on its Arctic territory was. On June 10, 1925, the Honourable Henry H.

Stevens (Vancouver Centre) stood up in the House of Commons, and with a recent dispatch from the *New York Times* in his hand, read that "high officials in Washington reiterated to-day that the Canadian Government has not yet raised the question or discussed with this government the matter of claiming all land between Canada and the Pole."[43] It went on to inform its readers that the MacMillan-Byrd scientific expedition, as they were calling it, had met informally with the Canadian commission at Washington, which had asked Byrd if he had obtained a permit to land on Axel Heiberg Island. The very act of Byrd having to request a permit from Canada would have implied that the United States government recognized the island as Canadian sovereign territory, and therefore this would have necessitated it making a decision "as to whether it considers that Canada has a valid claim to that region."[44] Stevens wanted to know from the prime minister whether Canada had made any representations to Washington, and suggested that failure to do so would place a large chunk of Canada's north in jeopardy.

Minutes later, the question was answered by the minister of the interior, Charles Stewart, who mentioned that only a few days earlier he had stated in the House of Commons that Canada owned "all the territory lying between meridians 60 and 141."[45] He had proposed that any foreign nationals passing over Canada's northern territory should not only advise Canada, but also seek permits from the Canadian government.

Although the United States did not formally recognize Canada's sovereignty in the Arctic at that time, nor would it do so for many years, the fact that it had a high standard for effective occupation over its own territory made it unlikely that it would ever claim any of Canada's Arctic assets without risking its own reputation.[46] The American threat was somewhat ameliorated later in the year when an eminent American lawyer, David Hunter Miller, wrote to William Cory asking for an interview "in order to discuss the Canadian claims in the Arctic regions."[47] Miller had some prominence, being a close advisor to President Wilson, and together with Sir Cecil Hurst of the British Foreign Office had drawn up the Hurst-Miller draft of the League of Nations. To have a man of this stature request an interview about Canada's Arctic was an important opportunity. James White took the interview, the result of which generated a favourable article in the American publication *Foreign Affairs* in October 1925. And, if this was any way reflective of how the rest of America was thinking—and apparently the average American had little concern over Canada's Arctic sovereign claims—then Canada was in good shape.

Miller wrote:

> The Canadian claims in the Arctic deserve special attention. They have very recently been definitely and officially stated by Mr. Stewart, and are outlined on a map laid on the table of the Canadian House of Commons. They include everything, known and unknown, west of Davis Strait and longitude 60°, east of the meridian which divides Alaska from Canada (141°), and north of the Canadian mainland up to the Pole.[48]

Although Miller stated that "there is of course no doubt of the perfect jurisdiction of Canada over these lands under Canadian law,"[49] he was at the same time conflicted about the international status of Canada's claim. Although he wrote that his doubt increased with every degree of latitude, he stated:

> On the other hand, whereas Canada makes a precise and definite claim of sovereignty, no other country (aside from the rather shadowy "discovery" rights of Norway to one or two islands) has announced any claim whatever. Furthermore, the appearance of these islands on the map as a seeming northern extension of the Canadian mainland is a visible sign of an important reality—namely, that many of them are quite inaccessible except from or over some Canadian base. With her claim of sovereignty before the world, Canada is gradually extending her actual rule and occupation over the entire area in question.[50]

He concluded his paper to say that if Canada, the United States and Russia agree with the way the Arctic has been partitioned, then "the rest of the world will have to be."[51]

Despite Stewart's public proclamation, MacMillan continued to thwart Canada's efforts to have him apply for permits. He did, however, acquiesce to a small degree. The Field Museum of Natural History had sent Finnie a letter requesting permits to collect ethnological material along the east coast of Baffin Island. Its three-man team would be hitching a ride with MacMillan. Finnie responded that their application would be looked upon favourably, but he wanted to know how MacMillan fit into the picture. The museum's letter was followed two weeks later by one from MacMillan himself, requesting the same permits. They were granted, but obtaining permits from MacMillan to over fly Canadian territory would still be a struggle.

To that end, in June 1925, the president of the Privy Council, Prime Minister William Lyon Mackenzie King, wrote to Governor General Byng. Attached to his letter were two secret dispatches that were to be forwarded to the ambassador of the United Kingdom in the United States. The first dispatch, marked "A", was for the ambassador to inquire of the US secretary of state whether it was true what MacMillan was planning, and the second dispatch, marked "B", explained extensively over nine pages "the grounds of Canada's claim to the territories in these regions and of the apprehensions of Your Excellency's advisors in regard to the activities of this expedition."[52] Buried in this latter dispatch was a statement that MacMillan had been sent all the relevant material regarding the Game Act and other regulations in January, but the government had yet to hear back from him. In fact, it had been this dispatch that prompted Minister Stewart to make his strategic "sector" speech in the House of Commons.[53]

The Northern Advisory Board decided that if the United States government failed to reply to the dispatches within a few days, then a telegram would be sent to request a response. This had hardly been decided when Henry Chilton, chargé d'affaires at the UK embassy in the United States, sent an "Urgent Secret" memo to the governor general suggesting that if Canada were worried about the United States claiming Axel Heiberg Island and "possibly" Ellesmere Island, then it had better declare to the US government that the islands belonged to Canada. He requested an immediate response from the governor general, given that the MacMillan expedition was about to depart. Skelton, after reading Chilton's memo, sent a missive to the governor general agreeing that a "more explicit statement should be conveyed to the United States Government."[54]

Two days before MacMillan's departure, Chilton sent a memo to Frank Kellogg, stating that he was informed, through the press, that MacMillan's scientific expedition was soon to depart. He advised Kellogg that Baffin, Ellesmere and Axel Heiberg Islands, as well as other islands, were located within the "northern territories of the Dominion"[55] and that the RCMP had detachments on Ellesmere and Baffin Islands. He further intimated that the US government had not yet communicated MacMillan's plans to Canada, but that the Canadian government was ready and willing to issue the required permits. He also advised Kellogg that the government requirement for all foreign scientific and exploring parties entering the Canadian Arctic was to apply for permits, a position that had just been "enacted by both Houses of Parliament this month."[56] It later came to light that the US government felt there was not enough time "before the MacMillan expedition departed to determine which island should be recognized as Canadian. Therefore, no application for permits was made."[57] A small concession, however, was granted when the US government advised the expedition to refrain from flying over Baffin Island, which it considered undisputed Canadian sovereign territory.

When it became obvious that the MacMillan/Byrd expedition was not about to apply for permits, Commissioner Starnes wondered how he should instruct Inspector Wilcox should he bump into the expedition on one of his patrols. He telephoned Oswald Finnie to request advice, and in turn, Finnie wrote to William Cory with his thoughts. The main concern was the integrity of the muskox herds on Ellesmere. Although MacMillan had denied killing these animals on Canadian soil the previous year, the RCMP, corroborated by Danish authorities at Thule in Greenland, disputed his claim and advised that he and three Inuit companions had shot three animals apiece. Cory advised Starnes to inform Wilcox that he was to keep close tabs on MacMillan, and were he to shoot muskox, then he should be "summoned in the usual way, under the North West Game Act and Regulations."[58] Wilcox would also be instructed to ask MacMillan about his permits to fly over Canadian territory as well as to conduct scientific and exploratory activities on Canadian soil.

On August 19, 1925, the *Arctic* arrived at Etah and anchored alongside MacMillan's two vessels, *Bowdoin* and *Peary*. Onboard the *Arctic* was the officer in command of the Canadian patrol that year, Commander George P. Mackenzie, the former Yukon gold commissioner. Mackenzie was well aware of the difficulty the Canadian government had had obtaining permits from MacMillan, and although Mackenzie had a couple of offside chats with Commander Byrd at Etah, the subject of the permits had not been raised. Byrd had mentioned, however, that he had made a few flights over Ellesmere Island and had dropped supplies of oil, gas and provisions at Flagler and Sawyer Bays on the east coast of the island, but ice had prevented landing on Ellesmere's west coast or on Axel Heiberg Island.

Mackenzie considered the situation delicate in that both parties were on foreign soil, Etah being in Danish territory. So instead of confronting Byrd himself, he sent his secretary, Mr. Harwood E. Steele, son of the famous NWMP superintendent, Samuel Steele, to politely suggest that if Byrd or MacMillan had not yet obtained permits to fly over Canadian territory or to establish bases on Canadian soil, Mackenzie was in a position to issue them for the Canadian government. Byrd thanked Steele and informed him that he would report to Mackenzie shortly. True to his word, he arrived aboard the *Arctic* within the hour, decked out in full uniform, and informed Mackenzie, who was on the deck at the time, that MacMillan had just informed him that the Canadian government had issued the requisite permits after the *Arctic* had departed from Quebec, and that it had been reported in the press.

Mackenzie advised Byrd that he did not think that could be the case because the Canadian government would have notified him if the permits had been issued subsequent to the *Arctic*'s departure—although the ship was having difficulty with its radio at the time. Byrd then mentioned that he had met William Cory in Washington where they had discussed permits, and Byrd had fully expected to travel to Ottawa to obtain them when his boss, William A. Moffett, chief of the Bureau of Aeronautics, United States Navy, advised him to stick to flying and that he had better leave the diplomacy to others. Moffett, however, wrote to the chief of naval operations to inquire whether the United States government recognized Canadian sovereignty over Ellesmere and Axel Heiberg Islands, and as a result of that memo, Curtis D. Wilbur, the secretary of the navy, requested advice from the State Department. And, on the same date as Wilbur's request for advice, MacMillan "argued that Canadian claims should not be recognized, and asked for permission to claim Axel Heiberg and the northern part of Ellesmere on behalf of the United States. No such permission was granted."[59]

On the deck of the *Arctic*, Mackenzie considered the conversation with Byrd of sufficient importance that he wanted a witness. He summoned First Officer Morin, who was pacing nearby. Mackenzie asked Byrd to repeat his assertion that the permits had been issued so that Morin could hear it. Byrd did so, before asking whether a Canadian had ever set foot on Axel Heiberg Island, to which Mackenzie replied that he did not think so, although Stefansson had visited Meighen Island to the immediate west of Axel Heiberg Island during his 1913–1918 Canadian Arctic expedition.

Mackenzie, Steele and Morin later completed affidavits corroborating their recall of the Etah discussion with Byrd. Byrd was also later questioned about the matter of the permits and whether the Canadian description of the events was accurate. He advised that it was. MacMillan, of course, denied ever telling Byrd that he had the permits, and suggested that he was lying to get out of a difficult situation. It was difficult to believe MacMillan, however, since he was known for arguing "strongly against us recognition of Canadian claims."[60] And, the State Department, in a bit of subterfuge, described the Etah event as a simple "misunderstanding based on an erroneous newspaper report."[61] This, however, was never communicated to Canada.[62] And, confusing the matter even more, it was revealed some time later that there was a possibility that the episode as relayed by MacMillan was true.

In January 1927, almost a year and a half following MacMillan's return, he was invited to Ottawa as a guest speaker of the Robert Louis Stevenson Chapter of the Imperial Order Daughters of the Empire. He had been invited there by Mrs. Bovey, the head of the organization, whose husband, Colonel Wilfrid Bovey, was the president of McGill University at the time, as well as a member of the same fraternity as MacMillan. Bovey, who was aware of the difficulty MacMillan had posed in the Arctic, requested advice from General McNaughton as to whether there was any objection to MacMillan's visit. He was informed that it was fine as long as no government officials were to chair the event or in any way to endorse it. McNaughton then asked Bovey to inquire of MacMillan about the "inside story" of what had happened in the Arctic. Bovey reported the intelligence he had gathered in a "Personal and Secret" memo to Major-General J.H. MacBrien, the chief of general staff, Department of National Defence, and who would four years later become the commissioner of the RCMP.

Without prompting him, MacMillan had opened up to Bovey about the Arctic affair. He advised him that first, although he was captain, he had no influence over where Byrd flew his aircraft after he had been dropped off. And second, that he had requested the Aeronautic Department in the US obtain a permit for him, but it had refused.[63] According to MacMillan, the department said that the Canadian government occupied the south end of Ellesmere Island and did not have sovereignty over the whole island. He also stated that it was Byrd who was untruthful to Mackenzie when he asked him if MacMillan already had a permit. Bovey, who believed MacMillan was telling the truth, advised MacBrien that MacMillan told him that he had sworn all in an affidavit—whereabouts unknown—and that it was the Aeronautic Department or higher that had blocked the permit.[64] Bovey believed that "the American Government had an eye on Ellesmere Land and had every intention of contesting our sovereignty over it, if it seemed desirable to do so."[65]

William Cory wrote to Finnie, enclosing a copy of the Bovey correspondence and his advice that "the whole thing is a nasty mess, but underlying it there seems to be little doubt that the State Department issued instructions that no permit should be applied for, or accepted, on any account and it looks as if the story told by MacMillan (if it was untrue) was to protect their own State

Department."[66] Cory concluded with a suggestion that it "might" be an idea for Mackenzie to write to Byrd to communicate the fact that MacMillan has stated that his comments to Mackenzie at Etah were untrue, but Dr. Skelton, who had been sent the Bovey letter, would have to be consulted first. Cory advised that he would be guided by Skelton but felt that nothing good could come from such a communication. Skelton agreed, and suggested that it would be helpful to hold something like this in reserve for future discussions with the US.

Fully a year later the issue was still percolating, and at a hotel in Sydney, Nova Scotia, where MacMillan had just given a talk to the Sydney Rotary Club, Dr. Rudolf Anderson, chief of biology at the National Museum of Canada had a chance encounter with him. The two had become acquainted years earlier. MacMillan was clearly eager to discuss what he considered to be a misunderstanding with Canadian officials over the Etah event. He volunteered that the whole affair was the doing of the United States government as well as Admiral Moffett, who had stated that no permits were required and that a request for one would be an acknowledgement of Canadian sovereignty. MacMillan even offered that the US government had prevented Canadian officials from visiting certain US officials in Washington to discuss the permits prior to the expedition's departure. With respect to Byrd's deception, it was considered diplomacy on his part, but MacMillan had considered it to be a lie and his assertion of such was what he believed had turned Canadian officials against him. Inspector Wilcox also happened to be in Sydney and ran into MacMillan that morning in the street, where MacMillan told him essentially the same story.

Anderson concluded his memo with a comment from MacMillan:

> He argues that it is foolish of the United States officials to protest Canadian jurisdiction in the Arctic, since by occupation Canada has so firmly established her title, and said he would argue the matter in Washington, DC every chance he had. He said he would be glad to have any Canadian publications on the subject as he needed some foundation stones.[67]

Finnie's response to the memo and MacMillan's comment was to advise that it was uncertain who was telling the truth, Byrd or MacMillan, and that "it is thought that as the whole matter worked out greatly to the advantage of our government in strengthening our claim to sovereignty over the arctic islands, we might let the matter rest."[68]

CHAPTER SIX

Axel Heiberg Island

Although the meeting with Byrd at Etah regarding the permits was unproductive, Commander Mackenzie could not delay his agenda to argue the case. He had a patrol to conduct, and so the following morning the *Arctic* raised anchor and made headway toward the Kane Basin sub-post to drop provisions there. While they were unloading, two of Byrd's aircraft impudently circled overhead. Something useful came from MacMillan's intransigence, however. Commissioner Starnes changed his mind about a detachment that far north, and so, a few months before the summer expedition season began, he had written to the minister of justice, Ernest Lapointe, who was in charge of the RCMP, to request the funds—approximately $20,000—to establish a post at Bache Peninsula on Ellesmere Island. It would be Canada's most northerly post. He stressed the urgency of the matter given that there were several foreign expeditions expected that summer. Starnes wrote that "the proposed detachment will have a personnel of one Officer or Non-Commissioned Officer, and two or three men, and as the stores have to be purchased, and delivered at Quebec, ready for shipment on board, by the end of June, the matter is of some urgency."[1]

Less than two weeks later, Starnes had a positive reply from the minister, his memo to Finnie dealing with the complications of landing the material to construct the detachment buildings at Bache if the ice that year prevented access. It was suggested that the material be deposited at Etah in Greenland, but the Danish government had not yet given its approval, and according to Rasmussen, there were insufficient Inughuit there to help transport the material over the ice from Etah to Bache.[2] A few days later, at a Northern Advisory Board meeting, Starnes suggested landing the material at Dundas Harbour until it could be transported to Bache. There it would be under the watchful eye of the constables at the post. Finnie later offered an alternative solution. The Northern Advisory Board had wanted a detachment in a more central location, so why not divert the Bache materials to either Cornwallis or Bathurst Island and a detachment could be established there. Starnes nixed the idea with the comment that the approval of the funds to purchase the materials for Bache was already underway but had not yet been passed by government. Despite the urgency, however, the Bache post would not be established until the following summer.

Meanwhile, by October, Mackenzie was becoming worried that no Canadian had ever set foot on Axel Heiberg Island. After discussing the matter with Inspector Wilcox, it was determined that a sled patrol should be organized to accomplish this as soon as possible. Staff Sergeant Joy, head of the Craig Harbour detachment, was queried about it and was "very keen" to make the patrol. He advised Wilcox to assure the government that he would patrol there at the earliest opportunity.

To say that Joy was keen on a lengthy patrol was an understatement. He lived for the moment that he could be out on the land, whether it was in pursuit of justice or to establish a Canadian presence on territory seldom or never visited by the Canadian government. Reading Joy's notes, his patrols were so much more than monotonous sledding across a trackless, frozen wasteland. They were replete with comments about game conditions and behaviours, ice conditions and weather, and oddly vacant about the seriousness of the privations that he and his team faced. He also mentioned various cairns that he passed. They were the mailboxes of the explorers who had been there before, and Joy was adept at spotting them and retrieving historical documents contained within, which he would forward on to Ottawa.

Joy made two noteworthy patrols in 1926, the first to pioneer a safe and efficient route from Craig Harbour on the south coast of Ellesmere Island to Dundas Harbour on the south coast of Devon Island. He had failed in his attempt to travel between Pond Inlet on northern Baffin Island and Dundas Harbour during a previous winter given the impossible ice conditions in Lancaster Sound that year, but now he was determined to prove that communication between the northern detachments was possible during the winter months. Joy was assisted in his endeavour by Constable Dersch and Nukappiannguaq, who was probably the most accomplished guide in the Arctic at the time.

Nuq, as he was known to many of the RCMP officers, was born in summer 1893 in the Thule District of northern Greenland. He was still a young man when MacMillan hired him in 1913 as part of his Crocker Land expedition. That expedition had travelled north from the northern coast of Axel Heiberg Island in search of land that the explorer Robert Peary said he had seen, or perhaps just imagined, in the Arctic Ocean. Nukappiannguaq had extraordinary powers of observation, spotting game with his naked eye when others needed binoculars, and reading the ice like no other (it is said that the explorers considered ice to be frozen water, while the Inuit considered water to be melted ice—a matter of perspective). He was also an accomplished hunter and according to MacMillan was always "in at the death."[3]

Joy and company departed Craig Harbour at 7:30 a.m. on March 22, driving through gale-like conditions. Blowing snow obliterated their view of the dogs racing in front of their qamutiit. Joy decided to carry on by keeping the gale to their backs. They made the shore of Devon Island by 5:00 p.m. where they camped, the gale continuing to blow all night and all the next day. At 2:00 p.m. on

Nukappiannguaq, one of the most accomplished guides in the Arctic, served the RCMP faithfully for many years. L.T. Burwash

March 24, they broke camp and travelled eastward, camping that night at a sheltered spot just southeast of Belcher Point. The following day the three split up to investigate the best possible route up onto the Devon Island ice cap, eventually finding one close to their camp. They broke camp early on March 26. At first the going was easy as they pursued a zig-zag course up the glacier. Joy described the surface as like a paved road, and by noon on March 27, they reached the divide, elevation 6,302 feet (1,920 metres). From then on the going was tough. Drifting snow concealed crevasses, some as wide as ten feet (three metres), into which the dogs plunged. Fortunately, no qamutiit were lost and all the dogs were rescued but one. Testing the way forward with a harpoon became a necessity. Joy decided to camp, and the next morning discovered a route with less crevassing. The party arrived at a glacier descending into Croker Bay on the south side of the island at 2:00 p.m. on March 28. The going was tortuously slow, and they travelled only ten miles (sixteen kilometres) that day.

On March 29, the men found a practical route between the glacier and the mountains, where Joy spotted several coal seams, but deep holes in the glacier necessitated relaying the qamutiit one at a time over them to prevent loss. They finally arrived at the sea ice at 1:00 p.m. and made the detachment eight hours later, where they were greeted by Constables Anstead, Maisonneuve and Makinson. They stayed there for three days, and since the detachment was short of stationery, Anstead and Maisonneuve, as well as Klishook, their Inuit companion, decided to accompany Joy back to Craig Harbour. A more convenient route was discovered over the ice cap on their return journey despite encountering immense snow drifts up which everything had to be conveyed by hand. Steps were carved into some drifts that were as high as a hundred feet (thirty metres). They reached the Craig Harbour detachment at 4:00 a.m. on April 9, having travelled 340 miles (547 kilometres) over nineteen days.

Although the journey between detachments was considered important, it was largely conducted out of a sense of curiosity to see if it was possible, while Joy's second major patrol that year had a much weightier purpose. It was unquestionably motivated by the threat that Byrd had posed by asking Mackenzie whether a Canadian had ever set foot on Axel Heiberg Island. Byrd had probably been aware that his colleague, MacMillan, had already been there, exploring parts of the island during his Crocker Land Expedition (1913–1916).

Joy departed Craig Harbour on April 22, 1926, his journey taking him west by way of Jones Sound. He was accompanied in his quest by Nukappiannguaq. Constable Bain and his companion, Panikpah, would tag along for the first seven days of the journey to convey dog food and fuel to be cached for Joy's return journey. Panikpah, a Greenland Inughuit who had been hired by the RCMP to serve at Craig Harbour, had accompanied Robert Peary on his first attempt to reach the North Pole.

Fresh off their Dundas Harbour adventure, Joy and Nukappiannguaq once again found themselves urging their dogs forward on a patrol that would see them cover 975 miles (1,569 kilometres) over forty days. They made good time for the first two days from Craig Harbour, camping in the middle of Baad Fiord just along the coast from Grise Fiord on the night of April 24. But the going after that was tough: sledding through deep, soft snow that exhausted both men and dogs. On the 25th, they arrived at the cape between Baad Fiord and Musk-ox Fiord, where Joy discovered a cairn from Sverdrup's *Fram* party. In the cairn was an unopened cylinder from 1902, the last year of Sverdrup's expedition, which had been extended by a year when the *Fram* became icebound. Joy removed the record and left a note about his patrol.

Sverdrup's record was from his second expedition to the Arctic aboard the *Fram*. His first (1893–1896) had been with another Norwegian legend, Fridtjof Nansen, who had constructed *Fram* to his own specifications in 1892, her rounded hull built to withstand prolonged pressure from the sea ice. The ship was launched in Norway in October that year, and Nansen hired Sverdrup as its master. Nansen's plan during the expedition had been to lock the *Fram* into the pack ice and then drift near to his goal, the North Pole. The slow and erratic pace of the drift, however, motivated him and a companion to leave the ship after eighteen months. They travelled over the sea ice by ski and dogsled, admitting defeat at 86°13.6′N latitude—approximately 208 nautical miles (385 kilometres) short of their goal—due to a combination of cold, difficult terrain and a southerly drift of the pack ice that frustrated his northward progress.

Despite his disappointment, Nansen and those aboard the *Fram* did prove that there were no significant land masses between the northern continents and the North Pole. Nansen then retreated to the Russian Archipelago, Franz Joseph Land, where he was eventually rescued by a British expedition led by Fredrick Jackson aboard his ship, *Windward*. Sverdrup, meanwhile, completed the expedition's planned Arctic drift, which eventually ushered the *Fram* into the North Atlantic near Spitzburgen, just as Nansen had predicted. Nansen was dropped off by Jackson at Vardo on Norway's north coast on August 13, eventually making his way south to Hammerfest on the 18th. Upon hearing about *Fram*'s almost simultaneous emergence from the ice, he quickly sailed the 131 miles (211 kilometres) farther south to meet the ship at Tromso. Both Sverdrup and Nansen arrived back at Christiania (now Oslo) together on September 9, 1896.

It was *Fram*'s second expedition, however, with Sverdrup in command, that was causing Canada so much anxiety. That anxiety emerged because Sverdrup's initial plan, which had been to sail up the west coast of Greenland and then circumnavigate it by dogsled, was thwarted by ice in Nares Strait. He then pivoted to explore Ellesmere Island and environs. This must have been in the back of Joy's mind as he and Nukappianguaq travelled along the coast where Sverdrup had spent the last three winters of his four-year expedition aboard the *Fram*—Sverdrup's first winter had been spent off Ellesmere Island's east coast near Pim Island in a bay he called Fram Haven. The following summer, Sverdrup anchored the *Fram* at Havne Fjord (Harbour Fiord) next to Grise Fiord on southern Ellesmere where he spent the ensuing winter, and then farther west at Goose Fiord for two subsequent winters. After anchoring at Harbour Fiord, he sailed and rowed the *Fram*'s pinnace along Ellesmere's southern shore. He wrote: "We passed one perpendicular headland after another, and after each one we thought we should see the land trending northward; but in this we were mistaken. Westward, always westward, went the coast-line as far as we could see, with high bluffs and precipices falling straight down to the narrow strip of shore."[4]

Joy too passed by this rugged terrain, sledding through deep, soft snow until toward the middle of Musk-ox Fiord the snow surface began to get harder, causing Joy to report that the travelling had improved somewhat. By late evening they arrived at Cape Storm where Joy discovered another cairn—this time with an open cylinder inside—from Sverdrup's expedition; he also lifted this cylinder and replaced it with a note explaining his actions. Just past Cape Storm, Joy and company stopped to examine some ancient fox and bear traps constructed of stone and by 5:00 p.m. came abreast of Goose Fiord, where they camped just inside its entrance. Constable Bain was troubled by a mild bout of snow blindness. The party carried on up the fiord the next morning, and Joy spotted several small cairns on both sides, further evidence of Sverdrup's presence. Then he sighted two six-foot (two-metre) cairns, one on either side of the fiord, that he determined marked the location of Sverdrup's winter camp. Nukappiannguaq shot four caribou, but they were in such deplorable condition that they weighed no more than sixty pounds (twenty-seven kilograms) each.

The following morning, Constable Bain, whose snow blindness had improved, and Panikpah, began their return journey to Craig Harbour after caching the dog feed and fuel for Joy's return journey. Joy and Nukappiannguaq, meanwhile, sledded to the watershed at the end of the fiord where for the first time they sighted Axel Heiberg Island in the distance to the north. They broke camp at noon on the April 29, and travelling overland, made for Little Bear Cape on the southwestern shore of Ellesmere Island opposite Graham Island. They entered Eids Fiord at the base of the Bear Peninsula on the 30th, crossing overland to Baumann Fiord to the north. The following day, they skirted the southern shore of Hoved Island located in the middle of the fiord. Turning north at its western extremity, they immediately encountered deep snow and "patches of rough ice."[5] Fresh bear and wolf prints were abundant.

Joy wrote:

We broke camp at 6 p.m. on the 4th, and reached the mouth of Trold Fiord at 5.30 a.m. the following day. The travelling during this march was of the worst kind; deep snow that reached above the knees on the even surface and much deeper in the rough ice, so that we had to rest the dogs every two hundred yards or so. I had intended to proceed via Eureka sound from here, but on account of the deep snow and rough ice I decided to try Trold fiord instead.[6]

While they were establishing their camp, a gale continued to blow, but Nukappiannguaq decided to explore the travelling conditions in the fiord, while Joy remained at the camp to look after their equipment. He packed light and advised Joy that he would be back within twenty-four hours, but he did not return until the evening of May 7, having travelled the length of the fiord as well as crossing overland close to Bay Fiord. He reported that the wind had been calm at the head of the fiord and beyond in contrast to the fluctuating gale that Joy experienced at the camp located at the mouth of the fiord. One of Nukappiannguaq's dogs died during his journey.

They decided to continue their journey up the fiord that evening, but the gale continued relentlessly, delaying their departure until 10:00 p.m. But only eight miles (thirteen kilometres) into the fiord the wind abated, giving way to excellent sledding over old ice. They rested at the head of the fiord for two hours to give the dogs a breather before they tackled the upland portion of their journey. Sverdrup had become excited upon entering the same fiord twenty-five years earlier, but near its watershed he wrote:

> Here, then, was an end to this fjord also, and our hope that it would lead us to the promised land in the north sank many degrees. It was a horrible hole that we had got into; the fjord became narrower and narrower the farther we went, with high threatening walls of rock on both sides. At its actual head it was as narrow as a gut. The mate dubbed it "Troldfjord" (Troll Fjord), a name we thought so suitable it has not been changed.[7]

Continuing on to the upland portion of the journey, Joy wrote that they "soon ran into the most difficult kind of travelling; deep, soft snow with frequent bare patches of rocky ground, and several steep climbs. One of us worked constantly at the qamutiik to assist the dogs, while the other walked ahead dragging a piece of meat to encourage them. They endured this repeated fooling process, and were ever ready to be fooled again, for nine hours."[8] Between the end of Trold Fiord and their camp five miles (eight kilometres) short of Bay Fiord, Joy spotted several beds of coal, one of which was seven feet (two metres) thick. These deposits and those close by would many years later be identified as significant fossil beds.

On May 11, Nukappiannguaq complained of a sore back, which he had suffered manhandling the qamutiik over the upland portion of their journey. They decided to take a day of rest, which also afforded them an opportunity to dry their clothes. In the late afternoon of May 12, they broke camp and three hours later arrived at Bay Fiord. Joy wrote that on either side of the large river-bed down which they had descended, as well as on the adjacent ravines, there existed the most abundant growth of vegetation that he had ever seen in the Arctic. Along the southern shore of the fiord, rolling hills rose up from the ice, and Joy estimated that they must be teeming with game. Several muskox were sighted. (Sverdrup referred to these animals as polar cattle.) In the afternoon of May 13, they crossed Eureka Sound to camp just south of Stor Island on the ice in the middle of the sound.

Sverdrup had been there in 1901, in what was a productive year for him. During that year he had sledded north between Axel Heiberg Island and Ellesmere Island to clarify whether Axel Heiberg was actually an island or just a peninsula of Ellesmere. While he was doing that, two members of his crew were mapping Amund and Ellef Ringnes Islands to the southwest, the eastern part of King Christian Island, and the northern part of Cornwall Island. He passed by Stor Island again in 1902. His great concern that year, which was the fourth and unexpected year of his expedition, was to make sure that their whereabouts were known in case a ship arrived in Jones Sound while they were away. He sent a party of three eastward from their winter camp at Goose Fiord to build cairns and leave records of his expedition along Ellesmere's southern coast and on Cone Island, located off its extreme southeast corner. He and another member of the crew, making up a northern party, sledded north to map tracts of land west of Greely Fiord on Ellesmere's west coast, travelling 963 miles (1,550 kilometres) over seventy-seven days. Accompanying him north to Stor Island were two other members of the crew who were to put down a cache to be accessed by Sverdrup on his return journey.

Following everyone's eventual arrival back at the ship, further excursions were to be conducted; one to Beechey Island "to correct our chronometers according to place-determination of the English"[9] (resetting a chronometer using place determination was a way to calibrate longitude; Greenwich Mean Time would be compared to local time calculated through observations of celestial bodies) and partly to investigate the stores that had been laid down there in 1850 during the search for Sir John Franklin. Sverdrup also wanted to see if the sloop *Mary*, that had been left there by Sir John Ross, one of the many

Franklin searchers, was still in reasonable condition. If so, he planned to use it to sail to Greenland if the *Fram* had the misfortune of again becoming ice-bound. The officials there would forward messages to the families of the crew in Norway about the expedition's predicament. Sverdrup also wanted to send another party to complete mapping the part of Devon Island that had been missed the previous year.

On the morning of May 14, Joy turned west to complete the crossing of the sound to Axel Heiberg Island. This was Joy's, and Canada's, first visit to the island that had so frustrated Canada's sovereignty efforts. Turning south, the men sledded along the eastern shore, arriving at Bjornesundet at 6:30 p.m. They camped for the night on the south side of the fiord's entrance. All along their journey, the men had spotted bear tracks and caribou tracks that had exited one ravine on Axel Heiberg and entered another a few miles (kilometres) north. Joy lifted a note in an envelope from a cairn that evening. It was from MacMillan's Crocker Land expedition, dated 1916. Joy left a note in return, identifying the route of his patrol as well as leaving a proclamation claiming the land for Canada.

The following day, after seven hours of travelling through deep snow, the men reached Wolf Fiord where they camped at 3:30 p.m. There they shot a large bear that the dogs had brought to bay on the ice. While they were skinning it, another bear came within a few feet of them, which they also shot, but cached the meat from this bear for future use. The following day they rested, but from their camp they observed an abundance of game. Heading west across Wolf Fiord the following day, the snow was so deep that the dogs had difficulty pulling the qamutiik. They camped just inside the entrance to Gletcher Fiord where Joy discovered another cairn and record from MacMillan's expedition, this time encased in a soap box.

On May 19, Joy constructed a small cairn on Hyperite Point on the island's extreme southeast coast. He left a note explaining the route of his official patrol as well as another proclamation. They then departed from Axel Heiberg Island and struck off in a southeasterly direction for the Bear Peninsula on Ellesmere. Joy noted that a bear visited their camp that night. The following morning, they remained in camp because both were "badly snowblind."[10] They reached Little Bear Cape on May 22 and reported that travelling conditions were much improved. Joy decided to travel overland to the head of Goose Fiord, which they reached on the 24th. Travelling down the fiord, they picked up the cache deposited by Constable Bain and Panikpah. It had been visited by bears but left undisturbed. They continued down the fiord, reaching the west side of Cape Storm in the afternoon of the 26th. The following day, on the east side of the cape, they came across Constables Dersch and Bain, who had only just arrived from Craig Harbour to meet them. On May 29, at Sydkap, Joy spotted another cairn with a note from Sverdrup dated 1899. Sledding was excellent for the remainder of the journey, which saw them arrive back at the detachment on May 31. Joy concluded his notes with an observation that the ice conditions around Ellesmere that year were unusually good and that they did not encounter the pressure ridges and rough ice that he had heard others speak of. Game was also abundant.

Ten days prior to Joy's return to Craig Harbour, Oswald Finnie had received a letter from MacMillan requesting permits to collect ethnological material on Baffin Island for the Field Museum of Chicago. He would be accompanied in his quest by three of the museum's scientists. Despite his disappointing expedition with Lieutenant-Commander Byrd to discover "new land" in the Arctic Ocean north of Axel Heiberg Island the previous year, MacMillan was still motivated to return to the Arctic. And although the Canadian government was fed up with his antics, at least he was now asking for permits, despite the fact that they were only for Baffin Island, already considered undisputed Canadian sovereign territory by the United States. Finnie wrote to Commissioner Starnes less than a month before MacMillan was to depart from Wiscasset, Maine, to ask his opinion on how he should be handled. It was obvious from the tenor of Starnes's response that he was fed up with the recalcitrant explorer as well.

He wrote that "unless we are prepared to see this thing right through to the bitter end, if necessary, in so far as Doctor MacMillan is concerned, or any other foreigner, it is of no use taking any action at all, and for this reason I presume it will be necessary to ascertain how far the Dominion Government is prepared to proceed in any action taken by your Department."[11] Starnes suggested that should MacMillan not comply with Canadian regulations, then Immigration and Customs Officers should be instructed to board his ship at Sydney, Nova Scotia, to report on his eligibility to enter Canada. And, should MacMillan continue to ignore Canadian regulations and proceed north without its permission, then Starnes suggested that "it might be possible to give orders to our men to seize his ship under the Customs Act."[12] This would necessitate appointing Inspector Wilcox and some non-commissioned officers as immigration and customs officers. Starnes noted, however, that this might very well blow up into an international incident, and he was not sure that the government wanted to take it that far. Given that such an action might involve the Canadian Navy escorting MacMillan's ship out of Canadian waters, it did smack somewhat of payback rather than a practical manoeuvre to rein in an errant visitor.

The government, however, had a new weapon at its disposal to prevent future issues with the likes of explorers like MacMillan. On July 19, 1926, Prime Minister Meighen's government passed into legislation an order-in-council referred to as the Arctic Islands Preserve. It basically replaced another earlier act known as Backs River, but the revised version added significantly more territory to be administered under the act. In addition to outlining the regulations guiding the establishment and operation of trading posts, it permitted First Nations and Inuit hunters to hunt and trap at will—except for muskox, which could only be taken to ward off starvation—but it restricted "white men" from the same privileges without the express permission of the commissioner. What made this order-in-council very different and somewhat of a global declaration was that it stated that the act would be administered along Canada's previously established sector lines all the way to the North Pole.[13] It was hard to find a better demonstration of effective occupation than the administration of this preserve, which would also serve to protect Canada's diminishing population of muskox as well.

With MacMillan taken care of for the time being, there still remained the issue of the Norwegian inquiry. Just before Joy had departed for Axel Heiberg Island and almost a year from the date that the first correspondence was received from Norway's acting consul general requesting Canada's position on the Sverdrup Islands, another polite note was sent to the Canadian government through the secretary of state for external affairs, William Lyon Mackenzie King. This time, it came from Ludvig Aubert, the permanent Norwegian consul general, who repeated the previous inquiry as to whether "certain specified islands situated between the Canadian mainland and the North Pole regions belong to the Dominion of Canada, and if so, on what basis such claim of sovereignty is founded."[14] The Norwegian government was still waiting for a reply to what was frequently referred to by Canadian officials, and others, as their "shadowy" claim.

A draft was prepared under the direction of Oscar Skelton by Jean Désy, also of the Department of External Affairs, and it was read into the minutes of the next Northern Advisory Board meeting on May 11. It dealt with the Norwegian inquiry in a general way, reserving more detail for future discussions, but it was not sent,[15] thus prompting another polite, but this time edgy, missive from the Norwegian consul general a little more than four months later. What triggered this communication was a story about the Arctic Islands Preserve that had been featured in the July 1926 issue of the *Canada Gazette*.[16] The Norwegian government would persist with their inquiries regarding the Sverdrup Islands, and in diplomatic fashion, the Canadian government would continue to politely fend them off or to ignore them altogether.

At the next meeting of the Northern Advisory Board, on January 13, 1927, the Norwegian inquiry was not even discussed. The meeting was essentially taken up with a discussion of Cornwallis, Bathurst and Melville Islands and whether Canada was on solid ground with respect to British sovereignty over them. Finnie assured the group that British sovereignty had never been questioned in that area. The consensus was that it was time to place an RCMP detachment on one of them. The three islands were smack dab in the middle of the Canadian sector and they had not received much attention. Although they were difficult to reach from the west due to heavy ice conditions, it was acknowledged that the Pond Inlet and Dundas Harbour detachments did offer some measure of control in that they were located at the eastern entrance to Lancaster Sound.

Commissioner Starnes advised that if it was not that important for sovereignty reasons, then he would prefer to establish a detachment there the following year, since he had his heart set on a detachment at Lake Harbour on southern Baffin Island that year. It was suggested that as a start, the commander of the next ship patrol north would be instructed to proceed west through Lancaster Sound to reconnoitre the three islands for prospective harbours— ice conditions, etc. Unfortunately, the next ship north was forced to turn back due to impenetrable ice when it got close to Cornwallis Island, the first major island to the immediate west of Devon Island.[17]

At the meeting's conclusion, Deputy Minister of National Defence George Desbarats brought up the issue of the use of aircraft to augment government expeditions in the Arctic. The cost would be shared with the Departments of Marine and Fisheries, National Defence, and Railways and Canals, the initial goal being to conduct an aerial photographic reconnaissance of Hudson Strait. The government had decided to complete the Hudson Bay Railway, which ran from The Pas, Manitoba, to the northern part of the province at Churchill on Hudson Bay, to facilitate the shipment of grain to Europe, and aircraft were needed to report on the length of the shipping season through the strait. As well, in addition to determining the feasibility of establishing air bases in

Hudson Bay, on a test case basis, aircraft were also to be used to aid marine navigation.[18] There was no doubt that the RCMP would benefit from such a convenience in addition to the bonus of a permanent rail link from Hudson Bay south, although complications and delays would not see it operate until September 1929.

Despite the Northern Advisory Board not discussing the Norwegians and their repeated inquiries, the issue was not going to go away on its own. Communication was now becoming tense, and on March 26, 1928, Consul General Aubert wrote in frustration that "I am now instructed by my Government to inform you that they reserve to Norway all rights coming to my country under International Law in connection with the said area."[19] The Canadian government had communicated with Aubert on October 9, 1926, in response to his September 27 inquiry of that year, informing him that the matter would be taken up when the prime minister, who was in England at the time, returned to Canada. Aubert stated that he had yet to hear from the Canadian government, despite sending another note on April 27, 1927, and after speaking with Dr. Skelton in Ottawa on January 25, 1928. A detailed draft was prepared on August 16, 1928, for Skelton's review that mirrored Minister Stewart's 1925 "sector" press release, but Skelton was off to Europe, so it was up to his secretary, Marjorie McKenzie, to advise Aubert that the matter would be delayed until his return.[20]

Meanwhile, in Norway, Otto Sverdrup, who was not only extremely frustrated, but also unwell, wrote a letter to his government on February 28, 1928, threatening to approach the Canadian government directly for compensation if his government failed to make a claim to the Sverdrup Islands. Complicating and delaying matters, the Norwegian government was in the process of annexing a small island in the South Atlantic, which they named Bouvet Island. Only 1,100 miles (1,770 kilometres) from Antarctica, it was considered to be one of the most isolated islands in the world, a mere spit of volcanic rubble burdened with glaciers and an odious deposit of guano. Having little to no vegetation or animal life and no natural harbour, it was coveted by Norway nevertheless, contradicting the adage that it was only the English who hungered for desolate places.[21]

The island had first been sighted in 1739 by a French commander, Jean-Baptiste Charles Bouvet de Lozier, while on an expedition to discover a large southern continent. A succession of others sighted the island until 1825 when a British whaler, Captain George Norris, master of the *Sprightly*, landed on it, named it Liverpool Island, and claimed it for the British Crown. Following Norris's claim, others sighted and landed on the island, but it was not until 1927 when the Norwegian Norvegia Expedition, led by Harold Horntvedt, landed on the island for an extended stay that it was claimed again, this time for Norway. Norway was unaware that the British had annexed it a hundred years earlier, and rather than acquiesce to Britain's claim, Norwegian parliamentarians met in secret on March 16, 1928, to devise a plan. They all recognized that their claim to the Sverdrup Islands was weak, so why not use Bouvet Island as a bargaining chip?[22]

While that plan was developing, Captain Bernier was giving a talk to the Rotary Club at the Windsor Hotel in Montreal. Finnie caught wind of Bernier's speech in which his ego was once again on display. Bernier declared that he had laid claim to all the islands in the region, "planting the flag on the islands in the years between 1904 and 1911 and later during 1922 and 1923 and 1925 and 1926."[23] Finnie, in a memo to Roy Gibson, the acting deputy minister, Department of the Interior, stated that:

Many students of Arctic geography, including the late Mr. James White, were firmly of the opinion that such utterances, from a retired officer of the Department of the Interior, were injurious to the British claim. His statements make it appear that we had some doubt as to the validity of the Imperial Order in Council of 1880, and that it was necessary to supplement that by planting the flag.[24]

Finnie continued: "I know Captain Bernier is firmly of opinion that if it were not for him the entire Arctic would be in foreign hands."[25] Deputy Minister of the Interior William Cory suggested having a talk with him the next time he was in Ottawa.

Given Norway's secret plan to trade Bouvet Island for the Sverdrup Islands, the negotiations began quietly between Benjamin Vogt, the Norwegian minister in London, and Francis Lindley, representing the United Kingdom in Norway. Vogt called Lindley to arrange a meeting, and within a short time steered the conversation in the direction of Bouvet Island. The Norwegians, he said, had no knowledge of the British claim despite extensive efforts to determine its sovereignty. Complicating matters were Britain's negotiations with a Norwegian company, Johan Rasmussen and Co., to occupy the island to facilitate its whaling enterprise.

Vogt advised that it was doubtful that the Norwegian government, "after having officially annexed the Island, would feel able to withdraw their claim to it."[26] Lindley replied that he understood that, had Norway known that the island had been annexed by Britain a hundred years earlier and that the British government was just in the process of negotiating a lease with a Norwegian company, it would not have annexed it. Furthermore, the negotiations had begun with Johan Rasmussen and Co. months before Harold Horntvedt planted Norway's flag on the island. Vogt argued that Sverdrup had planted the Norwegian flag on the Sverdrup Islands twenty years previously and "that the Norwegian title to these islands had never been recognized by the Canadian Government."[27] Furthermore, several approaches by Norway's consul-general in Montreal to the Canadian government to determine Canada's position on the Sverdrup Islands had been unsuccessful. Now, were Norway to surrender its rights to these islands "on the grounds that they had not been utilised since the Norwegian flag was hoisted, it was difficult for them [Britain] to act in precisely the opposite manner in the Antarctic and admit a claim on the plea of prior discovery when more than a hundred years had passed without that discovery being put to any practical use."[28] Lindley informed him that he understood the difficulty that presented but advised that an isolated island in the South Atlantic could not be treated in the same manner as a group of islands "which might be said to belong geographically to the mainland to which the Canadian Government was in undisputed possession."[29]

Some months later, Lord Cushendun, acting secretary of state for foreign affairs, received a call from Vogt who wanted to express his government's views regarding Bouvet Island following a meeting he had had with Sir Ronald Lindsay, permanent under-secretary of state for foreign affairs. The two had discussed Bouvet Island as well as a couple of other items. Lindsay had advised Vogt that his government was not averse to abandoning their claim to Bouvet Island, but that there were two other issues that he wanted to discuss, and which, he offered, were not conditional. The first was co-operation between their two governments through an international agreement regarding whaling in the Southern Ocean and the second had to do with the annexation of land in the British sector, within the Antarctic Circle, by foreign powers. This latter condition was based on a resolution that had been passed at the 1926 Imperial Conference. Vogt advised that it was unlikely that his government would want to sign an international agreement over whaling in the Antarctic since such an agreement would quickly attract foreign whalers when the British and Norwegians were presently the dominant players. On the second matter, Vogt stated that that matter should be kept quite distinct from any discussion of Bouvet Island.

Lindsay had advised Vogt that, although his Majesty's government "did not want to establish any direct connection between the two questions, they nevertheless felt that, in view of their readiness to relinquish all claims to Bouvet Island, they were entitled to expect, more or less simultaneously, some such assurance that would set their mind at rest on the other matter."[30] Vogt quickly changed tactics by stating that if "there was to be some *quid pro quo* for the renunciation of the British claim to Bouvet Island, such a one might be held already at the opposite extremity of the globe. There were... certain regions in the Arctic circle that were indisputably Norwegian by priority of discovery—discovery [of a date] much more recent than that of the British discovery of Bouvet Island—where the Canadian government was exercising some sort of administrative authority."[31] Without mentioning the names of the "certain regions in the Arctic circle,"[32] it was obvious that they included none other than Axel Heiberg Island among others explored and mapped by Sverdrup. Lester B. Pearson, first secretary of the Department of External Affairs, wrote in a September 23, 1929, memo that, unfortunately, "Lord Cushendun sheared off from this suggestion, and an excellent opportunity to settle the whole matter was lost."[33] Vogt's implication of a *quid pro quo* arrangement, however, was not an explicit offer, and later, when the Norwegian minister in Paris learned of Vogt's discussion with Cushendun, he was astonished, because if it was an offer, it had been made without the knowledge or consent of the Norwegian government.[34]

On November 14, 1928, however, Vogt again met with Sir Ronald Lindsay, with Vogt reading out two memos that essentially solved Lindsay's "other matters." The Norwegian government would co-operate with Britain on the conservation of whales in the Antarctic and Norway would not occupy territory in the areas referred to in the resolution passed at the Imperial Conference of 1926. Professor Janice Cavell commented:

> After reiterating that the British action had no formal conditions attached, Lindsay withdrew his government's claim to Bouvet Island. He then emphasized that the British still attached great importance to the issue of whaling regulations and to the avoidance of any foreign claims in the Antarctic sectors claimed by the United Kingdom. The Sverdrup Islands were not

mentioned, but British officials assumed that logically Norway must cease to pursue this claim."[35]

Bouvet Island thus became a dependency* of Norway.

Roughly two months later, Roy Gibson wrote to Oscar Skelton, advising him that he had read all the correspondence with respect to the Bouvet Island affair, and that

> from the subsequent despatches it appears that it was thought desirable to withdraw any claim to Bouvet Island as an act of grace and to rely on the good will that such an action would be likely to inspire, to move the Norwegians to reciprocate and give the assurances which His Majesty's Government desires.[36]

The issue went dormant for several months while Vogt retreated to consult with his government.

Meanwhile the Communist Party newspaper, *Norges Kommunistblad*, wrote about the satisfactory conclusion of the Bouvet Island issue with the following: "Norway's acquisition of Bouvet Island is thus neither a victory for Norwegian diplomacy nor Norwegian military force, but for the grovelling of capitalistic Norway before the 'British predatory Imperialism'."[37] At that point, the Communist Party had never held a seat in the Storting.

Meanwhile, it was business as usual in the Arctic. Three years earlier, a new supply ship, the 2,700-ton (2,449 tonne) ss *Beothic*, a sealer owned by the Job Brothers of St. John's, Newfoundland, had been chartered to replace the aging CGS *Arctic*. It was a modern steel vessel and would serve Canada's Arctic supply needs admirably for the next five years. It was now gearing up for its next voyage north, and on board was a roster of fresh-faced RCMP officers, many of whom were eager to experience what they had only read or heard about. For some, the adventure would smack them smartly in the face, while others would relish their northern assignment.

---

* A dependency defines a territory that is not fully independent or sovereign, but is dependent upon that state to a certain degree.

CHAPTER SEVEN

Dundas Harbour

On April 27, 1926, Reginald Andrew Taggart, born December 31, 1904, posted a handwritten note to the RCMP's headquarters at Ottawa requesting a position with the force. A little more than a year later, he was accepted into its ranks at the modest salary of $2.00 a day. He had applied two years earlier, but scrawled across the bottom of that letter was the note: "No Vacancies." Following training, on February 14, 1928, he applied for northern service and was accepted three months later after acknowledging that he had volunteered for the position and after passing a review by his superior that consisted of answering "Yes" to the following questions: "Is the applicant cheerful, even tempered? Is the applicant resourceful and handy? Has the applicant paid his income tax to date?"[1] C.H. Hill, commander of "N" Division, recommended Taggart with the following succinct comment: "I consider that this applicant would be a very suitable man."[2] Taggart, who would be assigned to the Dundas Harbour detachment on Devon Island, had previously indicated that he had extensive farming experience, that he could ride a horse and that he was adept at handling a rifle—all positive attributes for an RCMP recruit as well as for a northern assignment.

Taggart and the three other officers who were to replace the existing staff at the Dundas Harbour detachment were to be transported north on the SS *Beothic*, which would depart from North Sydney, Cape Breton Island, sometime in July 1928. Taggart's colleagues consisted of Inspector Alfred Herbert Joy, Corporal Maurice Mason Timbury and Constable Robert Warren Hamilton, also known as "Paddy." Every one of these four men had been born overseas: Joy in Bedfordshire, England; Timbury in Hampshire, England; Taggart in Killeen just outside of Belfast, Ireland; and Hamilton in Castlefinn, Ireland. Inspector Joy, recently promoted and already an Arctic veteran, was sent to the detachment for one winter only, given that two officers had died there by gunshot over the previous two years, one by suicide and one by "misadventure."[3] Following that posting, Joy was to replace Inspector Wilcox at Pond Inlet, who was scheduled to go out with the *Beothic* that summer.

On July 3, 1928, Taggart and Corporal Timbury were issued orders by the officer in command in Ottawa to proceed east by rail to North Sydney for the purpose of checking the stores for the Eastern Arctic detachments that would shortly be loaded aboard the *Beothic*. They arrived there on the morning of July 5, and since the stores had yet to arrive from Ottawa, Taggart and Constable Ashe, who had been picked up in Montreal, had time to take in the sights. Taggart noted that North Sydney was old and none too clean, and that it had more than its fair share of bootleggers and rum-runners, all of whom shied away from the pair, who were dressed smartly in their new uniforms. Two

Constable Reginald Andrew Taggart.
Photo courtesy of the Taggart Family

days later, Taggart and his colleagues began checking the stores that had just arrived from Ottawa, and that task consumed them until the ship's arrival from Newfoundland on July 16, at which point loading began. Loading the stores occupied two days, with Taggart writing to his mother that: "Well, we couldn't put all the stores on in half a day, so this morning we were got out of bed at 4:30 a.m. At 8:00 a.m. we had breakfast and finished loading at 11:45 a.m."[4]

The officers waved goodbye to civilization at noon on July 19 after attending a dance held in their honour at the Nova Scotia Yacht Club a couple of nights earlier. The Canadian Government Arctic Expedition of 1928, commanded by Mr. George P. Mackenzie, was officially underway. Mothers, wives and girl-friends dressed in summer frocks and sun hats crowded the dock on the day of departure to see their loved ones off, their warm embraces and tears hardly dampening the palpable excitement of the young men about to experience the adventure of their lives. Constable Hamilton wrote: "With a long blast from the ship's siren and an answering salute from other ships in the harbour, moorings were cast off, a clang of bells heard faintly in the engine room, and the sturdy little vessel slowly moved out of the harbour and headed north."[5] The excitement, however, was quickly scuppered when the *Beothic* cleared the shelter of the harbour and entered the Gulf of St. Lawrence. The ship was immediately buffeted by heavy winds and rough seas that broke through the railings, flooding the rolling deck. Taggart wrote that "the old mast was swaying from 50 to 60 feet from one side to the other."[6] Three of the officers were seasick, the rest managing to appear for supper that afternoon.

And, as if it was a taste of what was to come, the men soon saw their first icebergs and ice floes, a scene that would quickly lose its allure. The cold soon crept into the ship, causing the men to don sweaters and heavy underwear. On July 21, the ship cruised through the Strait of Belle Isle, the narrow passage between Newfoundland and Labrador, and entered the Northwest Atlantic, where it encountered nothing but the grey, bleak wall of impenetrable fog and endless rolling seas punctuated by the occasional iceberg.

The sea later calmed and the men could be seen relaxing in civvies on deck, taking photos, smoking their pipes and roughhousing with each other, but as the ship sailed north and the temperature began to sink, they instead huddled around the funnel for warmth. Inspector Joy, garbed in dress pants, dress shoes and a cozy woollen hoodie, looking somewhat pensive in his deck chair, held court with a suited Captain L.D. Morin, the ice pilot, a stylish fedora-hatted Doctor L.D. Livingstone, the government medical officer, a plaid-shirted Dr. R.M. Anderson, the chief of the Division of Biology, National Museum of Canada, and a plethora of young RCMP officers who were avidly soaking up the stories of these seasoned Arctic veterans. While they talked, Captain E. Falk, master of the *Beothic*, was seen on the outer bridge, sextant raised to his eye to fix the ship's position.

At 10:00 p.m. on July 24, Greenland was sighted in the far distance, Taggart noting that there was "no darkness at night here."[7] At 11:00 a.m. the following morning, the ship crossed the Arctic Circle, the men celebrating the event "in the usual way"[8]—which most certainly involved an alcoholic beverage or two. A polar bear was sighted on the ice, and although Doctor Livingston wanted to shoot it, Inspector Joy prevented it, cautioning him that the bear might one day save the life of a hungry traveller or even an RCMP patrol in need of a meal.[9] At 3:00 a.m. on July 26, the ship arrived at the Danish settlement of Godhavn on Disko Island, located off the southwestern coast of Greenland. It was considered a goodwill gesture to drop in and say hello.[10] As soon as the ship dropped anchor, a puff of white smoke emanated from shore followed closely by the welcoming report of a small canon.[11] A party led by the director of the Danish Arctic Station, Dr. Morten P. Porsild, a contingent of Danish officials in tow, arrived at the ship by rowboat where they were received by Commander Mackenzie and Captain Falk. As they came aboard, local Inughuit women and men dressed in a mixture of traditional and western garb looked on curiously from shore. A kayak slipped by the ship and on shore a dog team pulled a wheeled cart carrying two large canisters of what looked very much like milk cans. Just outside the harbour, the sea was populated with dozens of jagged "bergy bits,"* highlighting the almost monochromatic palette of the environment. Taggart commented disappointedly in his diary that he did not see any green in Greenland.

The officers, in full uniform, were invited ashore, although the crew remained on board. After mailing a few hastily written letters, the men were toured around the local school, museum, bakery and printing office. Hamilton noted that "the houses, European in style, had long slanting roofs with low walls, and were painted in bright colours."[12] Later that evening the whole community turned out to be treated to tea, biscuits and jam by Chief Steward MacCrudden aboard the ship before several movies, including a couple of Mickey Mouse cartoons, were played on deck, to the delight of the locals. Taggart wrote to his mother that the locals "were 'tickled' with everything on board, especially the pigs and chickens as they never see them up here."[13] This was a big event for the community, which according to Taggart, consisted of about 18 Europeans and about 200 Inughuit. The Danish men were smartly attired in suits, their wives adorned in the finest of European fashion. Taggart noted that

> the Eskimos were very clean and tidy—their clothes are something unusual to us, the women wear long sealskin boots reaching nearly to the hips, a pair of small fox-skin pants and a print blouse embroidered with beads. The men have sealskin boots reaching to the knees, sealskin pants, knee length, and a short pullover blouse with a hood sewn on which hangs down their back.[14]

Following a final walk around the community with the Danish officials, the men boarded the ship at 5:00 p.m. and by 7:00 p.m. were underway, the next stop being the RCMP detachment at Pond Inlet on northern Baffin Island. The ice in Baffin Bay was heavy in places, causing the captain to frequently telegraph "dead slow" to the engineer in the engine room. Meanwhile, the men

---

* Smaller than an iceberg but larger than a growler. They also come in various shapes.

settled comfortably in the salon playing cards, reading and writing letters—a level of comfort that would soon be nothing but a fond memory.

At Pond Inlet, the men gathered at the rail to look over the tiny settlement, which consisted of a few small buildings clustered away from the shore: the detachment, a Hudson's Bay Company store, and two missions, one Catholic and one Anglican. At the top of the hill behind the settlement was a larger than life sign with the letters RCMP embedded into the hillside with whitewashed stone. The men watched as the two officers being relieved made haste toward the ship by rowboat while Constables Ashe and McBeth quickly gathered their gear together for their two-year assignment. All were tasked with transferring the annual stores from ship to shore, and following a long catch-up session at the post that extended well into the early morning, the men lay down on the floor for a three-hour nap before the ship raised anchor and turned north toward Dundas Harbour on Devon Island.

Once past Bylot Island, the *Beothic* entered Lancaster Sound, encountering heavy pack ice and menacing icebergs, one of which upended as they steamed past it. Just before the ship arrived at Dundas Harbour, Hamilton noticed Inspector Joy, the captain and others outside on the bridge with their field glasses trained on the detachment. They were pointing at the flag, which was at half-mast, and speaking in muted tones.[15] The flag had now attracted everyone's attention. Someone had obviously died, but who was a mystery. Soon, a rowboat issued from shore. Aboard were Constables Urquhart and Wilson, and two Inughuit. Once on board, the two constables were quickly and quietly ushered into Inspector Joy's cabin.

As the men waited for information, they heard about another death at the detachment, a stark reminder of the risks inherent in a northern assignment. Up the hill behind the post was the grave of a constable who had died tragically two years earlier. Constable Victor Maisonneuve, aged twenty-seven, took his own life at Croker Bay by gunshot on June 16, 1926, only a couple of months shy of his departure; now his remains were interred in one of the loneliest graves on the planet. The men soon learned that the flag was flying at half-mast in mourning for Constable William Robert Stephens (aged twenty-five), another constable who had died by gunshot. Hamilton learned that on August 26, 1927, Stephens, who had just begun the second year of his two-year assignment, had been out hunting walrus with the Inughuit and after shooting two, he went up the hill to see if he could spot more. He sat down on a rock with his rifle between his legs to roll a cigarette when his rifle went off unexpectedly, killing

The graveyard at Dundas Harbour; the last resting place of Constable Victor Maisonneuve (27) and Constable William Robert Stephens (25). Photo courtesy of the Taggart Family

him instantly. His body was cached in the rocks at the base of the hill behind the detachment awaiting an investigation.

Inspector Joy, however, reported on the incident somewhat differently in his annual report for that year. He wrote that

> the year was marked by a distressing accident which on August 26, 1927, caused the death of Constable W.R. Stephens. On the date mentioned, soon after the ship had left, walrus hunting being in progress, Constable Stephens went out with his rifle to look for game. He saw some walrus, fired at them, wounded one, returned to the detachment for more ammunition, and left for the scene of the hunt, and on his way in some way discharged his rifle; the bullet entered his head and killed him instantly. A careful investigation went to show that the death was due to misadventure.[16]

The late Dr. Shelagh D. Grant, however, suggested that perhaps something more sinister occurred with both Maisonneuve's suicide and Stephens's "misadventure." In 1928, the first Canadian Inuit to serve at Dundas Harbour arrived aboard the *Beothic*. Previous assistants to the RCMP there had been Inughuit men and their families from Greenland whom the RCMP recognized were more willing to serve in the isolated locations where the detachments were located than their Canadian counterparts. Dr. Grant interviewed many Inuit preparatory to writing her book, *Arctic Justice, On Trial for Murder, Pond Inlet, 1923*, about the killing of the trader, Janes; one of these was Samuel Arnakallak, whom she spoke with at Pond Inlet on September 27, 1994. He was a senior at that point, his family having been sent to Dundas Harbour in 1928 when he was three. Samuel was about six by the time he left Dundas Harbour, just old enough to understand the stories being told about the deaths of the two constables.[17] During the interview he informed Grant that: "I think they were shot by Greenlandic husbands. I think they were just saying they shot themselves. I suspect this because they wanted to exhume them. They wanted to know where they shot themselves and where the bullet entered and left the bodies."[18] The deaths were indeed unusual given the mandatory firearm training received by all members of the force and the officers' general familiarity with many kinds of weapons and the risks associated with using them.

Dr. Grant explained:

> Arnakallak admits that he was the only one who thought the two policemen might have been shot by Greenlanders, but if his suspicions were correct, it would explain the absence of any official report. For obvious political reasons on both the domestic and international scene, it would have been unwise to open the case to further investigation if there was even a remote possibility that a jealous Inuk, particularly a native of Greenland, had killed a police officer. Instead, the record shows that there were no further suspected murders in the vicinity of North Baffin through to the Second World War.[19]

Given the lack of understanding of how the two men died, a few suggestions popped up. One was by murder/suicide. It was said that the two officers could not stand each other and had built a wall down the middle of the detachment to prevent them from interacting with each other, but that explanation falls apart when one learns that Maisonneuve and Stephens did not serve at Dundas Harbour at the same time. And then there is the story that Maisonneuve had an incurable sexually transmitted disease and his despair over that led to his suicide, or that he had been ridiculed by the other two officers. And lastly, that both men had gone "mad." Given that there were no witnesses to either death, the mystery of their tragic endings has never been solved.

Following Dr. Livingstone's inspection of the body, Stephens's remains were interred beside Maisonneuve's. The men from the detachment later placed white crosses at the head of each grave and erected a white picket fence around what had now become a small graveyard. It then became the duty of the officers at the detachment to maintain the gravesite. Even later, in 1973, professionally carved granite headstones were shipped in to replace the white crosses. Hamilton wrote: "This certainly was not the kind of welcome I had anticipated to the post which was to be my home for the next two years."[20] He was therefore relieved for the distraction when he was approached by Inspector Joy to accompany him on the ship to the Craig Harbour and Bache Peninsula detachments to assist with the collection and evacuation respectively of stores there. The ship would then return to Dundas Harbour where Joy and Hamilton would disembark.

The *Beothic* sailed early the next morning, leaving behind Corporal Timbury and Constables Taggart, Urquhart and Wilson. The latter two would rejoin the *Beothic* once it arrived back at Dundas Harbour in a couple of weeks for its trip back to civilization. Two Canadian Inuit families from Pond Inlet had also disembarked from the *Beothic*. They consisted of Qamaniq and his wife, Muckpainuk, their adopted daughter, Qanngualuk (Qamaniq's sister's daughter), their daughter, Anna Ataguttiaq, her husband, Kipumii, and their two children—son Samuel Arnakallak and daughter Inuutiq. The Inughuit that they were replacing were taken aboard the *Beothic* to be transported back to Greenland. Samuel Arnakallak, in a 2012 interview at Pond Inlet regarding his time on Devon Island, reflected on why local Inuit were then favoured by the RCMP: "well, only the RCMP officers lived down there, they had Greenlandic Inuit as guides. People kept going down there and in the end only Canadian Inuit would work for the RCMP.... That was how it was, since then they would not use Greenlandic Inuit, perhaps due to the RCMP's sovereignty agenda, yes."[21]

The Inuit women would assist the young constables with cleaning, laundry and sewing their winter clothing, while the men would assist with hunting, guiding, travel and general cleanup/maintenance around the detachment. Samuel Arnakallak also informed Shelagh Grant in his 1994 interview that the women were constantly making skin boots (kamiks) for the officers because they wore them out so quickly. Inspector Joy even wore them on board the ship when in dress uniform, because they were so comfortable, although the officer's boots were made from sheepskin rather than the caribou hide that the Inuit used. When not in uniform, the men wore what the Inuit men wore, clothing made from caribou skins that had to be sewn by the women, the skins softened by them as well. When it came to washing clothes, some of the men would do

The population of Dundas Harbour, Devon Island. Back Row (L to R) Corporal Maurice Timbury, Constable "Paddy" Hamilton, Joanasie Kipumii and Qamaniq (far right). Middle Row (L to R) Qanngualuk, Anna Ataguttiaq and Muckpainuk. Front Row (L to R) Constable Reginald Taggart and Samuel Arnakallak. Photo courtesy of the Taggart Family

their own, but for the most part the women performed this task. When it was time to do the laundry, they would arrive at the detachment and kneeling on the floor would scrub the clothes by hand in hot water with a washboard and basin. In the summer months, they would transport the washboard, basin and dirty laundry by rowboat to the local creek for cleaning. Samuel Arnakallak recalled that there they would light fires to heat the water for washing, the soot marks from the fires still staining the rocks sixty-five years later.[22]

After grabbing a few hours' sleep in his new home, Taggart—who would be nicknamed Muqsaatuq (meaning tight curls) by the Inuit—organized his gear until about noon when Kipumii, who would become his loyal hunting companion, spotted some walruses about two miles (three kilometres) from the detachment. Walrus meat was essential for feeding the dogs during the winter, the edible yield from a reasonably sized animal tipping the scales at about a quarter of a ton. Taggart, Kipumii and the rest of the constables piled into the motorboat and sped toward the walrus, towing the rowboat behind. Once they arrived in the vicinity of the animals, they tethered the motorboat to the ice and transferred to the rowboat, stealthily stalking the walrus. They shot two, cutting one of them up immediately while the other was tied to the motorboat to be towed to the detachment. En route, an errant rope became entangled around the propellor, stopping the engine. Taggart stripped down and jumped overboard with a knife to free the prop, but the water was so cold—estimated at about −1.8°C (29°F)—that he failed to complete the task. Hamilton wrote that Taggart was almost paralyzed with cold and that it took the better part of an hour to warm him up. The walrus was then cut adrift and the rowboat used to tow the motor boat to shore where it was later hauled up to remove the rope and replace the damaged key in the propellor shaft. It was early the next morning before the job was complete.

Constable Hamilton, meanwhile, was on his way to Craig Harbour and Bache Peninsula, but the ice in Smith Sound was especially bad that year, causing Captain Falk to divert the ship to Robinson Bay on the southwestern coast of Greenland to drop the Inughuit off there. Inspector Joy had another reason to travel to Greenland. He wanted to re-engage the services of Nukappiannguaq to assist with the marathon sled patrol across the Eastern Arctic islands that he planned to start late the following winter. He learned that Nukappiannguaq had relocated to Etah, so Captain Falk decided to visit the Bache Peninsula detachment first and then cross Smith Sound to find Nukappiannguaq at Etah.

At Etah, Joy soon located Nukappiannguaq, who agreed to guide him on his patrol, but he was in a state. He had just quarrelled with his wife, who now refused to accompany him to Dundas Harbour. Nukappiannguaq then tried to persuade the young wife of his father to join him, but she too rejected his advances (a few years later, Nukappiannguaq was successful in luring away his father's wife, leaving his daughter in her place to take care of the old man). Other frantic attempts to find a wife also failed, but he was assured by Joy that the Inuit women at Dundas Harbour would take care of his clothing needs. Resigned to his bachelorhood, Nukappiannguaq loaded his dogs, kayak and hunting gear aboard the *Beothic*, which steamed away toward Craig Harbour, its final destination before returning to Dundas Harbour.

At Craig Harbour, rudimentary repairs were made to the buildings. These had been unoccupied for some time and had suffered significant damage from bears, which had broken up the blubber tanks, squashed several empty forty-five-gallon (170-litre) drums that had contained seal oil, and smashed in the door of the detachment. The post was being officially closed, one of three such openings/closings at the site.[23] Taking advantage of the constant daylight, the men worked through the night, loading everything aboard the ship that they could carry. The equipment and stores would be redistributed to other Eastern Arctic detachments. A day and a half later, the ship arrived back in Dundas Harbour where Joy, Hamilton and Nukappiannguaq disembarked, Constables Urquhart and Wilson taking over their bunks on the *Beothic* for their long and welcome voyage south. Taggart, who had engaged in a flurry of letter-writing to friends and family during the ship's absence, in his final letter wrote to his mother: "We haven't any cook books here so please send one to me for next year."[24]

After final farewells, the ship departed, but it had one small diversion to make before it made its way south. The crew was to lay down a cache at Beechey Island, located off the southwestern corner of Devon Island, that Inspector Joy could access on his upcoming patrol. It was still undecided who would join Joy, but it had likely been narrowed down to either Hamilton or Taggart, as Timbury would remain at the detachment as officer in command. Time would tell who Joy would choose to accompany him and Nukappiannguaq on this memorable and significant sovereign mission. The men were now left to their own devices, but before they had time to reflect on their circumstances, there was plenty of work to do. Winter was fast approaching and already freezing squalls of rain were foreshadowing what was soon to follow.

Constable Taggart had quickly settled into the rhythm of detachment life. In the two weeks before the *Beothic* returned, he and Kipumii had shot several walruses and had spent the good part of one morning cutting up the meat preparatory for caching. Stores that had been temporarily deposited in the detachment were moved to the nearby storehouse where a rudimentary inventory of stores was taken. Taggart painted the inside of the detachment and spent two evenings tinkering with the outboard motor on the gas boat to make sure that it would run smoothly. Upon Joy's and Hamilton's return, efforts were stepped up to move the rest of the stores to the storehouse and any perishables were relocated back to the detachment so they would not spoil in the cold. And the cold was certainly upon them, for the first snowfall of the season arrived on August 16.

Enough lumber to construct an addition to the detachment for Inspector Joy's use had been unloaded from the *Beothic*, but Joy was content to bunk with the men, so the lumber was available for other uses. Taggart was therefore in his element, seizing the opportunity to relocate the kitchen door and construct a new kitchen cabinet. A new outhouse was also constructed, much to the Inuit women's delight, and the detachment roof recovered with a new layer of rubberoid. The men were in the process of doing just that on August 18 when they heard and then spotted a small motorboat approaching. Hammers were dropped and the men quickly scrambled off the roof and down to the shore to greet the visitors. Aboard were Corporal McBeth, Constable Margetts and their Inuit companion, Penneiou (Paniloo). They had motored about 160 miles (258 kilometres) over twenty-four hours from Pond Inlet in the police boat, *Lady Laurier*, a feat that had never been accomplished before.

Despite this being McBeth's first year in the Arctic, he had grown up on Prince Edward Island and had gone to sea as a youth, but this errand was beyond anything that he had ever accomplished or even imagined. After the *Beothic* had departed Pond Inlet earlier that month, he realized that a bale of caribou skins had been left behind. He knew that the men at Dundas Harbour would be needing the skins for winter clothing, so despite the threat of a rough crossing, he wasted no time in getting the skins to them. The boat had no navigational aids, but McBeth's years at sea had him improvise a rudimentary compass from a rag tied to a pole in the bow for wind direction in combination with the sun's location. The boat had engine trouble partway over, forcing the trio to tie up alongside an iceberg for repairs. The berg capsized almost as soon as they moved away from it, almost swamping the boat. The bale of caribou skins was delivered safely as well as fifty pounds (twenty-three kilograms) of fresh arctic char, which the men erroneously assumed were salmon. Taggart wrote to his mother on July 3, 1929, that the fish was "very acceptable and made for a pleasant change from seal meat."[25] Four days later the *Lady Laurier* was refuelled and loaded with walrus meat (hunting walrus around Pond Inlet was prohibited) before the threat of inclement weather prompted McBeth to begin his homeward journey. Taggart et al. wondered if they had made it back safely, but a radio message soon after confirmed that they had. Pond Inlet had full radio communication, in contrast to Dundas Harbour, which only had a receiving set. Otherwise, communication between Dundas Harbour and the other detachments was either through the annual ship patrol or a winter dogsled journey.

Two days after McBeth departed, the inclement weather that had prompted his speedy return to Pond Inlet arrived in the shape of full-scale gale from the east. Taggart wrote:

Securing everything that is liable to blow away—gale got worse about 5:00 p.m. Pebbles were coming through the windows, their velocity was so great they wouldn't break the windows, just leave little round holes. We watched the blubber shed blow over and our new toilet was blown over also. We threw a one inch rope over the house and tied about one ton of coal in sacks at each end; that saved the house, though we thought she was going to blow away in pieces.[26]

The motorboat was also swamped and tossed up on the rocks, but Taggart and Hamilton managed to salvage it. Surprisingly, it was not damaged too badly, but still it took two days for Taggart to repair its sprung planks and get the motor—which had been saturated with salt water—running again.

On August 25, Taggart wrote: "Overcast, gale still blowing. Smashed a row boat, blew down our radio aerial, house is trembling pretty bad. We can't do anything, just have to wait till the wind goes down."[27] The storm abated two days later, at which point debris, including barrels and empty boxes, were scattered about the yard and as much as half a mile (804 metres) from the beach. The blubber shed needed replacing as well as much of the tarpaper roof on the storehouse. The next few days were occupied with cleaning up the debris and repairing the various buildings. Taggart also planned to construct a small shed, but during its construction he stepped on a nail which pierced an artery in his right foot, sending him to his bunk.

Although Taggart's injury restricted him to light duty for several days, he still managed to carry on with chores around the detachment, such as repairing the broken kitchen table, making some pans to bake bread in and compiling a list of all the books at the detachment. The men also spent much of their time hunting, with Inspector Joy and Taggart shooting five geese with rifles, three of which were set aside for Christmas dinner. Kipumii shot a hare, and Taggart and Hamilton shot an eider duck in the harbour. Taggart wrote that Timbury and the Inuit shot four walruses, one white whale (that would now be called a Beluga, a term not used historically) and a bear, and that he witnessed a stunning migration of white whales and seals in the harbour following an immense school of small fish to the east. Taggart shot and killed one of the whales and towed it to shore with a canoe. A small school of fish fled in front of the towed whale and when Taggart got to shore he was able to scoop a good quantity of them out of the water with his hands. Ice was now forming in the harbour and therefore a new chore was added to their daily routine. Water was now only available in the form of ice from a few small icebergs in the harbour, because the small creek emanating from the glacier that had been serving their fresh water needs was now frozen.

The frenetic activity that occupied the first few weeks at the detachment had calmed somewhat, permitting the men to reconnoitre their surroundings. Despite Taggart's foot injury, he and Hamilton walked three miles (five kilometres) to the glacier, scouting the area and looking for game. Hamilton wrote about the harbour in his diary, calling it one the best harbours in the Arctic. It had an ideal anchorage, except for a reef that prompted Captain Falk to navigate the *Beothic* well to the west when approaching the detachment. It was also large, being three miles (five kilometres) wide and one-and-a-half miles (2,400 metres) deep. Although the detachment was located in the shadow of the Cunningham Mountains, it had no protection from the incredible winds that swept through the area, contradicting Commander Craig's comment about the harbour being protected from the wind after he reconnoitred the site in 1922. The men also very quickly learned that travel was complicated by open water at Cape Warrender just to the east of Dundas Harbour, so travel along the coast to the west or north across the ice cap were the safer options if one was hunting or patrolling away from the harbour.

Now that winter was on the horizon, travelling meant learning how to handle a dog team. This essential skill was as familiar to the Inuit as driving a car was to the young constables, but the sleds and dog placement were a great deal different from what they had read about or even seen in the south. The dogs were not tethered to their sleds by the tight formation of a gangline hitch which kept the dogs running in pairs beside each other. That placement was employed on the narrow trails and forested areas of the south, while the Inuit employed a fan hitch which allowed the dogs more freedom to find their way around the many obstacles on the ice.

Taggart wrote that he

didn't find it so difficult to drive dogs though they are fresh and want to fight everytime [sic] they get a chance. The method of driving dogs in this country is different to the method employed in Northern Saskatchewan: up here they are all hitched abreast on long traces, one trace to each dog, traces are about eighteen feet long. This is the Greenland (North) method. The Baffin Island Eskimo has no two traces the same length; they range from fifteen feet to thirty-five feet, each dog is about half a length behind the other. If the lead dog is no good then they are hard to manage. I am using the Greenland method as the driver has more control over his dogs.[28]

Hamilton also wrote that the men spent the late fall learning how to use their long driving whips, his first experience leaving him with two black eyes. Walrus hunting was also on the agenda, which Hamilton noted

was a new and exciting adventure and at times can be very danger-ous, especially when they travel in large herds. On [sic] day in the fall, Nookappeungwak and Keppomee went out hunting in the bay in front of the detachment. They were on a large ice pan, which was quite safe, and were shooting at a herd of walrus in the water. Nookappeungwak decided to go after a wounded animal in his kayak. However, when he and his frail little craft came within range of the walrus and he was poised ready to throw his harpoon, another walrus came up right behind and charged his kayak. He dropped his harpoon, grabbed his paddle and made all possible speed to return to the icepan. I am sure he would not have been success-ful had not Keepomee hurriedly pushed out in a row boat to meet him. Nookappeungwak was just crawling into the boat when the walrus struck his kayak and took it completely under the water.[29]

They later found the kayak ripped to shreds.

And, as if to further emphasize the danger of hunting walrus, Hamilton, Qamaniq and the other men were out hunting one day on foot. They usually hunted along the edge of the shore ice, which was reasonably safe since the ice was now about six inches (fifteen centimetres) thick in places. On their way back to the detachment, they spotted a dead walrus frozen into the ice and pro-ceeded to chop it out. Nearby they heard walruses beneath the ice, and before they could react, a large walrus broke through, knocking Qamaniq down. They all scrambled to shore, but when things calmed down again they resumed chopping out the dead walrus. Qamaniq, believing that the walrus that had knocked him over would reappear, waited patiently beside the hole with his harpoon. Sure enough, it re-emerged, permitting him to harpoon it. He then mentioned to the others that he had seen this happen before where walruses were attracted to other walruses' blood in the water.

The ice continued to grow in the bay until by early November the ice edge was about two miles (three kilometres) from shore. The departing members of the detachment had offered Taggart and the others some parting advice to be wary of the stability of the ice, which would often sweep out to sea without notice. Complicating matters, the sun was showing for only an hour a day, and by November 6, had disappeared altogether, although there was still a sliver of light rimming the horizon. The men were constantly on the lookout for game, but it was in short supply, and except for a couple of bears that were killed because they were raiding the meat caches, the men often returned to the detachment empty-handed. Taggart wrote that at least the dogs were getting exercise.

Trapping arctic fox became the officers' main diversion, and although it was not officially sanctioned by the RCMP, Inspector Joy made an exception to keep the men occupied to combat boredom and to supplement their meagre wages. Each member who wanted one had his own trapline and were good about respecting each other's territory, often bringing in their colleague's foxes when they came across them and re-baiting the traps with blubber. The pelts were then scraped clean, dried and bundled. Over a two-year period, the men accumulated about fifty to sixty fox pelts each that would be sold upon their return to the south. Although the sale of these pelts would normally mean a significant boost to the men's incomes, by 1929 the worldwide depression had devalued furs as well as other commodities, a state that would persist well into the 1930s.

The darkness and cold that soon settled over the land tended to draw the men back to the detachment for indoor activities such as reading, playing cards, or in Taggart's case, repairing and making new dog harnesses. Joy and Taggart put up a batch of beer and wine for Christmas day, and one evening they broke out a bottle of whiskey, which left all the officers with aching heads the following morning. One of the main enjoyments, however, was listening to the radio, which offered both a mixture of entertainment and information. In some detachments in the Eastern Arctic—Dundas Harbour was one—radios were receiving sets only because transceivers were considered too expensive.[30] Commissioner Starnes wrote in his 1928 report that

> broadcasting is resorted to for communicating with detachments like Baillie Island, Bernard Harbour and those on the Eastern Arctic islands, which have no access to wireless stations. All our northern detachments are provided with efficient receiving sets, and at times previously arranged they listen. At those times instructions, personal messages, etc., are broadcast from a

suitable broad-casting station. Again I must acknowledge the cordial reception by various sending stations of all our requests for assistance of this sort. Most of our messages have been sent by station KDKA at Pittsburgh, and our relations with Mr. G.W. Wendt, the Canadian manager of the Westinghouse Company, have been most agreeable.

The foregoing remarks refer to official communications, but it need hardly be added that these sets have been of advantage in alleviating loneliness in these isolated posts.[31]

Superintendent Ritchie, in his annual report for "G" Division, reiterated the commissioner's comments, adding that "these sets are an unending source of amusement and enable the men to keep in touch with world affairs."[32] He went on to report that, although the men would like to receive news and entertainment from a British source, American stations were more easily accessed. Reception, however, was not always good, prompting Commissioner Starnes to report the next year that "an important message about the voyage of the *Beothic* was received by the two northern posts, Bache Peninsula and Dundas Harbour, but not by some of those farther south."[33] He stressed that the reception was both "irregular and often disappointing."[34] Constable Harry Stallworthy, stationed at Bache Peninsula a couple of years later, however, indicated no such issue with reception when he wrote that "the radio was also the source of news, especially the evening newscast from KMOX in St. Louis that ran from 8:00-8:15 every night. They even managed to pull in news broadcasts from two English stations. But perhaps more importantly, they received personal messages either from CKY, Winnipeg (Northern Messages) or from KDKA, Pittsburgh."[35]

Taggart, when writing to his brother John, wrote that "our best station is KDKA of course but we get the other stations fairly good at times if static is not too bad (the guy who says that there are no static in this country doesn't know what he is saying)[.] I get most of the messages sent to me at least I think so."[36]

KDKA was created by the Westinghouse Electric Corporation after World War I, and ran a program called "Northern Messenger" beginning in 1922. Its existence was the direct result of a suggestion from George Wendt that the station initiate a program for Canada's far north residents. In 1928, it was cohosted by Freddie Rogers and Louis Kaufman, and it broadcast messages to the RCMP, the Hudson's Bay Company and various missions between November and May each year, after the annual ship patrols had stopped for the season and until they started up again the following year.

Constable Hamilton wrote in his diary that everyone was excited to receive messages, even the Inuit, and when it was time for the Northern Messenger broadcast, which usually occurred around 11:00 p.m. EST on a Saturday night, everyone would lie on the floor with a pencil and paper and copy down as much of the message—which would be delivered in the form of direct broadcast and code—as they could hear. Then they would all compare notes. First, a commercial announcer

> dubbed "Winchester Bill" would start off with a commercial for Winchester rifles. He would invariably say theat [sic] Winchester arms were used by the Royal Canadian Mounted Police who were men who knew their firearms, especially those in the far north, where they depended for their living and sometimes their lives…. Next, Freddie Rogers would come on the air with the messages. He would read for about an hour and be relieved for coffee by a Mr. Koffman. This would go on for hours until all the messages for the week were cleaned up.[37]

There were two radios at the detachment, one belonging to the RCMP and a shortwave set owned by Corporal Timbury that had been presented to him by a Westinghouse executive. Timbury's shortwave set often picked up more of the messages than the other radio, permitting most of them to be successfully deciphered.[38] Timbury's set proved to be valuable for another reason as well. Only a week after his arrival at Dundas Harbour, he tuned in to a conversation between an American Arctic expedition and its handlers in Washington, DC, complete with excellent first-hand accounts of the ice conditions along the Greenland coast. Timbury's 1929 report reflected the value of this one-way communication:

> Radio reception during the winter was very good, and the majority of the schedules to the Far North from Westinghouse stations were received clearly on loud speakers. Many other Canadian and United States stations were heard, CNRW being the outstanding station in Canada; this reception continued to be good until the May 25, when on that date an address was heard from station KDKA by Mr. Wendt to the Far North. News of all kinds

and items of interest were obtained in this manner and much appreciated by members of this post.[39]

The Northern Messenger program was scheduled a year in advance, with the broadcast dates for the upcoming year delivered by ship to its listeners in the Arctic. As an added service, emergency notifications were broadcast on any Saturday at the same time as the published schedule. KDKA, Pittsburgh, PA, was the most prominent station. It boasted that it was "the Pioneer Broadcasting Station of the World."[40] On the ship's return from the Arctic, it carried a plethora of letters of appreciation for George Wendt: "These come from as far west as Alaska, as far north as Bache Peninsula, which lies within 760 miles of the North Pole, and as far east as Greenland."[41] Louis Kaufman, of KDKA, was also celebrated, earning the sobriquet "The Friend of the Arctic," and the *Canadian Jewish Review* noted in 1929 that he was probably "the best known personage north of 55 degrees."[42]

The RCMP were now beginning to realize the value of radio, and so equipped its new patrol schooner, *St. Roch*—which Commissioner Starnes referred to as a floating detachment—with a state-of-the-art shortwave set in 1928, the same year that the ship was launched by the Burrard Dry Dock Company in North Vancouver. According to Gilbert and Proc, "the use of shortwave in the Arctic had been pioneered by Tom Mix of the American ship, *Bowdoin* in 1923. Canadian Jack Barnsley, in Prince Rupert, BC, provided vital communication support to the *Bowdoin*."[43] Barnsley was an amateur radio enthusiast, using a Paragon Type RA-10 Regenerative Receiver and a Paragon Type DA-2 Detector-Amplifier, and broadcasting from his experimental Prince Rupert radio station, 9BP, when he answered a challenge from the Chicago Radio Laboratory (CRL) in 1923 to make contact with the ship, *Bowdoin*, which was locked in the ice at Refuge Harbour, Greenland, during Dr. Donald MacMillan's Arctic expedition. The CRL had lost contact with the ship just north of Disko Island, and was worried about its safety. Barnsley managed to make contact with the ship and became its proxy messenger, forwarding over 500 media and personal messages that were skipped to his station from the *Bowdoin* over a two-month period.[44] (The *Bowdoin* was the same vessel that two years later was used by the MacMillan/Byrd Arctic expedition that would cause the Canadian government so much grief.)

Four years before the *St. Roch* was equipped with its shortwave set, the Canadian government had already started experimenting with the new technology. In 1924, Captain Bernier had welcomed aboard the CGS *Arctic* a young radio operator, Bill Choat, whose position had been arranged by Commander C.P. Edwards, head of the radio branch in Ottawa. Choat's duties were nothing more than to experiment with the *Arctic's* radio equipment. The radios, however, at some of the remote Eastern Arctic detachments would remain as receivers only for many more years, expense and technical issues being the main barriers to upgrading them to full service stations.

Constable Robert Warren Hamilton, also known as "Paddy." Photo courtesy of the Taggart Family

Despite the bitter cold, which encouraged the men to seek refuge indoors, they were surprised to discover that the three months of winter darkness did not always mean that outdoor activity, including winter travel, had to be restricted. There were times when it was impossible to venture out, but when the weather was favourable they found it easy to surveil their surroundings under either the moonlight or the northern lights, which bounced off the snow with the brightness of klieg lights.

Winter also meant learning how to build an igloo to protect themselves when out on the land. It was an essential skill that could mean the difference between life or death. On one of his first overnight trips of the winter, Taggart, accompanied by Kipumii, sledded to Croker Bay to check his fox traps and to scout the area for game. Since they would be away for the night, Kipumii showed Taggart how to build an igloo. First, the right snow had to be located, so they searched for a wind-blown drift with tightly compacted snow that would be rigid enough to form the walls of the structure. Using a long metal snow knife, blocks were cut, each about two feet wide by three to four feet long (sixty-one centimetres by approximately one metre) and about eight inches (twenty centimetres) thick. These would be arranged in a circle, each concentric layer narrowing toward a dome at the top. The structure was both convenient to build and surprisingly warm, although heat from the occupants and the small oil lamps or kerosene stoves that they used within would melt the inside of the igloo somewhat. When the moisture froze, it would both seal the inside and strengthen the structure. Hamilton wrote that when he had the opportunity to help build an igloo he made a nuisance of himself, but the Inuit were tolerant, eventually accepting one of his blocks.

The men were beginning to venture out on the land by themselves, which was both rewarding and at the same time dangerous. One day in late November, Taggart was checking his fox traps by himself when he slipped, seriously spraining his ankle to the point that he could not stand. Crawling to his qamutiik, he almost froze to death as he painfully got aboard and negotiated his dog team home. Running beside a qamutiik was what usually kept the men warm. It would be several weeks before his ankle was healed enough for him to regain full movement.

It took only a split second of inattention to find oneself in trouble, as Hamilton discovered a month later to the day of Taggart's misadventure. His unnerving experience occurred on the return from one of his trips with Taggart. Taggart wrote about it three days before Christmas:

Cold and clear, strong wind N. Hitched up the team. Hamilton came along with me today to the harbour as he wanted to see where my traps were, but we didn't get anything. When I was coming back he stopped off at the storehouse to get some supplies. I waited while he went inside. I saw him strike a match. A minute or two later he suddenly shouted "Fire!" Sure enough the storehouse was on fire inside. He called me in to put it out but it was too hot and I only succeeded in burning three fingers on my right hand. He stayed at the building while I drove the team to the Post to get help. When everyone got back with fire extinguishers and snow shovels the interior was full of smoke but very little flame. I guess the smoke must have choked the fire as the building was nearly airtight. We got the fire under control after about three hours. Saved all the stores but lost a lot of foxes and deerskin clothing, tents, sleeping bags, sails, etc. Fire occurred at about 1:30 p.m. We left the storehouse at 10 p.m. with all our stores outside and one native to watch in case a spark should create another fire. Everyone was black and dirty; some of our clothes were partly burned, and of course my ankle was swollen worse than ever, but we didn't mind as our stores were safe. Cleaned the dirt off ourselves, had a good meal, also a drink of whiskey to celebrate the shortest day, and went to bed.[45]

Taggart estimated the damage to be about $1,500 and commented in a letter to his mother that the "storehouse is a wreck inside. Bob was fined $20 for negligence and got bawled out."[46]

Although not as devastating as the Craig Harbour fire that had destroyed the detachment building five years earlier, the loss of any equipment and stores was cause for concern, especially when replenishment could be months away. Throughout the balance of Hamilton's service in the remote Arctic, he was very cognizant of the damage his inattentiveness had caused and was ever so vigilant with himself and others to avoid a repeat of that experience. It was obvious that others had had the same experience, and it was one of the reasons why the storehouse was located at arms' length from the detachment. A fire at one building could very easily become a fire at two. Fortunately, the Inuit were close at hand at these remote detachments, for given the worst case scenario, they would know how to survive.

Christmas Day in these remote Arctic detachments was always an event. It was a tradition born from the isolation, hardship, cold and deprivation experienced by men in challenging environments. All thoughts of that would be set aside, however, when the best of food and humour materialized, suspending their plight for at least one day. It was a time for socializing, for games, for merry-making and reminiscences, and it was perhaps the one time in the year when the men would be comfortably and nutritionally replete. Taggart wrote:

Christmas Day. Clear and bright, lovely moon—lights up the whole country. I never saw moonlight so bright before except here in the Arctic. The Eskimos had on new clothes and were very clean and neat. We gave them a wonderful feed at noon—roast goose, ptarmigan and eider duck, all kinds of pies, cakes, fruit and puddings. They slept all afternoon in their igloo. We had another good meal about 7:00 p.m., then we brought out our liquor and smoking material and had a spree. At 11:00 p.m. we got KDKA coming in very good. Everyone got messages; even the Eskimos heard the announcer trying to speak their language when sending a message to them. I guess they had a good time. We shut off the radio at 7:30 a.m. and went to bed.[47]

On December 31, Taggart celebrated his twenty-fourth birthday, with the new year dawning dark and cold. The ice in the bay was showing signs of stress, manifested in mountainous pressure ridges, evidence of the tectonic-like collision of ice floes driven against one other by unseen tidal forces. And to cap that, a perpetual shroud of sea fog boiled off the open ocean, drifting across the ruptured ice before a steady onshore breeze, obscuring both danger and direction. Taggart reported that his forays onto the ice were short and cautious. The ice was dangerous as Kipumii was soon to discover.

On January 24, Taggart and Kipumii sledded to Home Bay to check Taggart's traps. Taggart found two foxes in his traps at Croker Bay and Kipumii, one. They stayed in the igloo for two nights, making inroads toward the detachment on the morning of the 26th. Taggart and Kipumii travelled in tandem until Kipumii stopped to fix his dog traces. Taggart wrote:

> I went on, keeping to the trail. About two hours later I thought he should be coming along so I waited awhile, then went on as we often split up and come home separately and I wasn't worrying about him. After I left Croker Bay I noticed fresh cracks in the ice, then I came to open water where the trail should have been. I started for the shore. About five hundred yards away the cracks were getting wider; about two hundred yards from shore they were three feet wide. I began to be afraid that I wouldn't make the shore. The last hundred yards was risky. When I came to the shore there was twenty feet of water to cross. Luckily I found a small berg which was touching the shore ice so I got on land without much trouble. Travelled to the harbour over land. Ice has all gone out from the shore except the bays and fiords. Got back to the Post at 6 p.m.... Kiponee has not arrived—guess he went out on the ice and couldn't get back.[48]

The next day, Taggart wrote that "about 8 a.m. Nuqaqpainguaq and I hitched a team to a small boat and went back to look for Kiponee who was lost yesterday.... Found Kiponee's tracks where he had passed us in some rough ice. Turned back and found him at the Det. He had drifted back to Cape Home during the morning—was on the ice all night."[49] Hamilton wrote that Kipumii was travelling to the west while the ice, at low tide, was moving east, which was drawing it away from land. Kipumii stated that he had manoeuvred his team as close to the ice edge as possible, so that he could make a dash to land if the ice butted up against the shore. He had passed the detachment three times during the night and at one time was as far east as Cape Warrender. Another ten miles (sixteen kilometres) east and he would have been swept out into Baffin Bay, where he would most certainly have been lost. As soon as the tide turned, however, the ice was pushed up against the shore which afforded him the opportunity to get to land. With two deaths at the detachment already, Hamilton wondered if there was to be a third. But Kipumii, who had an adequate supply of food—he had killed two foxes, which he ate—and plenty of experience on the ice, had suffered no serious hardships.[50]

CHAPTER EIGHT

Beechey Island

The sun's return was a cause for celebration and on February 3, 1929, about noon, Taggart, who had been sledding across the new and somewhat unstable ice in the harbour—at one point he almost fell through—happened upon an iceberg that he climbed for a vantage point. Looking south and east toward Baffin Island, he spotted the edge of the sun peeking over the horizon. Although it lasted only a tantalizing ten minutes before its radiance once again slipped into the void, it was a joyous occasion nevertheless. The return of daylight, welcome for many reasons, also signalled that packing could start for Joy's patrol west to Melville Island.

Taggart, of course, was especially pleased, since Joy had chosen him eleven days earlier to accompany him on his historic sovereign journey. He was the natural choice, however, and although all the men were competent, Taggart had adapted quickly to the rigours of Arctic life. He had befriended his Inuit companions and had formed a special bond with Kipumii. He was a quick study, showed initiative, was a natural hunter/trapper and was adept at travelling over land, sea and sea ice. Of equal importance was the fact that he was handy; he could make his own dog traces, repair his qamutiik, repair the boat and the outboard motor as well as construct and repair buildings. He was, in fact, the ideal Arctic travelling companion, and it seemed that he had been born into the role. Inspector Joy, when later writing to Taggart's mother, Florence, wrote that "I can assure you that you need have no more than a mother's emotional concern for your son's welfare. He was in splendid health when I left him; he knows how to take care of himself; he likes the country really well and he finds it not so bad as it is described in most literature."[1] Hamilton, although disappointed that he had not been chosen, was somewhat mollified when "Inspector Joy told me that Kominick and I would accompany the patrol with one team to help carry supplies as far west as Beechy Island."[2]

But planning for the mission would initially involve more than just Joy, Taggart, Nukappiannguaq, Hamilton and Qamaniq. Joy needed to know how the cache that had been laid down at Beechey Island by the *Beothic* the previous summer had fared over the winter. Taggart wrote that Joy feared that the coal oil, biscuits and dog pemmican had been disturbed by bears. To that end, he instructed Corporal Timbury to travel to Beechey Island to check the cache as well as to observe the ice conditions in Lancaster Sound. Timbury was to be accompanied by Kipumii and Nukappiannguaq. Taggart wrote on February 12 that they "left for Beechy today thought [sic] they might not get there as there may be no ice on the Sound further west. In that case they will have to go over the ice cap to Jones Sound and travel to Beechy around North Devon Island."[3]

Timbury wrote:

On the 13th, we were forced by the rough conditions of the ice on the Sound to travel on a narrow strip of snow between the ice pressed up against the shore and the base of the hills until within two miles of Cape Bullen. Here we were able to return to the ice again, but soon encountered open leads too wide to be crossed with a komitik. All the ice about us was in motion, and moving in our favour; so we waited and crossed the leads as they closed until we reached Cape Bullen. The ice across the mouth of Cuming Creek was set fast, and in splendid condition....A short distance west of the mouth of Cuming Creek we passed a small glacier about a mile broad. At the end of the glacier we met with thin ice badly broken and pressed up, and large stretches of open water could be seen in all directions only a few hundred yards from shore. Here we took observations from the adjacent hills, about fifty feet above sea level, and saw a heavy black mist to the west, indicating open water; and to the south open water and moving ice could be seen as far off as the horizon, and the constant grinding and cracking of breaking ice could be heard in all directions.[4]

The following day they observed that the new ice was too thin to support a qamutiik, so they decided to reconnoitre the coast on foot. There they observed a female bear and two yearling cubs ambling along the shore. Timbury was amazed at the strength of the adult which, while they watched, discovered the concealed lair of a seal, and rising up upon its hind legs, plunged downward into the lair, crushing it, although it appeared to be empty. The trio killed all three bears for dog feed. The next few days was a repeat of the first, where they carefully negotiated long stretches of rough ice, and at one point were forced to chop their way through a formidable ice barrier along the shore to gain access to the snow corridor. Timbury wrote that "soon after leaving camp on the 19th,

The Franklin Cenotaph. Photo courtesy of the Taggart Family

we crossed over an extensive stretch of very flat land, only a few feet above sea level, which gave us a short cut to Beechey Island. We arrived at the cache at 2 p.m. and found the contents intact."[5] Despite bear tracks all around the cache, Timbury was surprised that it had been left undisturbed, but Kipumii informed him that bears will not touch a cache with coal oil in it.

Timbury described what he had understood to be an island:

Beechey Island is apparently not an island; but is connected with North Devon Island by a long narrow strip of land almost at sea level. The south side of the so-called island ends in a vertical cliff several hundred feet high, and tapers off to the connecting beach on the north side. Near the cache are the remains of a good-sized boat, an old wooden shack, broken barrels, and much other rubbish. Further back from the water line stands a small memorial tablet in memory of the late Sir John Franklin and his men.[6]

The return journey was complicated by difficult ice conditions, significant open water in Lancaster Sound and a persistent wind from the southwest that quickly blossomed into a raging blizzard that did not abate until noon on February 23. Timbury wrote that visibility on the 22nd was restricted to only a few yards. The men arrived back at the detachment on the night of the 28th, having travelled 400 miles (644 kilometres) over seventeen days.

Meanwhile, preparations at the detachment were well underway. It was only a matter of days before departure, and there was still much to do. Taggart and Kipumii hauled in a load of meat from a cache at the glacier that had to be specially prepared for Joy's patrol. Taggart wrote that "we have to have twelve hundred pounds of lean meat for the patrol to Melville. As it is now the meat has to be thawed out, the lean cut off and put in boxes, about eighty pounds to the box, frozen again and then the box is broken off, leaving a square block of lean meat to be packed on the kometic when we leave on patrol in March."[7] While Taggart and Kipumii were travelling to the various meat caches, some of which were miles away, to retrieve enough meat for the patrol, Hamilton remained behind to assist in preparing the meat blocks.

The return of the sun, which was now visible for about two hours each day, made these preparations all the more enjoyable, but despite the psychological lift it offered, the temperature, which had sunk to a frigid 50° below zero, managed to check the men's exuberance somewhat. Even the Inuit complained of the cold. The women, meanwhile, were focussed on sewing new outfits for Joy and Taggart, with Taggart anticipating a new pair of sealskin boots and mitts. It was also important that the dogs receive special attention, given that they would be hauling extraordinary loads, so Taggart made sure that they were well fed and in top form. Taggart's qamutiik also needed additional scrutiny to make sure that it would stand up to the heavy loads and the interminable stresses placed upon it by travel over the rough ice. And in order to reduce the sled's friction, he polished the shoeing on the runners. On another day, he, Joy and Nukappiannguaq walked to the base of the Cunningham Mountains behind the detachment to stuff a bag with dried grass for use as makeshift insoles in their footwear. Kipumii, as well, was not idle. He made an eighty-foot (twenty-four-metre) long lashing rope for Taggart's sled as well as fifteen rings for his dog traces.

It was a sled lash line that had saved Hamilton only a few days earlier. He was travelling over ice broken by numerous open leads when his dogs came upon an unexpected breach in the ice and to avoid it bolted sideways for the shore. Due to the long traces, the sled continued to move forward on its original trajectory until it and Hamilton were unceremoniously driven into the water. Hamilton recorded that:

I managed to hold on to the sled lash line and the dogs were able to pull both the sled and myself to the firm ice and then to shore. I had to run along side the sled for the remainder of the short journey to keep from freezing. A knoght [sic] in armour had nothing on me and deerskin clothing. I was a walking ice statue, and when I arrived at the detachment, Timbury and Taggart had to cut me out of my deerskins. I was not frost bitten, but it would no doubt have been a far different story had I not been so close to home.[8]

On March 6, Taggart wrote: "Collecting pots, kettles, plates and primus stoves, tent, sleeping bags and deerskin robes for use on patrol. There is quite a pile of necessities to be taken on a trip of this kind."[9] Four days later, and two days before departure, the three qamutiit were loaded with the bulk of the supplies required for the journey. The day before departure, Taggart wrote that there was not much to do; everything was ready. He noted that his and Nukappiannguaq's sled would be loaded with 1,000 pounds (450 kilograms) of supplies each, while Qamaniq's would be loaded with 500 pounds (227 kilograms). Taggart, following Inspector Joy's lead, had earlier bundled up his fox skins and other gear, and wrote of Joy's advice: "He says anything might happen to any of us while we are away so we are leaving everything in order in case of accidents."[10]

Taggart wrote that the Inuit "were all over during the evening. We opened our last bottle of whiskey and killed it in one round."[11] The following morning, March 12, dawned bright and cold. Leaving the detachment at 7:00 a.m., the men made for the storehouse to finalize loading the qamutiit. In a letter to his mother, Taggart wrote: "We each had 600 lbs of walrus meat for dog feed, 100 lbs of biscuits, 80 lbs of beans, about 100 lbs of coal oil, 80 lbs of walrus meat for our own use, rifles, sleeping bags, deerskins and a lot more necessary articles, such as stove, pots, cups, etc."[12]

Two-and-a-half hours later, the journey began in earnest. Taggart's qamutiik was pulled by twelve dogs while Nukappiannguaq's employed fifteen. For the first two hours the travelling was slow through deep, soft snow—there had been no wind to compact several recent dumps—with progress reduced to one mile (1.6 kilometres) an hour. Immediately upon leaving the harbour, they encountered rough ice, which stayed with them until they stopped on the east side of Croker Bay to make coffee and eat some biscuits. The going after their break was much better, but they stopped again after sighting a bear on the far side of the bay. Stripping Nukappiannguaq's qamutiik of its load, Taggart and he set off after the bear. When they were close, Nukappiannguaq released his dogs and they brought the bear to bay. Taggart shot it and they loaded it aboard the qamutiik to return to the outfit where it was immediately butchered and fed to the dogs. They camped at 8:00 p.m. at Cape Home.

Taggart wrote that

everyone was cold and hungry by the time the igloo was built. We soon got warm when we were all inside eating our supper, which consisted of thick broth of walrus meat, pemmican and Julienne [compressed vegetables] followed by coffee, biscuits and cheese. We soon got into our bags; and though the igloo was small for five men, we were too tired to let a little thing like that bother us.[13]

They broke camp at 11:00 a.m. the following morning, Joy writing that

from here onward for several miles rough ice compelled us to travel almost constantly on the ice-foot, where deep soft snow was met with. Late in the afternoon we came abreast of drifting ice and open water extending to the ice-foot. Here repeated pressure from the sound had built up a wall of ice, varying from twenty to one hundred feet high, all along the shore line. Huge cakes of ice had been forced over the wall and lay thick and loose in the narrow passage, between the ice-wall and vertical cliffs forming the coastline, where we had to travel. Our progress then became more difficult and demanded the utmost exertion of men and dogs, although one or more of the party was kept constantly in advance of the teams chopping a road.[14]

Taggart added that

sometimes two or three dogs would be away on top of a block of ice ten feet high while others would be scattered about among other blocks. They have a rough time. If anyone from outside could hear the noise of dogs yelling and the language of the men they would wonder what it was all about.[15]

Travelling the following day was similar to the day before until they reached Cuming Inlet where across the mouth the ice was in excellent condition. But shortly thereafter, they had to once again resort to the ice-foot—a wall of ice frozen to the shore—Joy writing that "several times during the afternoon we came upon places where the ice-wall had broken off and drifted away, leaving only a sloping snowdrift, so narrow that we were unable to drive the dogs across it."[16] Here, they had to carve a track for one of the qamutiik's runners so that the sled would not slip into the sound and carefully haul the heavy sleds across the passage by hand, all the men participating due to the weight of the loads. Joy wrote that "just before dark we found our path obstructed by pressure ice a full one hundred feet high lying hard against the cliffs for about three miles."[17] Forced to retrace their steps until they found the lowest access point to the mountains, they camped at 7:00 p.m.

The following morning, Nukappiannguaq and Qamaniq repaired Taggart's qamutiik, the lashing of which had become loose from the previous days' exertion, while

Inspector Joy, Hamilton and I [Taggart] portaged our loads up a steep snow-bank. We had to cut steps all the way up—guess the drift was about one hundred and fifty feet high. The land was very rocky and rough. During the afternoon Joy and I walked along to a deep inlet about a mile away and I was lucky enough to get three ptarmigan coming back. We put them in the broth for supper. We have two meals each day with a cup of coffee and a biscuit for lunch.[18]

The following day, they were forced to drag the qamutiit over bare rock for four miles (six kilometres) until they could return to the sea ice. The going was good for the first hour, but then open water and pressure ridges once again forced them up against the shore on the ice-foot with worse conditions than they had previously experienced. At 9:00 p.m. they camped, too exhausted even to build an igloo. The tent was not as warm, but it would have to do.

For the next two days the going was rough, and at one point the dogs had to be unhitched so that the men could push the qamutiit over a snow drift to prevent it from slipping into the sea. Joy had planned to send Hamilton and Qamaniq back to the detachment at this point but decided to keep them on for another day to assist them over the rough spots. Joy wrote:

Shortly after leaving camp on the 18th the ice-foot became impassable. Here, however, rough land-fast ice extended out in the sound a hundred yards or so, and through this we chopped our way all morning. In the after-noon we ventured out on thin ice which lay across the mouth of a small bay and the face of a glacier, where the ice near shore was exceedingly rough for about five miles.[19]

Taggart wrote: "The worst part of the trip to Beechy Island is over. Our clothes are wet with perspiration and of course when we take them off they freeze stiff. The inside of my fur parka is coated with frost."[20]

On March 19, the men redistributed Hamilton's and Qamaniq's load between Taggart and Nukappiannguaq, and bade them farewell as they turned back toward the detachment at Dundas Harbour. The snow was hard packed toward the west and Taggart wrote that the dogs flew across the surface at the mouth of Graham Harbour and Maxwell Bay as if they didn't have a load. The men camped that night in an old igloo on the west side of Maxwell Bay. The weather was clear and they could see Somerset Island to the south. The hills of Devon Island, now free of the ice cap, were diminishing in height the more the trio travelled west. On the 21st, Taggart wrote: "Clear and cold, strong wind. Headed for a gap in the hills down in a large bay and climbed up a low ridge when we got to the gap. We could see Beechy Island in the distance across two little bays."[21] Taggart and Joy also spotted four hares about a mile distant through their field glasses and set off after them. Taggart wrote that he shot two while Joy missed his, and was amazed at the speed and fashion with which they ran.

> They run on all four feet until they get up speed, then they raise their fore-legs off the ground and leap along on their hind legs alone. They go very fast. The ones I killed weighed about fifteen pounds apiece. We went back to the kometics with our load of hares and started down to the first bay, crossed it, climbed a low ridge, then down onto Erebus Bay and across to Beechy Island.[22]

Sir William Parry had been the first European to visit Beechey Island while searching for the Northwest Passage in 1819. The island was named by his lieutenant, Frederick Beechey, after his artistic father, William Beechey, and thirty-one years later became one of the most historic meeting sites in the history of Arctic exploration. Although it is but a trivial dot on the map, unremarkable in physical attributes in that it is only a diminutive 1.5 miles (2.5 kilometres) across and rises to only 800 feet (244 metres) in elevation, it still punches much higher than its weight in the arena of important Arctic sites. After all, it was Sir John Franklin's first overwintering site, and was therefore the natural gathering point for a legion of Franklin searchers sent by the British Admiralty, Lady Franklin herself, and an American financial interest, Henry Grinnell, entreated by Lady Franklin to help with the search for her husband whose undertaking to discover the last un-navigated stretches of the Northwest

Passage had clearly met with disaster. In all, no less than a dozen ships were headed toward this rallying point in 1850, and within the decade, as many as forty expeditions would be launched, many no doubt consciously or unconsciously aware that they were participants in a macabre contest to be the first to discover the fate of Franklin, and therefore lay claim to the £20,000 sterling reward offered by the British government.

On August 27, 1850, in the Union Bay harbour just west of the island (aptly named by one of the British Admiralty's Franklin searchers, Captain Horatio Austin), ships from three expeditions lay at the land ice—De Haven, Penny and Ross—and others were making progress through the ice to join them. The flotilla was as disparate as it was a transitionary reflection of the time, running the gamut in size from a mere twelve-ton yacht *Mary*, towed to the site by the *Felix* under the command of the aging Sir John Ross (RN), a Lady Franklin conscript, to large brigs, and in propulsion from sail to a combination of sail and modern steam. Lieutenant Edwin De Haven was the commander of two small vessels, *Advance* and *Rescue*, both purchased by Henry Grinnell and turned over to the American navy for use in the Franklin search. Captain Penny was only there at the insistence of Lady Franklin. He was not the British Admiralty's first choice to command an expedition given that he was merely a whaling captain, but he had as much ice experience as the most seasoned Royal Navy veteran. He commanded two brigs, the *Lady Franklin* and the *Sophia*. Sir John Ross was there with two vessels: *Felix*, and the smaller of the two, the aforementioned *Mary*, which he planned to leave at Beechey in case any Franklin survivors needed a means to escape the Arctic.

Lieutenant Edwin De Haven described the scene on that most unusual day:

> The vessels were made fast to the land-ice on the northwest side of the island on the 27th of August. The schooner Felix, Captain Sir John Ross, RN, and the squadron under Captain Penny, joined us at that point. Consulting with these gentlemen, a joint search was instituted along the adjacent shores in all directions. In short time one of Captain Penny's men returned and reported that he had discovered several graves. On examination, his report proved to be correct. Three well-made graves were found, with painted head-boards of wood....
>
> Near the graves were also other unmistakable evidences of the missing expedition having passed its first winter here. They consisted of inummerable [sic] scraps of old rope and canvas; the blocks on which stood the

The yacht, *Mary.* Photo courtesy of the Taggart Family

armorer's anvil, with many pieces of coal and iron around it; the outlines of several tents or houses, supposed to have been the site of the Observatory and erections for sheltering the mechanics. The chips and shavings of the carpenter still remained. A short distance from this was found a large number of preserved meat tins.[23]

Seventy-nine years later, Taggart, Joy and Nukappiannguaq arrived at the same site, now further deteriorated. Taggart wrote that "Joy and I wandered around looking at the ruins of the cache left by the Franklin Search Expedition during the year 1850, but there wasn't very much to see as the bears and Eskimos between them had made away with anything of value."[24] Taggart commented that an old boat was there, presumably the *Mary*, as well as "the ruins of a wooden house and lookout mast, old meat tins and a few old casks, also a tablet erected to Franklin and his men by Capt. McClintock in 1858."[25]

Joy had decided to remain at the site for a few days to rest the dogs and to dry clothing, but on March 25, the planned day of departure, cold, heavy fog over Wellington Channel influenced him to not risk the crossing. Taggart took the opportunity to explore the island and later that day discovered the three graves of Franklin's crew members: William Braine, RM, of the *Erebus*; John Hartnell, AB, of the *Erebus*; and John Torrington of the *Terror*. The had all died in 1846. Taggart also climbed the highest point on the island, and as the fog lifted, he had a commanding view to the west, and was surprised to find open water between Beechey and Cornwallis Islands. Joy wrote that "from the top of Beechey Island the floe edge was observed to trend northwest for about fifteen miles inside Wellington Channel, and beyond this for another ten miles lay an impenetrable mass of rough ice, which reached almost to the coast of Devon Island."[26]

The next morning, Taggart took one last look at the graves, snapping a picture before they retraced their steps across the tombolo—a gravel bar connecting Beechey to Devon Island—and moved north along Devon's west coast up Wellington Channel. Four miles (6.4 kilometres) up the coast they encountered a bear that showed no fear and even some interest in them, but since they had no need of the meat and were in a hurry to cross Wellington Channel to Cornwallis Island, Taggart and Nukappiannguaq chased it off by cracking their driving whips at it. It was a long day, the last few hours navigated by moonlight until they camped ten miles (sixteen kilometres) short of the Cornwallis coast at 11:30 p.m. Reaching Cornwallis at noon the next day, they travelled south, and at 3:00 p.m., they spotted a cairn with a tall pole at about 800 feet (244 metres) in elevation and half a mile removed from the shore. Leaving Nukappiannguaq to look after their outfit, Taggart and Joy reached the cairn to discover a note from Captain William Penny dated August 8, 1850. The message, which was directed at the lost Franklin expedition, provided directions to three caches: one at Mary Point, North Devon Island;* one on Leopold Island located off the northeast corner of Somerset Island; and the third at Cape Hotham, located on the southeast corner of Cornwallis Island. The message also requested that the finder of the note forward it on to the Admiralty Office in London, England. Joy packed it away to present it to the appropriate authorities in Ottawa. Upon visiting the latter cache, Joy and Taggart found it to be totally ransacked, with empty, rusting tins and broken equipment scattered about.

Joy had hoped that the ice conditions along the coast of Cornwallis Island would have improved somewhat from their experience along the coast of Devon Island, but the trio was once again consigned to travel the ice-foot. Taggart

---

*   Devon Island was referred to as North Devon Island until the end of the nineteenth century.

wrote that "the ice looks rotten on the Sound and the shore ice looks worse. We are going to have a lovely time tomorrow."[27] The next day, necessity determined that they travel along the new ice formed in the sound. Joy wrote that it "bent perceptively under our komitiks."[28] They travelled on this new ice for five miles (eight kilometres) before the surface transitioned into old ice. Taggart considered that it was the "best day's travel we have had so far."[29]

Joy wrote of Cornwallis that

> the configuration and the nature of the east side of Cornwallis Island is similar to the west end of Devon Island. It consists of steep hills, approximately 800 to 1,000 feet high cut through by narrow irregular ravines, and is entirely covered by small, loose limestone rocks. Towards the west, however, the hills gradually decline and become more undulating, and reach almost to sea level around the largest indentations of the coastline. The first vegetation observed by us was on the small cape at the west side of Allen Bay, but here it was minute and very scarce.[30]

On the 29th, Taggart wrote that they shot a starving bear, but the temperature was so cold that they almost froze their hands skinning it. They left the hide due to its weight and fed the meat to the dogs. That night they camped at Cape Rosse, located on the southwest corner of Cornwallis Island, Taggart noting that "we were very glad to get in the igloo and get something to eat."[31] They decamped at noon the next day and almost immediately spotted a bear and two cubs in the distance. Taggart and Nukappiannguaq unloaded their qamutiit and moved quietly toward the bears. When a half mile distant, they released the dogs, which put the adult bear up on a small berg. The dogs, not satisfied, began to fight the bear and the whole bunch rolled off the berg. Taggart, alarmed that one or more of his dogs would be injured or killed, rushed up to the melee. At that point the bear jumped up and Taggart shot it through the heart, and then ran around the berg to dispatch the cubs before they could run off. He and Nukappiannguaq then skinned the animals, leaving the hides on the ice. Following that, the trio departed Cornwallis Island and began to cross McDougall Sound toward Bathurst Island. They camped at the mid-point at 8:00 p.m., the intense cold freezing Taggart's fingers and Joy's face and hands.

On April 1, Taggart commented in his diary: "We are surrounded on all sides by storms—we counted four during the morning."[32] Early that same morning, Taggart had been woken to the low nervous bark of only one of his dogs,

Buster, his best bear dog. He woke Joy and Nukappiannguaq and all concluded that there was a bear outside. Nukappiannguaq cautiously left the igloo and quickly informed the others that the bear was "right here." He shot it and to make sure that it was down, set Taggart's dogs upon it as they were nearer to the bear than his own. The three wondered why all the dogs, except Buster, had failed to react. In the morning they skinned the bear and gave the dogs a good feed, but later, when they sighted another bear the dogs were uncharacteristically disinterested. Taggart wrote in his diary that: "We are living on bear hearts and steaks these days. The dogs are having lots of warm meat and all the sleep they want."[33] He also noted, however, that well fed dogs tend to be lazy. Joy made the decision not to travel that day.

The following day was overcast and cold, but the storm that had plagued them calmed about noon. That night, Taggart loaded his rifle and left it outside the entrance to the igloo in case another bear visited them during the night. The men did not take their rifles into the igloo with them at night in the winter because they tended to develop condensation in the warmth and then freeze, making them useless.

Taggart wrote:

We are sleeping very lightly these nights. A dog whined sometime during the early hours of the morning. We were awake right away. Nothing could be heard except the snow sifting past the igloo outside. I cut a hole to see if the dogs were all tied and to find out which one was whining. When I looked out at them they were all sitting up and looking towards something beside our igloo. I told Joy what I saw. Newcapungwah cut a hole on his side and looked through it and he saw a bear not six feet away, pawing over some of our grub on the kometic. We decided to cut a hole beside my sleeping bag, farthest away from the bear, and I was to crawl out and shoot him. Joy started to cut the hole while I pulled on some clothes. The bear must have heard us for he came over to the igloo and sniffed at one or two holes that were cut in the wall. He then tried to climb on top of the igloo after some meat which we had placed there out of reach of any dogs that would happen to break loose. By this time I was dressed. The hole was not completed so I picked up my butcher knife and finished it; then I put my head through the hole to see where the bear was before I would venture out. I looked one way and he was not there; I glanced the other way and here he was diving for my head with his mouth wide open. I didn't lose any time in drawing my head out of harm's way. He shoved his head in the hole after me. I gave him a crack on the nose with my knife which I was still holding in my hand. He snorted and drew back. He tried to get in again and again but every time he tried I cracked him on the nose with the knife. After about a minute of this he backed up about four feet and stood watching the hole. I looked through the hole and could see my rifle half buried in drifting snow. I crawled close to the hole with the bear watching me—I guess he thought I was coming out. Anyway, I made a quick snatch for the rifle and got it; the bear made a quick grab for my arm, but I was too quick for him or else he was too slow. He missed my arm but came down on the rifle and hooked his claws in the cover. I tried to draw the gun inside but I couldn't even move it. He started to pull the rifle from me and nearly dragged me through the hole. He tried to get inside again but each time he put his head in the hole I hit him on the nose with my knife. He quit after awhile, though I was afraid he would have the igloo down, then he would do some damage. He sniffed at something on the kometic close by though he still watched the hole. I crawled half out of the igloo and recovered the rifle where he had left it. He was just turning back to the igloo while I took the cover off the gun. I lay down at the hole and put a bullet through his brain. Then I discovered my hands were nearly frozen. Joy said "shoot him again." I went to him and gave him a second bullet though he didn't need it. He had not done much damage to our stuff on the kometic (sp), tore some clothes, destroyed a small bearskin, spilled some beans, nothing else.... I don't remember anything about it myself, but Inspector Joy said everyone of us was shouting and yelling at the top of our voices. I remember the dogs barking while the bear was attacking the igloo. He could easily have got into us if he had hit the igloo with one or two slaps with his paw. Lucky for us he didn't as he certainly would have got one or two of us. He was starving and very thin, of about average size, with a beautiful coat. Skinned and cut up the bear right away. We wondered why the dogs didn't give us warning sooner. I guess they were so full of meat and sleeping heavily, and the storm drowned any noise the bear made till he got right into camp. Walked about for an hour or two during the morning. Dried my foot gear and mitts over the Primus after we had lunch. Gathered together all my gear as we are going to go on tomorrow. Inspector Joy and Newcapungwah are slightly ill. Joy says we are eating too much bear meat. Turned in after fixing the dogs 4 p.m., talked till 6 p.m., had our supper and went to sleep. We are hoping to get a night's rest without being disturbed by any more bears.[34]

They broke camp at 10:30 a.m. on April 4, and on the west side of Dyke Acland Bay, which was in the middle of Bathurst Island's southern coast, they once again were forced onto the ice-foot where they found the snow to be soft and deep. Joy noted that the island was both low and almost flat at this point, which afforded them the option of travelling over the land when the shore ice became too obstructive. They counted eleven caribou in a five-mile (eight-kilometre) stretch. Nukappiannguaq set off to get one while Taggart and Joy stayed with the outfit on the ice. He shot one and then sat down to rest while Taggart stalked two others. When he was 250 yards (228 metres) distant, they sensed his presence and began to move off. Taggart lay down and took careful aim, killing them both. Skinning them out, he brought the carcasses back to where Nukappiannguaq had killed his caribou and the trio set up camp. The quality of what little snow there was around was inadequate to build an igloo, so they erected the tent in minus fifty-plus degree temperature. Taggart almost froze his hand and Nukappiannguaq complained of frozen feet. He had to tie a caribou skin around his feet to keep them warm. Taggart wrote: "We had caribou tongues, briskets and tenderloin for supper, followed by biscuits, cheese and coffee. The inside of the tent was coated with a half-an-inch of rime from the steam of cooking and our breath."[35]

That night, Taggart wrote that he was cold in his eiderdown sleeping bag, so he threw one of the raw caribou skins over his feet and a piece of canvas over that to keep warm. In the morning he commented that "everything above freezing point steams as though it was warm; cold water steams and hot water fills the tent with a dense fog."[36] The next morning they were greeted by drifting snow and intense cold, which necessitated running beside their qamutiit to keep warm. Joy and Nukappiannguaq both complained of cold feet. Arriving at Cape Cockburn on the southwest corner of Bathurst Island later that afternoon they spotted a cairn, but it was empty. On arriving at the cape, Joy wrote that "we found that the rough ice extended as far as the eye could reach to the south, west and northwest, with no possible chance of getting into it with a komitik; the only visible improvement being inside the bay towards Harding Point."[37]

The trio departed Bathurst Island at Cape Cockburn, turning toward Harding Point, and made good headway toward a small island in the middle of Austin Channel. Taggart wrote: "Heavy drift, so we camped early in the lee of

On patrol to Melville Island. Photo courtesy of the Taggart Family

an iceberg, built a big igloo and were mighty glad to get inside. We were warm and comfortable and quite cheerful once we had some supper under our belts."[38] The following day they had been travelling for about two hours when one of Taggart's qamutiik runners split from end to end. They made camp immediately, erecting the tent despite the cold, and built a snow wall around it to keep out the wind, which was blowing strongly. The dogs were tired and hungry, but there was no game to be had at that moment.

Joy wrote: "We dismantled the komitik, ripped the runners, and rebuilt it, which took us until 2:30 a.m. the following day."[39]

On April 8-9th, Taggart described the travelling conditions.

Very cold, heavy drift. We shouldn't be travelling in such weather but we can't afford to lose too much time. We struck what we believe to be Byam Martin Island. I have never experienced such cold weather even with our heavy parkas, bearskin pants and fur stockings, not to mention heavy underwear, sweaters and blanket parkas we nearly froze. We saw a halo around the sun and three sundogs—more cold weather coming. When the CGS Arctic wintered at Melville Island 21 years ago the thermometer measured 76 degrees below zero. We attempt to get out on the sound to cross to Melville but ice is too rough. Froze my nose slightly as did Joy. He also has great trouble with his feet and hands. Wish we had a thermometer to see how cold it is—our coal oil froze up today—looked like condensed milk. Guess we are on Byam Martin Island somewhere."[40]

Taggart later commented to a reporter with the *Vancouver Sunday Province* that they had broken all three thermometers on the trip so were unable to record their daily temperatures.

Early the next morning, the dogs gave warning that there was a bear around. Taggart quietly removed the block of snow that was at the entrance to the igloo and crawled outside to retrieve his rifle, which was leaning up against the wall of the shelter. He immediately spotted the bear, which was standing between the dogs and the igloo. He killed it and Nukappiannguaq came out to help him skin it and feed the dogs. They then retreated from the cold, which had once again frozen their coal oil, had a cup of coffee and fell back to sleep until 3:00 p.m. But when they woke and looked outside they had a surprise. It was a clear and cold day and for once they could see into the far distance. They had thought that they were on Byam Martin Island midway between Bathurst and Melville Islands, but they quickly discovered that they were nowhere near Byam Martin Island. Byam Martin was to their southwest and Melville was to their west. They had become disoriented in the storm and had been travelling north up Austin Channel to their present camp at Longford Point on Bathurst Island. Had the storm not abated, they would still be travelling north. They would try for Melville Island the next day.

Joy wrote:

We left camp at 4:00 a.m. on the 11th, and in less than an hour one of the runners of Constable Taggart's komitik broke. The old ice was found to be very ridgy, and covered with several inches of unpacked granulated snow which kept the dog's feet constantly bleeding. Towards the west side of the channel, however, we met with new ice and excellent travelling for about two hours, then old and new ice alternatively [sic] until we reached Melville Island a few miles north. During this march Constable Taggart's dogs showed unmistakable signs of weariness.[41]

Camping a few miles south of Richardson Point, they built an igloo. Taggart wrote that

> while we were eating our supper Joy said that if he had even dreamed that the ice was in such condition he would never have thought of the trip. We have had rough ice and deep snow all the way from Dundas Harbour to this place. We certainly can't go back the same way as the ice would be gone out to sea from Lancaster Sound and Barrow Straits. We are going to try to reach Winter Harbour on Melville and pick up supplies from the Government cache there, cross over Melville to Sabine Bay from Bridgeport [sic] Inlet, travel to Borden Island and then turn east and make for Bache Peninsula on Ellesmere Island. We have two weeks dog feed to carry out that programme; if our luck fails and we get no more bears we are going to be up against it.[42]

A storm sprang up early the next morning with the wind scouring several holes in the igloo. After repairing the holes and removing the drift that had sifted in over their belongings, they decided to spend the day resting. They talked all day and Taggart got up at midnight to feed the dogs and straighten the traces. He commented that the dogs are "getting thin—the severe cold and hard work is telling on them."[43] The following morning, with the cold and blizzard still raging, Taggart discovered that one of his dogs was frozen and couldn't rise. It was quickly dispatched. He wrote: "We waited about an hour and then decided to go on and travel on the shore ice. We did so and had a tough time facing the wind and drift from the south."[44] After crossing two points that they suspected were King Point and Rae Point, they spotted two caribou through the haze. Nukappiannguaq went after them while Joy and Taggart waited in the lee of a snow drift. Nukappiannguaq returned empty-handed three hours later. Taggart wrote that he

> walked about all the time to try to keep warm. Was chilled clean through—my hands nearly froze. I never had such a miserable three hours in all my life. I don't think I shall ever forget this day as long as I shall live.... We drove on about two or three miles, built our igloo and camped. The dogs are very hungry and tired—they feel the cold nearly as much as we do. We had our supper at 6 a.m. It was just eighteen hours since we had last eaten.[45]

Taggart taking a monthly wash at camp on Dealy Island. Photo courtesy of the Taggart Family

On April 16, the sun rose at 2:00 a.m. and by 6:00 a.m. the trio were travelling the shore ice around Arctic Point. Joy wrote that: "Five brilliant mock suns were visible in the east when we left camp at 6 a.m. Rough ice conditions compelled us to follow the coastline again all day. All our dogs were now very poor and suffering from sore feet, and although well fed they deteriorated daily."[46] The following morning, Nukappiannguaq rose early and informed Joy and Taggart that he was going to look for game. He returned at noon with the news that he had shot five caribou, and quickly departed with the dogs to retrieve them. Taggart helped skin them, and following a good feed for the dogs, the three enjoyed a hot meal of caribou tongues and kidneys. After a few hours' sleep, they departed camp at 10:00 p.m., passing Ross Point shortly after. There they spotted twenty-one muskox up on a hill. They left them undisturbed and at noon camped on the west side of Skene Bay, sleeping until they broke camp at midnight.

It began to snow almost immediately after they left camp, reducing visibility and forcing them back to the shore in order to continue their travel. Crossing a low point of land, they turned north and saw Dealy Island vaguely through the driving snow. About a mile off, however, they spotted a large bear that they pursued through the rough ice. Taggart's team was flagging so he dropped back and waited for Nukappiannguaq, who released his team to bring the bear to bay before he shot it. The dogs were immediately given a meal of warm meat before the men took a short rest. When they began again, they spotted a tall mast with three barrels nailed to its top on one of the highest hills of the island, and looking closely, they also spotted a building near the shore. They made haste toward it and Joy wrote that

> the cache on Dealey Island was deposited during the winter of 1852-53 by Commanders Kellett and McClintock, then in search of Sir John Franklin. The structure is 45 by 20 feet, built in lean-to style, the highest wall being ten feet high and the lowest seven feet. The sides and one end are built with neatly laid slabs of sandstone, the other end is composed of three large iron tanks surmounted by meat tins filled with sand and all the walls are still firm and intact. The roof was obviously made of canvas and has long since disappeared. The surface of the interior is a confusion of broken barrels, rotten clothing and fermented food. It is possible, however, that some of the casks beneath this chaos contain food yet of edible quality; for while in search of something to augment our supply of dog food for the homeward journey, we found a full two hundred pounds of perfectly good canned meat which was used with the utmost satisfaction.[47]

Taggart wrote about the place that it was

> full of snow inside but we could see all kinds of casks, two coal oil cisterns, a stove and some tools. The bears and foxes had accounted for all the salt pork. We smashed open several casks and found underwear, mitts, stockings, boots, coats, sweaters, etc., also found flour, raisins, potatoes, etc., and a big stack of canned meats and vegetables.[48]

Taggart also discovered two 303 rifles at the cache, but since they were manufactured in 1896, it was a puzzle, as the cache had been laid down in 1852–53. He surmised that they must have been left by another party. Taggart also tried some of the ammunition, which he deemed unreliable.

The following day it was decided that Joy and Nukappiannguaq would travel to Winter Harbour, thirty-five miles (fifty-six kilometres) to the east, while Taggart would remain at the cache to rest his dogs. Taggart took the opportunity to rummage through the cache and wrote: "I am wearing a suit of new underwear now and it is very warm. I believe all the woollen goods are hand knit."[49]

He also had time to reflect that by the time Henry Kellett's and Francis Leopold McClintock's storehouse on Dealy Island had been erected in the summer of 1853, there was really no hope that it would provide aid to any survivors of Franklin's lost expedition—too much time had elapsed. The reason for the storehouse was to provide succour to the many search expeditions that followed. Kellett and McClintock themselves were part of the last official fleet sent by the British Admiralty to solve the mystery of Franklin's fate, but there would be other unofficial expeditions that would follow. Kellet captained the HMS *Resolute* and McClintock the HMS *Intrepid*, both ships being under the leadership of Sir Edward Belcher, who commanded a total of five ships. Kellett and McClintock followed Belcher as far as Beechey Island where the two split off to spend the winter at Winter Harbour where Sir Edward Parry had wintered in 1819, but heavy ice stymied their efforts to enter the harbour so the two retreated to Dealy Island, located at the mouth of Bridport Inlet.

Belcher, their commander, had not only been instructed to determine the fate of Franklin, but also to discover the whereabouts of two other Royal Navy captains, Richard Collison aboard the HMS *Enterprise* and Robert McClure aboard the HMS *Investigator*. Both these ships were part of the British Admiralty's Franklin search fleet, but they had been instructed to enter the Arctic from the Pacific. Off the coast of Chile, the two ships had become separated and McClure beat Collinson to the Arctic. His ship became trapped in the ice at Mercy Bay on the north coast of Banks Island and during the winter he sledded to a high vantage point on the island's north coast where he had a commanding view to the east of Melville Island and Parry's winter quarters at Winter Harbour, thereby discovering the missing section of the Northwest Passage. That knowledge, however, did little to improve his plight. His ship was still locked in the ice, and desperate to save himself and his severely compromised shipmates, he sledded across the ice to Winter Harbour to leave a message there. Lieutenant Bedford Pim of Kellett's *Resolute* discovered McClure's note the following spring and travelled over the ice to find him at Mercy Bay. McClure then followed Pim back to where the *Resolute* and *Intrepid* were wintering at Dealy Island, and later sledded on to Beechey Island to join Belcher's *North Star*, which ferried him back to England.

While Joy and Nukappiannguaq were at Winter Harbour, Taggart relaxed at the cache, feeding the dogs bear meat until they were replete, and cooking his breakfast over an open fire made from barrel staves. A snow bunting made an appearance. Taggart wrote that: "I am very hungry for sweets and have been since leaving Beechey Island. None of us are getting enough sugar and grease to keep out the cold.... I noticed the silence for the first time today. I have often read about the silence that could be felt, but this is the first time I ever experienced it—there is absolutely no noise of any description."[50]

CHAPTER NINE

Bache Peninsula

On September 24, 1819, Sir William Edward Parry sailed the HMS *Hecla*, and his lieutenant, Matthew Liddon, sailed the HMS *Griper* into a protected harbour on the south shore of Melville Island that Parry would name Winter Harbour. He noted a prominent feature on the beach that would become as identifiable with him as Beechey Island is to Sir John Franklin.

He wrote that

> near the south-western point of this harbour there is a remarkable block of sandstone, somewhat resembling the roof of a house, on which the ship's names were subsequently engraved by Mr. Fisher. The stone is very conspicuous in coming from the eastward, and when kept open to the southward of the grounded ice at the end of the reef, forms a good leading mark for the channel into the harbour.[1]

This was the same sandstone boulder, known as Parry's Rock, that Captain Joseph Bernier affixed a plaque to on July 1, 1909, thus introducing the sector principle, the plaque reading: "This memorial is erected today to commemorate the taking possession for the Dominion of Canada of the whole Arctic Archipelago lying to the north of America from longitude 60 degrees west to 141 degrees west up to the latitude 90 degrees north."[2]

Two days after Parry's arrival, he wrote:

> At half-past one P.M. we began to track the ships along in the same manner as before, and at quarter past three we reached our winter-quarters, and hailed the event with three loud and hearty cheers from both ships' companies. The ships were in five fathoms' water, a cable's length from the beach on the north western side of the harbour, to which I gave the name of Winter Harbour.[3]

He also named the island Melville, after his sponsor, Robert Dundas, Second Viscount of Melville, who was also First Sea Lord at the time. Parry and his crew were locked in the ice for the next ten months. They endured three months of total darkness, which afforded the officers an opportunity to put on plays and publish a small newspaper. To ward off the cold, each crew member was issued a wolfskin blanket, and appropriate measures were implemented to stave off the scourge of these Arctic expeditions: scurvy.

When Parry left his winter quarters on August 1, 1820, after having to saw a passage through the ice to permit his release, and continued his journey west, he was forestalled by heavy pack ice at Cape Hay on Melville Island, longitude 113°48'22.5" west. That longitude would mark his farthest west position. Had he not been obstructed by ice, he would have sailed through what is now McClure Strait and into the Beaufort Sea, through the Bering Strait and on into the Pacific, thus becoming the first to transit the Northwest Passage. It was not to be, however, but one thing Parry did accomplish was to recognize that Lancaster Sound was the entrance to the fabled passage.[4]

Joy and Nukappiannguaq arrived at the government cache at Winter Harbour in the early morning hours of April 20, 1928. The cache had been established by Captain Bernier during his 1908-1909 expedition to aid any parties that were stranded or in need of supplies. Joy wrote:

> We found the door of the shack partly open, and the floor at the north end of the building covered by a full two feet of soft snow. The shack is a well-built structure and is in good repair. The contents of the shack were as follows: 7 tins of flour, each about 50 pounds; 25 pound tin of tea, sealed; 12 10-pound tins of bovril, tins are corroded and contents spoilt; 1 double-barrel hammerless shotgun; a few rounds of shotgun ammunition, spoilt by moisture; 1 303-cal. rifle; 1 case 303 rifle ammunition, unopened; 3 large oars for rowboat; 1 wooden komitik runner, manufactured, and miscellaneous articles of cast-off clothing. An 18-ft clinker-built rowboat, apparently in good repair, was lying bottom up at the back of the shack, frozen down and partly covered by snow. Inside the shack I picked up a note dated July 8, 1917, left by Vilhjalmur Stefanssen [sic], Commander of the Arctic Expedition 1913–18, which I replaced with a note of our visit.[5]

Taggart later related Joy's surprise that Stefansson had taken so much from the cache.

The patrol returned on April 22, after having been away four days, and said that they had found a note left by Vilhjalmur Stefansson, the explorer, who had been in these waters several years before, saying that he had taken most of the supplies. As we were expecting to renew our own supplies from the cache, in which only some hundred pounds of flour and seven pounds of compressed tea were left, we were rather disappointed to find that there was little for us.[6]

Joy wrote:

We camped in the shack and although our stay here extended well over 24 hours, we failed to get a view of the adjacent coast line through the thick falling snow. We set out on our return journey at 9 a.m. on the 21st. Within half an hour of leaving the shack we passed two bears travelling west. Nookapeeunggwak [sic] presaged the appearance of a bear early in this march while we were having breakfast. He has done this with uncanny accuracy on five other occasions during this patrol. His premonitions, he tells me, invariably come through dreams which he sees a woman stripped to the waist.[7]

Joy and Nukappiannguaq arrived back at the Dealy Island cache on April 22 under stormy conditions that did not abate until the evening of the 23rd. It was a short intermission, however, highlighted by seven mock suns, a first for Taggart who had only ever seen four or five before, and Joy noted that it was followed almost immediately by a "fierce gale from the northwest, which prevailed until noon the following day."[8] Then, clear, calm and sunny weather interceded, which permitted the trio to dry their clothing and have their first wash in six weeks. They boiled up some of the currants they had discovered at the site and they were so good that they consumed another pot. The following day they opened about fifty tins of the canned meat, about 150 pounds (68 kilograms), Taggart noting that it was "similar to corned beef."[9] They placed it in sacks for dog feed, with Taggart writing that "some of the meat is as good today as it was when it was canned eighty or more years ago."[10] He later added that "this cache was laid down eighty years ago, and the directions for opening (the meat) were to use a hammer and chisel. We used an axe instead, and found the meat very good, although we did not use very much of it."[11]

The tins were labelled Fortnum & Mason, the principal supplier of Sir John Franklin's expedition, which purchased an astonishing 65,000 pounds of "tinned, dried and bottled foods, including 18 oxen."[12] In 1853, Lady Franklin also provisioned her rescue ships with Fortnum & Mason goods, and it was her tins that were likely found at Dealy Island by Taggart and Joy.

Joy wrote that night that

> early in this patrol I realized that should it occupy more than two months, it would be difficult if at all possible to return to Dundas Harbour along Lancaster Sound; and from the constant prevalence of fog over Devon Island and other atmospheric signs, I concluded that Jones Sound was unfrozen, and that our return to Dundas Harbour by that route would be equally difficult and uncertain. I therefore determined to proceed to Bache Peninsula by way of the north end of Melville Island, and await the arrival of a ship there.[13]

They departed Dealy Island at 9:00 a.m. on April 26, loaded down with so much dog food that they had to abandon their polar bear hides. Taggart wrote in explanation: "We expect to pass over a starvation belt of country on our way to Bache."[14] Before that, however, they travelled "over a low peninsula into Bridgeport [Bridport] Inlet and reached the head of the Inlet two and a half hours after leaving Dealey [Dealy] Island, a distance of twelve miles. Travelled in a general direction north, along river beds, over ridges and across lakes, through valleys and over hills."[15] They camped about halfway to Sabine Bay, and Taggart wrote that the weather was so fine that for once the dogs were too warm. Nukappiannguaq shot three caribou where they camped and they all, including the dogs, enjoyed a meal of fresh meat. Upon arrival at Sabine Bay early in the afternoon of the 27th, Taggart noted that the ice there was over a hundred years old and free of pressure ridges, so that they made good progress all that afternoon and into the evening.

They camped at 10:00 p.m., and before turning in, Taggart gave the dogs a good feed of fresh caribou meat. Breaking camp at noon on the 28th, by 2:00 p.m. they had reached the head of Hecla and Griper Bay and now set their sights on Cape Mudge, midway up the Sabine Peninsula. Joy noted that it was obvious that the ice had not gone out for several years. It was ridgy and covered with a significant layer of loose snow, thigh deep in places, that made travel for both man and dog difficult. As well, the snow was granular and lodged between the dogs' toes, causing their feet to bleed. They camped late that night midway across the bay with Joy writing that the sun did not set. Taggart fed the dogs their last share of the fresh meat and noted that they had only twelve days supply of pemmican left. After that they would have to source some game. As they were now entering what Taggart termed the "starvation belt," that might prove difficult. However, in contradiction, Joy noted that they had passed six caribou just before reaching the coastline and there was still a modest amount of vegetation about.

Joy then wrote that "the following afternoon we reached Cape Mudge. Near the cape we passed some large food tins filled with gravel standing on a knoll. These bore the name of Fortnut, Masson and Company [Fortnum & Mason] of London, and were dated 1852."[16] That night they made camp midway up Eldridge Bay and were forced to consume an old piece of walrus meat that was embedded with small pebbles and coated with coal dust that they had rescued from the dog's feed. On top of that, they consumed a few salted sea biscuits that had been inadvertently soaked in seawater while on Timbury's journey to check and restore the cache on Beechey Island. Their food, as well as the dogs', was running dangerously low.

On April 30, they broke camp at 5:00 p.m. with cold and heavy fog to the northwest. They struggled through rough ice until they were past MacDougall Point, where the ice became smoother. Off Roche Point, at the end of the peninsula, a high fog bank blotted out the sun, but they had occasional glimpses of Vesey Hamilton Island to their north, which kept them on track. They travelled on good ice until, within about four miles (six kilometres) of the island, they encountered rough ice through which they struggled to reach the shore before they camped. Joy noted the physical features of the island:

> The nature and formation of Vesey Hamilton Island is remarkable. The whole of it is composed of loose and conspicuously dark soil with occasional outcrop of pumice, and is devoid of vegetation. The hills, several hundred feet high, are serrated, with knife-like peaks and edges and very steep slopes; the ravines are deep, and narrow down to a mere groove, which gives the island the appearance of a miniature Rocky Mountains.[17]

The following morning, they climbed to the highest point of the island and looked to the north toward Borden Island, their axis point. The ice between Vesey Hamilton and Borden was impossibly pressured. Taggart wrote that: "It looks very bad; piled up in every conceivable shape and form, anywhere from twenty-five to seventy-five feet high."[18] Joy wrote that at 5 p.m. the same day, in fairly clear weather, we set out northward for Borden Island. When well away from the land we were for once materially assisted by the existence of enormous snowdrifts, on some of which we were able to travel through and over the rough ice for a quarter mile. The runners of both komitiks were split on this march; the front of one runner on one komitik and both on the other were so badly broken that only the heavy metal shoeing held them together. On the 3rd we made good progress over new ice for about 9 miles, and then met with old ice similar to that of the previous day. Here I relinquished the intention of visiting Borden Island, and turned southeast for the south end of Lougheed Island.[19]

Taggart noted that the ice was so rough that they had to stop every hundred yards or so to climb a pressure ridge to map their way forward. Joy, whom Taggart described as in "tough" shape, wrote:

We continued to travel over old ice, sometimes rough and sometimes moderately even, the remainder of this march and all the following one, at the end of which we reached Edmund Walker Island about 8 a.m. on the 5th, and camped. Scattered small herds of caribou numbering over 40 animals could be seen on Edmund Walker and Lougheed Islands. Our provisions were then almost exhausted; our dog feed was low, and we therefore killed ten of them.[20]

Taggart woke early the next morning and looking through a hole in the tent, observed that the dogs, now well fed, were still sleeping soundly. He had something to eat and went back to bed. It was overcast and snowing. He later noted that: "We are sleeping like animals. Joy says everyone does the same on a trip, especially a long trip where a person is exposed to the cold and works hard."[21] Taggart later mentioned this fact in a letter to his brother, John, where he wrote that "it's wonderful how a person can sleep in this country in winter time when he is sleeping in an igloo[.] I have been in the sleeping robe for fourteen hours go out and look at the traps and get back into bed… and sleep again for another fourteen. I guess the cold is the cause of it."[22] The cold and exhaustion influenced their decision to rest for a couple of days. Both men and dogs needed to re-energize, and burdened with the weight of the fresh caribou kill, their sleds were expected to weigh as much as they did when they left Dealy Island.

They departed in the late evening of May 8, travelling up the east coast of Lougheed Island until at the twenty-mile mark they struck off in a northeasterly direction across Maclean Strait for King Christian Island, the monotony of the journey wearing on them. Taggart later noted that "you get so that it seems you have been mushing forever, and that you will never stop. Slowly one scene merges into another, but somehow the landscape is always the same."[23]

They were now approaching Sverdrup's domain, with whom, coincidentally, Ottawa was still wrestling over ownership of the eponymously named group of islands. They soon got into heavy ice, Taggart freezing two of his fingers and Joy, his cheek and nose. They camped at 9:00 a.m. in the rough ice. Early in the morning on the 10th, they broke camp, Taggart writing that the

ice was very bad for the first four hours. After sighting King Christian I. 5 a.m. the ice got much worse. We struck some old pack ice which had been drifting around the Arctic Ocean for no one knows how many years. I thought we had been through rough ice but this beat everything; harness breaking, traces breaking and kometic breaking, we had a merry time for the next five hours. The dogs would pull for everything they had while I pushed behind up a steep slope thirty feet high, then shoot down the other side, up another one and down again, soft snow, hard snow, all kinds of snow, over blocks of ice, under some and around others.[24]

They camped, exhausted, and slept all night with the tent flap open to gain some benefit from the ever-present sun.

Breaking camp at 5:00 a.m., they immediately discovered a smooth stretch of ice that took them right to King Christian Island. They moved north up the island's shore for four miles (six kilometres), turning northwest along its coast for another six miles (ten kilometres) until they reached its northern extremity. Taggart noted that they saw no game, but did see some old signs; as well, they spotted some coal on the beach. Hugging the island's north coast for eight miles (thirteen kilometres), they launched across Danish Strait from its northeast corner, crossing to Ellef Ringnes Island in two-and-a-half hours. Taggart noted that the last run was the best they had had for some time. He also observed that the island was flat with no fresh signs of game. They camped at 6:00 p.m., departing camp at 8:30 the following morning. Then they had three hours of good sledding until they were just past Cape Nathorst on the island's southern extremity where they met rough ice through an old section of piled up ice floes.

Complicating matters, a heavy fog descended, and the biting cold returned in the early afternoon. They camped at the mouth of Hendriksen Strait, the narrow body of water separating Amund Ringnes Island from Cornwall Island.

On this leg, Joy wrote that

> during the latter part of this march we passed several bear tracks, and although not fresh they put spirit into our dogs for several hours. These were the first bear tracks we had seen since leaving Bridport Inlet. Bears as a rule do not frequent areas covered by old ice, that is ice more than one season old, particularly where no open leads exist, because it is almost impossible for them to capture seals there. This accounts for the total absence of all signs of these animals between Bridport Inlet and our present position, and the presence of so many of them on Lancaster Sound, Barrow Strait, and Melville Sound.[25]

On the 14th, they set off in perfect weather along the north coast of Cornwall Island, skirting the shore, and at a couple of points, passing over low points of land. Taggart noted that they came abreast of a very high cape on the island's north coast, the highest point of land they had seen since leaving Devon Island. Joy wrote that they then turned northeast toward Axel Heiberg Island, camping three hours later approximately twelve miles (twenty kilometres) from Cornwall. He observed that

> many bear tracks were passed, and lemming tracks were also very plentiful. Signs of the latter animal have been particularly abundant along the whole course of this patrol. We have seen great numbers of their tracks more than a day's journey from land on the tops of icebergs, in the roughest kind of pack ice, and in deep snow. These persistent little travellers obviously are not deterred in their migrations by such obstacles as rough ice and deep snow.[26]

The good weather was welcome, but at the same time a menace. All were suffering from various degrees of snow blindness; Taggart's eyes were streaming and his nose was running as well. He admitted that he had neglected to wear his snow glasses as much as he should have. The next morning his eyes were fine, but within two minutes of being exposed to the sun, they began weeping again to the point that he had difficulty seeing. They travelled for ten-and-a-half hours over smooth ice, reaching Cape Southwest on the southwest corner of Axel Heiberg Island a few hours past midnight where they camped. Departing camp at 9:30 p.m. the same day, they travelled along the island's southern coast, no more than half a mile (a kilometre) from shore, where they observed that the island was both mountainous and ice-bound inland. Taggart lamented that their provisions were running extremely low. Their coffee had been finished a few days earlier, they had eaten all their sea biscuits, and had almost consumed all of the caribou meat harvested at Edmund Walker Island. Dog feed was also running perilously low. The one saving grace was that both men and dogs were weaker, and thankful for the lighter loads.

An hour into their day, travelling along the southern shore of Axel Heiberg Island, they met soft snow, which slowed their progress considerably. They camped about ten miles (sixteen kilometres) west of Gletcher Fiord (Glacier Fiord) where one of Nukappiannguaq's dogs gave birth to a litter of pups that were promptly consumed by the rest of the dogs. An hour after leaving camp at 11:00 that evening, the soft snow abated and the sledding improved across the fiord, improving still more as they approached Hyperite Point at the fiord's eastern extremity. Almost three years to the day, Joy and Nukappiannguaq had left a note in a cairn at Hyperite Point explaining the route of their patrol, a patrol that had been unquestionably motivated by a query from the American commander, Richard E. Byrd, about whether a Canadian had ever set foot on Axel Heiberg Island. This patrol would now count as another official visit to the island.

While crossing the fiord, they were surprised to discover two sets of qamutiik tracks. Taggart wrote: "We all got excited, though the tracks were old, but we haven't seen any one for over two months so even tracks made by someone else is something to start a person thinking of other people."[27] Taggart guessed that Corporal Anstead from the Bache Peninsula detachment had been there looking for bears. Indeed, on the other side of Wolf Fiord on the west side of Ulvingen Island, they discovered a camp with the bones of three bears and some hares. Nukappiannguaq saw two seals on the ice and went after them. The dogs were grateful, since they were not too fond of the pemmican they were being fed.

Since the dogs were weak from exertion and tired from their big feed of seal meat, and because both Joy and Nukappiannguaq's eyes had not yet recovered from their bout of snow blindness, it was decided that they would take a day of rest. They spread their foot gear and mitts in the sun to dry and went back to bed. Taggart lamented that whoever had been hunting in the area had taken all the game. They decamped at 11:00 a.m. the following morning and headed in a northerly direction up Eureka Sound on wind-swept ice until they were abreast of Skaare Fiord where they saw and killed a brace of hares. Although they also saw three muskox, they let them be. Crossing the sound, they camped on Ellesmere Island opposite the southern end of Stor Island. Taggart reckoned that there must be a constant wind sweeping through Eureka Sound to keep the ice so bare. Joy wrote that soon after starting, however, they encountered deep snow at the entrance to Grethasoer Bay Fiord (now called Bay Fiord), which slowed their progress somewhat. He also observed an abundance of wolf, fox and hare tracks all along the shore for about ten miles (sixteen kilometres) and then saw a multitude of caribou and muskox tracks crossing Eureka Sound to Axel Heiberg Island. They camped at the eastern end of a small island approximately ten miles (sixteen kilometres) inside the fiord.

Breaking camp at 1:00 p.m. on May 22, they encountered more soft snow as they made their way toward a low point in the land between Strathcona Fiord and Grethasoer Bay Fiord. Nukappiannguaq saw a seal and went after it, but missed. Meanwhile, unknown to him, he was being stalked by four wolves. Joy and Taggart drove their qamutiik up to him and made him aware of the danger. The wolves disappeared over a hill, but not before Nukappiannguaq took a shot at one, hitting it in the back and killing it. Joy noted that it was an "exceptionally fat animal,"[28] and although it was fresh meat, the dogs would not touch it. They had no trouble consuming their own kind, but they shied away from wolf meat. Close by, the men discovered an old igloo that had likely been built by the hunting party. There was nothing in it, but it made for a convenient camp. That evening, Taggart and Nukappiannguaq went hunting and returned with four hares that would satisfy their needs for the next two days.

Rising at 3:00 p.m. on the 23rd, Nukappiannguaq went seal hunting again while Joy and Taggart sat on the qamutiit in the sun and discussed the vast difference in the temperatures between Melville Island, which was considered cold country, and where they were on Ellesmere Island, which was considered mild. Game was abundant and several herds of muskox were sighted about five miles (eight kilometres) away, one herd having twenty-five large animals plus some calves. Taggart estimated that the herds contained an accumulation of about sixty to seventy animals. The following day they elected to take another day of rest. Nukappiannguaq killed three seals, which gave the dogs and themselves a good feed. They also shot ten hares. Taggart noted that they had all been faithfully wearing their snow goggles and that all their eyes were in good shape.

On May 25, they broke camp at 6:00 p.m., and at the head of Grethasoer Bay Fiord, they found a tin of biscuits that a previous party had discarded. And a little further on, Taggart discovered a pound of butter and a jar of jam under a rock in a riverbed. This was fortunate given that they had only one pound of butter left, a little cheese and some sardines. Upon leaving the river bed, Joy spotted three muskox about a quarter mile off and instructed Taggart to go after one even though it was in contravention of the tenets of the Arctic Islands Preserve.* As soon as Taggart left his qamutiik, the animals moved off, forcing him to release one of his dogs to bring them to bay. He waited for them to settle and selected the youngest of the three, given that any muskox over two years old was considered tough eating. He felled it with one shot and waited again for the other two animals to move off. The larger one was mad, pawing the snow and shaking its head. Taggart called his dog off and the two muskox scampered up the hill. Taggart retrieved the downed animal and after butchering it gave the dogs a good feed while he, Joy and Nukappiannguaq feasted on the tenderest bits, which were still tough.

Breaking camp at 10:00 p.m., Joy wrote that they "followed the south side of the fiord until it turned northward. Near the angle on the east side we turned into a river-bed which leads part way to the inland ice, and camped about four miles further on at 7:30 a.m."[29] The next day they followed the tracks made by the other party, assumed to be members of the Bache Peninsula detachment, which led them to a lake they crossed in half an hour. They then began climbing through the hills toward the ice cap. Taggart wrote:

> We were four hours on the way before we reached the ice cap, but when we finally got there we had a lovely view of Grathson [Grethasoer] Bay Fiord. We could see all the little islands and bays all along its length. Here we ate some cheese and butter. Travelled about two hours on the ice then stopped again and made something to drink. Went on.[30]

They were travelling between two mountain ranges, crossing the peak of the ice cap at 6:00 a.m. on May 27. An hour later they camped within view of Beitstad Fiord on Ellesmere's east coast. Taggart wrote that the "dogs and men

---

*   In a letter to his brother John, Taggart wrote "I got one musk ox don't tell this outside the family of course, we needed the meat and had to get it some way."

are very tired—we crossed a lot of ground today."[31] The following day, they broke camp at 2:00 a.m., Taggart writing that they travelled

> five hours all down hill till we came to the end of the ice cap. We had a little trouble getting down on to a small lake but managed to do it without unloading.... We came to a place where a glacier had made its way through a crack in the mountains on one side, across the lake to the mountains on the other side. We couldn't get around it so had to climb up on top of it. We hadn't any trouble till we got to the other side where we had to get down over a straight wall eighty feet high. We were seven hours on the job, unloading the kometics and lowering everything with ropes. The dogs landed in a snow drift without being hurt when we drove them over. Then we had some tea and cheese, loaded up and drove to the ice in Birtstadt [Beitstad] Fiord.... Made camp beside a large iceberg 8 p.m. We were on the trail eighteen hours today.[32]

The men slept until noon, and after breakfast performed some personal hygiene in anticipation of reaching the Bache Peninsula detachment in a day or so. Taggart wrote that they

> broke camp 5 p.m. and travelled down Birtstadt [Beitstad] Fiord to Hays Sound. We passed over a lot of kometic tracks one or two days old and saw where several seals had been killed. Followed a well beaten trail which we found. On rounding a small point of land we saw a tent up on shore with a team of dogs tied to the ice. We drove up close. On arriving at the tent we were met by an Eskimo by the name of Ahkeoo. He was speechless with surprise and trembling like a leaf. He told us that he and McLean from Bache were out seal hunting. Mac was away hunting at the time so we made some coffee and ate up some of their biscuits and jam. Mac came in 10 p.m. I met him on the ice as he drove up. He didn't know me at first; he had to take his glasses off and have a good look before he recognized me. We had a long talk—all of us. It was funny to see the two Eskimos; they were sitting knee to knee, opposite each other, exchanging news.[33]

McLean also advised the trio that their dates were off by one day. Taggart and Joy had argued about that at Dealy Island, Joy now admitting that Taggart had been right. The two groups talked until 2:00 a.m. on the 31st and departed for the detachment an hour later, arriving at the post at 7:00 a.m. Corporal Anstead and Constable Beatty were still asleep when they arrived, but were soon roused by the strange voices in the detachment. They related to the trio that they had lost one of their Inuit companions to tuberculosis during the winter, and the summer before that, they had lost a young boy who had gone out in his kayak after a seal, but failed to return. Only his kayak was recovered. Ahkeoo then told them that his brother, who lived in Greenland, had been killed by a walrus while in his kayak.

Taggart wrote of the journey's conclusion on May 31, 1929: "This finished the patrol which lasted eighty-one days, covering a distance of approximately eighteen hundred miles. We hunted feed for sixty days as we left Dundas Harbour with twenty-one days dog feed on the kometics—the dogs never missed a meal during the trip. When we arrived at Bache we were minus four dogs which we killed when they became useless—I lost two and so did Nuqaqpainguaq."[34]

Joy summarized the journey in his diary as follows:

It might appear that the quantity of game killed on this trip would exceed our essential requirements; but in reality, such was not the case, for everything captured was needed and appreciated. Our phenomenal luck in securing so many bears, without losing time hunting, during the first half of the journey counteracted in large measure our misfortune in meeting with such bad travelling conditions over most of the route, enabling us to conserve our preserved dog-feed for the homeward journey, where otherwise it would have necessitated delay for hunting purposes. Our dogs were well fed all through the patrol, and did not miss a meal, except when it was thought expedient for them to do so.

As it happened, however, there was no necessity for so much haste on our part; for on arriving near Ellesmere Island, where in former years at an earlier date we had met with open leads, water on the ice, and snow-free land, there was yet no sign of a thaw having occurred. The spring had been an exceptionally cold one; the weather for over two months on this patrol was as cold as and sometimes colder than any we had experienced during the winter at Dundas Harbour.

A party travelling in the vicinity of Bathurst or Melville Islands need have no concerns about securing fresh meat for themselves and their dogs;

for, judging by the quantity of game and signs of it we saw, a day's hunting anywhere on these parts we touched at, I believe, would yield a substantial supply. Melville Island from a traveller's point of view, I would say, is the paradise of the eastern Arctic islands, and is equaled only in the occurrence of game by small areas on the west coast of Ellesmere island.

It would be difficult to compare the mileage of this patrol with any degree of accuracy owing to the necessity of our following almost every indentation of the coastline for hundreds of miles, and making great detours in the rough ice to take advantage of the best travelling conditions available; but from the number of hours spent on the trail each day, and the consistency of our daily marches, I would estimate the distance covered to be well over seventeen hundred miles. Time occupied, eighty-one days.[35]

Commissioner Cortlandt Starnes wrote in his report for the year ended September 30, 1929, that the patrol to Melville Island was the "most noteworthy event of the year."[36] Similar tributes were offered by others, both colleagues and admirers of Joy, using such terms as "one of the most impressive sledge trips ever achieved."[37] Later, Rear-Admiral Byrd (promoted to Rear-Admiral December 21, 1929) was so impressed with Joy that he invited him to accompany him to the Antarctic. Commissioner Starnes was agreeable, but Joy declined. Even Stefansson, who had caused the Canadian government so much grief, but whose achievements are still noteworthy, offered that Joy's patrol was "the finest sledge journey ever made by the RNWMP or the RCMP."[38] Although it appears in the literature that Joy received much of the attention and credit for the patrol given that he was its leader, were it not for the hunting and travelling prowess and the fortitude and determination of both Constable Taggart and Nukappiannguaq, the journey would not have been possible. Joy, himself, ever so humble and quick to give others credit, would have agreed.

The end of the patrol was by no means the end of the Sverdrup conflict, however, and while Joy, Taggart and Nukappiannguaq were demonstrating the ultimate display of effective occupation, Ottawa had only just begun its long and complicated negotiation with Sverdrup and the Norwegian government.

CHAPTER TEN

Sverdrup: The Final Chapter

Prime Minister W.L. Mackenzie King received a letter from Otto Sverdrup on May 7, 1929. The letter, which was passed to him by Eivind Bordewick, Sverdrup's proxy, was dated April 22, 1929, and laid out Sverdrup's case for compensation from the Canadian government for the "so called" Sverdrup Islands. The letter also served to introduce Bordewick, who would represent him in the anticipated negotiations. Bordewick, who was the general agent for Norway of the Canadian Pacific Railway Company, held Sverdrup's power of attorney and was authorized to make the best deal for him that he could. At the conclusion of his letter, Sverdrup had written: "I beg to add that the four years exploration of the so called Sverdrup Islands has taken the prime of the strength of the power of my life, and as this struggle and work has hitherto not given me any pecuniary return, I venture to hope that your Government will meet my wishes in connection with the cession of these lands to Canada, on the condition that suitable compensation is paid to me."[1]

Sverdrup's letter was preceded by one from the Arctic explorer, Fridtjof Nansen, supporting Sverdrup's plea, and a couple of weeks later by one from George Ferguson, premier of Ontario, who had just visited Norway, his letter endeavouring to pave the way for Bordewick to meet with the prime minister. It was Oscar Skelton, under-secretary of state for External Affairs, however, who took the initial meeting with Bordewick, not the prime minister.[2]

No more than a week before Sverdrup wrote his letter to the prime minister, the Norwegian government had offered him free rein to negotiate financial compensation directly with the Canadian government following Britain's recognition of Norway's claim to Bouvet Island. Sverdrup would receive no compensation from his own government. There was one stipulation, however, one that was never communicated to the Canadian government by either Sverdrup or his proxy, and that was that if the Norwegian government were to relinquish its claim, then it "would only be possible on the condition that if the Sverdrup Islands were opened for commercial activities, the rights of Norwegian citizens in such endeavours would have to be secured."[3]

And, as if that was not enough of a complication, on May 8, Norway had annexed another small island known as Jan Mayen Island, this time located in the North Atlantic between Spitzburgen and Iceland. The Norwegian government had established a meteorological station on the island in 1921 and claimed it by right of occupation even though the right of discovery lay with Britain. Laurence Collier, first secretary of the Foreign Office, United Kingdom, in a meeting of the Interdepartmental Committee on the Antarctic, mentioned Jan Mayen Island and the difficulty that the Norwegian annexation presented. Collier stated that the Norwegian government could not go about claiming any territory that it desired, and that it could not have it both ways, that is, claiming Jan Mayen Island under the right of occupation and then holding fast to the Sverdrup Islands under the right of discovery; it lacked consistency. He further stated that "with regard to this island there were certain grounds on which we could make trouble if we wanted to; we should prefer not to raise them but if we were not to do so they must really drop their absurd claims such as that to the Otto Sverdrup Islands."[4]

Alexander Leeper, first secretary, counsellor, Western Department, Foreign Office, United Kingdom, who was also at the meeting, suggested that the committee should first determine what stage of negotiation the Canadian government was at with the Norwegians, and depending upon that knowledge, decide whether to pursue the use of Jan Mayen Island as a pawn in the negotiation. In a coded and secret memo to the high commissioner of the United Kingdom on May 29, Leopold Amery, secretary of state for Dominion Affairs, wrote that "though not admitting the grounds on which the Norwegian claim is based we are not disposed to raise objection to the annexation, but it occurs to us that in return for our acquiescence it might be possible to insist on abandonment of extravagant Norwegian claims in other parts of the world, e.g., the claim to the Otto Sverdrup Islands."[5]

On May 30, the day before Joy, Taggart and Nukappiannguaq arrived at the Bache Peninsula Detachment, Charles Stewart, the minister of the interior, wrote an internal memo stating that he had closely reviewed Sverdrup's letter to the prime minister. He noted that Bordewick had called him some time earlier, and when he asked him if Sverdrup had left any "particular markings or officially taken possession of this territory,"[6] referring to the Sverdrup Islands, Bordewick was unable to determine from Sverdrup whether he had. Sverdrup, however, according to his book, (*New Land*), on May 4, 1900, while near Cape

North-West on the northwest coast of Axel Heiberg Island, decided that he and his companion, Ivar Fosheim, had reached their furthest north camp because of the poor condition of their dogs.

The following morning they found a spot on a "little Knoll" above their camp and proceeded to construct a cairn. Sverdrup wrote that

> on the top of the cairn we placed a tall stone, in which Fosheim made a hole with a chisel for a flagstaff, which bore the Norwegian flag. We then took a meridian altitude, which, when worked out on the spot gave a latitude of 80°55′ N., and placed under the cairn a record of our journey on the west coast, to which we added the latitude we had observed; finally we took some photographs of the cairn with its surroundings.[7]

Sverdrup believed that raising the Norwegian flag was adequate notification of a territorial claim and perhaps that is why he made no specific mention of a claim in his book the day that he and Fosheim raised his country's flag over the cairn. And, despite "several searches, this cairn has never been located."[8] However, almost as an afterthought, and again lacking any specifics, Sverdrup did write in the summary of his expedition two years later that he claimed one hundred thousand square miles in the name of the king of Norway.

Stewart concluded his memo with: "Before any action is taken, or consideration given, we should have from Mr. Sverdrup and the Norwegian Government full particulars as to their claims for consideration in connection with this territory."[9]

Later that same day, the Northern Advisory Board met at Stewart's office in Ottawa, the meeting being almost totally consumed by a discussion of the Sverdrup issue. Skelton reviewed much of the recent correspondence regarding the negotiations and then mentioned that the matter was very controversial in Norway. The reigning Liberal party, which was in a minority position, favoured granting the Canadian government sovereignty upon satisfaction of Sverdrup's compensation, while the Conservative party wanted the matter submitted to the League of Nations for review. The Communist Party was on the fence.

Meanwhile, Russia was stirring the pot, at least according to Norway. Britain's minister in Oslo, Sir Francis Lindley, had just received news that Russia had recently hoisted its flag on Franz Joseph Land, a group of 192 mostly glaciated islands located at 81°N latitude and directly north of the Russian coast. That action was the result of a decree issued by the Soviet Union on April 15, 1926, that claimed "as Russian territory all islands and lands, known or unknown, lying within that portion of the Arctic Ocean which is bounded on the South by the Russian Coast and on the east and west by meridians drawn from the North Pole to the Behring Strait and the Russo-Norwegian boundary respectively."[10] This had all the earmarks of Russia announcing its adherence to the sector principle, thus emulating Canada's sector announcement a year earlier. Of course, Norway objected to the flag raising, considering that it had economic interests in the area. But the Norwegian government was hardly in a position to complain, given its extemporaneous sovereign declarations over remote islands of late, but through its emissary in Britain, it still wanted to know what the British and Canadian governments' thoughts were of the Soviet action.

Canada was obviously reluctant to voice its opinion, given that the Sverdrup negotiations had yet to be concluded. More relevant though was that the decree issued by the Soviets had its roots in the Russo-American Treaty of 1867 when Russia sold Alaska to the United States. That treaty outlined the exact longitudinal boundaries of the purchase, and given that Canada had referenced the same treaty in support of its sector declaration, it was best to leave well enough alone.

This had also been the consensus of those attending the 1926 Imperial Conference in London where the Soviet decree was discussed. But the Antarctic Policy Committee at the meeting was in a quandary:

> By protesting against the argument on which the Russian claim is based we might be held to weaken the Canadian claim to Axel Heiberg Land and neighbouring territory (the Ringnes I[ds]) which was first explored by Sverdrup's Norwegian expedition in 1900-2 and which both Norway and the United States are known to covet.
>
> On the other hand, by accepting the Soviet argument we might conceivably stimulate other Powers (the Argentine; Chile; Norway [qua sovereign of Bouvet Island], France [qua sovereign of Kerguelen and the Crozet Islands]) to proclaim their annexation of Antarctic regions to which they are the nearest neighbours.[11]

The committee therefore "decided that the most satisfactory course would be to take no action."[12]

On May 31, the subcommittee of the Northern Advisory Board met to hear Bordewick's in-person request for Sverdrup's compensation. The subcommittee members consisted of Oscar Skelton, under-secretary of state for External Affairs, Oswald Finnie, director, Northwest Territories and Yukon Branch, Department of the Interior, Cortlandt Starnes, RCMP commissioner, and George Mackenzie, officer in charge of the Eastern Arctic Patrol. Bordewick first made it clear that he was acting for Otto Sverdrup who had, without success over many years until just recently, endeavoured to interest his own government in sovereignty over the islands. Bordewick also cautioned that he expected an imminent change in his government, which might very well upset the present favourable situation. He recognized that although the Sverdrup Islands had been transferred to Canada via the imperial order-in-council of 1880, which predated Sverdrup's explorations, Sverdrup was seeking compensation for the scientific and exploratory work that he had conducted over his four years in the Arctic.

Bordewick then asked for a few minutes with the prime minister, but Skelton, chairman of the subcommittee, advised him that their report would quickly be made available to the government. After Bordewick left, the subcommittee decided that they needed more information, in line with Stewart's memo advice, and since Oscar Skelton was due to visit England in the fall, he would "communicate with the British authorities in London with a view to securing a report on the standing of the Norwegian Government and on Commander Sverdrup's claims."[13]

Bordewick, however, still pressed for an audience with the prime minister, principally because he wanted to provide him with a current assessment of the political climate in Norway. As well, perhaps, he felt that he could not return to Norway and face Sverdrup empty-handed. To that end, Oscar Skelton wrote a memo to the prime minister with some background information, outlining the efforts of the government to date, which included Skelton having met with Bordewick on three occasions. Skelton had advised Bordewick that as "the Canadian Government considered that this territory was already in its possession, any discussion of the matter would be without prejudice to that understanding."[14] He also mentioned that Bordewick was expecting Sverdrup to be reimbursed for the whole cost of his expedition, which was in the neighbourhood of $200,000 (equal to about $400,000 in 1929 and, in context, about $7 million in 2023). In reference, he added that Canada's annual ship patrol cost was about $100,000 per year.

Skelton further advised the prime minister that

the attitude of the Norwegian Government in regard [to] its claims to these islands has been somewhat undecided. At intervals for the past three or four years the Norwegian Consul-General took up the question of Canadian jurisdiction. No definite reply was made pending an attempt to strengthen our title by further Royal Canadian Mounted Police administration. Last year the Norwegian Government informed us that they "reserved to Norway all rights under international law" in connection with the said areas.

Recently the Liberal Government in Norway considered the matter and indicated its readiness to relinquish any title they might have to these islands in favour of Canada, if the Canadian Government would reimburse Captain Sverdrup for the expenses of his expedition.[15]

Following Skelton arranging Bordewick's meeting with the prime minister, Bordewick wrote to thank him, but also to inform him of what he imagined were the next steps, steps that were included in an attached enclosure to be presented to both Skelton and the prime minister. It detailed three items, the first of which was an acknowledgment that the Canadian government recognized the value of Sverdrup's work and was willing to offer him compensation; the second was that a final settlement would be made in London on October 1, 1929; and the third was that the Norwegian government would offer full relinquishment of any claim they had over the land in question.

Skelton was likely a bit nonplussed, as Bordewick was obviously overreaching, or perhaps he had merely misunderstood the various discussions he and others had had with him. Skelton wasted no time in replying, advising him that the issue of compensation had not yet "received the consideration of the government,"[16] and that the meeting in London was not to offer compensation, but merely to inform Bordewick whether the government had come to a decision. Skelton did not mention that the London visit was to gather more information so that the government could make an informed decision.

Following the prime minister's meeting with Bordewick, Skelton wrote a letter to Bordewick for the prime minister's signature, commending Sverdrup for his wonderful work and the interest of the Norwegian people, but he concluded his letter with the following:

The question which has been raised as to whether the Canadian Government could recommend a grant to Commander Sverdrup in recognition of the achievements of the "Fram" expedition in 1898-1902 will be given most careful consideration by the Minister of the Interior, our other colleagues and myself. The proposal has been referred to the Northern Advisory Committee for preliminary enquiry, and, following its report, will be taken up by the Government at the first convenient opportunity.[17]

For the time being, Bordewick would return to Norway empty-handed.

A day after the prime minister signed his letter to Bordewick, Sir William Clark, high commissioner of the United Kingdom, sent a secret telegram to Lord Sydney James Passfield, secretary of state for Dominion Affairs, United Kingdom, outlining what had already transpired, that Norway might relinquish all claims to the Sverdrup Islands were Canada to compensate Sverdrup. But, in an attached minute prepared by Peter Clutterbuck, private secretary to the permanent under-secretary of state for Dominion Affairs, Edward Harding, five days later, Jan Mayen Island was again mentioned. He suggested that it be used as a pawn in the negotiations, but on condition that the Canadian government were to agree. He wrote that "evidently the Norwegians still regard their claim as a bargaining weapon.... In the circs. the C'dian Govt may welcome a proposal that the opportunity should be taken of the annexation by Norway of Jan Mayen Island to claim the abandonment of the Norwegian claim to the Otto Sverdrup Islands."[18] Harding, who had instructed Clutterbuck to prepare the minute, simply wrote: "Proceed as proposed."[19] On June 15, the Foreign Office notified Sir Francis Lindley in Oslo that the plan might work if the Canadian government was agreeable.[20]

Before the Canadian government could respond, however, Dr. Donald MacMillan announced his twelfth expedition to the Arctic. He would leave Wiscasset, Maine, on June 22 with two vessels, the *Bowdoin* and the *Maraval*. The latter was the mission ship of his companion on the expedition, Sir Wilfred Grenfell, who had spent his life as a medical missionary in the remotest corners of Labrador. MacMillan's goal was to explore and map 300 miles (482 kilometres) of heretofore unexplored northern Labrador coast, as well as conduct scientific inquiries around Baffin Island. Oswald Finnie wrote to Roy Gibson, acting deputy minister, Department of the Interior, to advise him that MacMillan had yet to apply for permits to visit the Canadian north and to conduct his explorations and scientific inquiries there. Finnie then wrote to Commissioner Starnes for advice, hoping that the RCMP could interview MacMillan when he put in to North Sydney Harbour for coal, but was advised by him that the most expedient way to rein him in was through the Department of National Revenue, Customs Division.

P.L. Young, the chief clerk, Correspondence Branch, Customs and Excise Divisions, Department of National Revenue, telegraphed his collector at Sydney, Peter Campbell, to instruct him that "if United States vessel Bowdoin calls at your port bound for Labrador vessel should report inwards and obtain clearance. If bound for any point in Baffin Island advise Commander MacMillan he must have permit to enter North West Territories in addition to Customs clearance. If vessel intends to proceed to North West Territories without permit advise department by telegram."[21] Starnes also advised that he would instruct his officers in the Eastern Arctic to board the *Bowdoin* should they sight it; they were to request that MacMillan state his purpose for being in the Canadian Arctic as well as show the officers his permits.

Campbell responded on July 2, advising Young that the *Bowdoin* had just arrived and that MacMillan was requesting permits to enter the Canadian Arctic. He had already obtained permits from James Harkin, commissioner of National Parks, to obtain scientific specimens for the United States Bureau of Fisheries, but now he needed entry permits. Finnie wired MacMillan on the same date, his wire serving as provisional authorization to proceed given that the official documents would take too long to prepare. That MacMillan had voluntarily requested permits was strong evidence that he, and in corollary, perhaps the United States government, were now recognizing that the Eastern Canadian Arctic was undisputed Canadian sovereign territory, although the United States had always recognized Baffin as such.

The *Bowdoin* was likely to cross paths with the *Beothic*, which departed North Sydney harbour on July 20 on its fifth annual ship patrol and resupply mission under Commander George P. Mackenzie. On July 31, it arrived at Dundas Harbour, expecting to find Inspector Joy there, but Mackenzie could not have known that Joy was waiting at Bache Peninsula. On August 3, the *Beothic* arrived in the vicinity of the Bache detachment. Taggart wrote that:

> we were startled about 3 a.m. by the ship's siren. I fired three rounds with my rifle to let them know we were around, then we all got in the row boat and went aboard. She was lying in Rice Straits when we first sighted her and looked tiny under the cliffs on Pim Island. After we went aboard she nosed

her way into Fram Haven and came to anchor. We all met the new men who are coming in to relieve the fellows who are going out. McKenzie [sic] invited us to his cabin and gave us a toast. That started the ball rolling—we had several after that. Anstead and I got the mail sacks out of the hold and opened them in the cabin. We spent two hours reading letters, then we had to clear out of the saloon for breakfast. Went ashore and brought back all our gear and the ship moved to Rutherford Point where she stopped as it is impossible to get through the ice to Bache Peninsula. Spent the morning and afternoon unloading stores. I brought my dogs and kometic aboard and said good-bye to the fellows who were stopping here. Left Rutherford at midnight.[22]

In a letter to his brother John, Taggart wrote that: "I haven't had a sleep for over thirty hours haven't time to sleep, got letters from some friends in the Force and have to answer some before the ship leaves to go outside."[23] Joy was headed for his long voyage south to civilization, while Taggart was destined for Dundas Harbour and the final year of his two-year assignment. Nukappiannguaq would remain at the Bache Peninsula detachment where he had been employed since 1925.

Joy and Taggart's patrol was a significant event in Canada's northern sovereign strategy and no one was more excited than William Cory, deputy minister, Department of the Interior, who on August 12 sent a letter to Oscar Skelton with the exciting news.

Perhaps you may have noticed in the press our news items on the progress of the Arctic Expedition, and the reference to Inspector A.H. Joy of the Royal Canadian Mounted Police. According to the wireless telegram from Mr. G.P. Mackenzie, Officer in Charge of the Expedition, Inspector Joy, Constable Taggart and native, with dog teams, started from Dundas Harbour on the 12th March last to patrol to Melville Island. They left word for Mr. Mackenzie that if not back within sixty days they would be either at Craig Harbour or Bache Peninsula. When the Expedition reached Rice Strait on the 3rd instant, Inspector Joy and the Bache detachment met the "Beothic".

From the brief wireless messages I have had the route taken by Inspector Joy traced on a small map which is enclosed for your information. When a full report of the patrol is received another map will be made in more

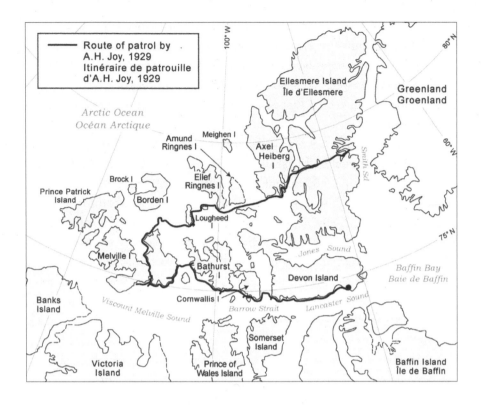

detail. Meantime, it would appear that this patrol was very successful, particularly with respect to the sovereignty of the Sverdrup group of islands.[24]

The full report would remain out of the public eye for the time being. Joy, when writing to Taggart's mother, Florence, to whom he had promised a copy of the report, wrote that "I have just heard from Mr. Lowdes, the editor,[25] to the effect that the Force would not give permission for the report to be published verbatim and as a result of this refusal the patrol has been only casually touched upon in the issue referred to, which I am enclosing herewith."[26] In fact, the casual reference amounted to a scant two paragraphs, but the government was likely withholding the complete report until it could be published in its September 30, 1929, annual report to be released the following year.

Meanwhile, there were new developments afoot in the Sverdrup negotiations. On September 7, 1929, Horace Seymour, head of the Northern Department, Foreign Office, United Kingdom, wrote a letter to Sir Charles Davis, permanent under-secretary of state for Dominion Affairs, United Kingdom, stating that he had read a dispatch from Sir Francis Lindley that Norway might be more inclined to relinquish its claim to the Sverdrup Islands were Britain not only to recognize Norwegian sovereignty over Jan Mayen Island, but Peter I Island in the Antarctic as well.* First Bouvet Island, then Jan Mayen Island, and now Peter I Island: it appeared that Norway's thirst for small foreign islands was unquenchable.

Peter I Island, first sighted by the Russian naval officer and explorer, Fabian Gottlieb Thaddeus von Bellingshausen, in 1821, is no more than a tiny volcanic dot located 240 miles (386 kilometres) north of continental Antarctica. The island is small enough to walk across in less than a day, but its difficult access (high cliffs and impenetrable pack ice during most of the year) and almost complete glaciation would make that a challenge. Norwegian citizens first set foot on the island on February 2, 1929, under the auspices of the Second Norvegia Expedition, whose Norwegian financier, Lars Christensen, coveted it because it would offer Norway sovereign territory in the Antarctic and therefore respite from paying whaling taxes to Great Britain.[27] At least any tax accruals would flow to his homeland.

Seymour further advised Davis that Lindley had since been informed that the government had no claim to Peter I Island, but Lindley had yet to communicate that to the Norwegian government. Seymour also mentioned that Arthur Henderson, secretary of state for Foreign Affairs, United Kingdom, "sees no objection in principle to making use of this recognition as a makeweight in the bargain which it is proposed to strike over the Otto Sverdrup Islands."[28] Seymour then questioned whether that information should be held in reserve pending the outcome of the current negotiations with Norway using Jan Mayen Island alone. Norwegian Prime Minister Johan Ludwig Mowinckel, however, three months later put an end to all talk of Norway annexing Peter I Island by advising that since the Norvegia expedition had been a privately financed expedition, not sanctioned by the Norwegian government, it had no authority to annex foreign territory such as Peter I Island; occupy it, yes, but annex it, no.

That response tellingly flew in the face of the Norwegian government's eagerness to annex Bouvet Island claimed for Norway by a previous Norvegia expedition, although that expedition had had the support of the Norwegian

---

* England's position in the Antarctic had been established as early as September 1839 with the Antarctic explorations of Commander James Clark Ross, who commanded both ships that Franklin would later sail to the Arctic, the bomb ships *Erebus* and *Terror*.

government. But this time the prime minster disavowed any interest in the small Antarctic island with its almost impossible access, although it would be annexed by Norway in 1931 and become a dependency in 1933.

For all the fuss that Norway was causing the British and Canadian governments, that country, according to Lester B. Pearson, first secretary, Department of External Affairs, whose memo of September 23 offered an extensive analysis—which leaned heavily on James White's 1925 notes[29]—of the Sverdrup issue, had never actually made a "public assertion of ownership"[30] of the Sverdrup Islands despite the Norwegian government advising Canada a year earlier that it "reserved to Norway all rights under international law in connection with the said areas."[31] That it rescinded that statement a year later suggested that Norway was merely trying to goad the Canadian government into responding to its many unanswered enquiries about Canada's status over the Sverdrup Islands. Perhaps its failure to make its claim "public" was also because Norway recognized that Sverdrup's expedition was not an "official undertaking" and had been privately financed, and similar to the response offered by Prime Minister Mowinckel over Peter I Island, had not been sanctioned by the Norwegian government to annex foreign territory. That, according to Lester Pearson, was one of the reasons why the Norwegian attitude was so "undecided." Furthermore, Pearson wrote that under international law " 'there must be some formal act of appropriation on behalf of the occupying state, either one by its authority or subsequently adopted by it and either publicly notified or done under the circumstances reasonably sufficient to bring it under the notice of other states.'"[32] Something that Norway had failed to do.

Pearson's memo also highlighted new developments in travel that were expected to increase the importance and value of Canada's Arctic islands. Air routes were anticipated to arc across the frozen wasteland, taking advantage of a shortened route between Europe and Asia, and Pearson wrote that "the fabled North West Passage is becoming once again the goal of mariners[;] mariners, now, of another element."[33] If air travel was to be a success, he wrote, then airfields, hangars, anchoring masts and fuel depots must be established, and the "strategic position of the disputed islands in this connection, especially Axel Heiberg, can be appreciated by a glance at the map.... It would seem wise then, for the Dominion to make every effort to establish internationally her title to the land north of her coasts, including the Sverdrup islands."[34]

Pearson concluded his memo by stating that any claim Norway were to make over the Sverdrup Islands could not be substantiated by international law, and therefore he questioned paying Sverdrup $200,000 in compensation, especially since Norway's rights to the islands had already lapsed. He suggested that a grant might be made to Sverdrup out of grace, and not out of right. Pearson wrote that the only other possible challenger to the islands would be the United States, but then the United States would have to abandon its sector rights north of Alaska that had been granted to it through its 1867 treaty with Russia, made when it purchased Alaska.

Great Britain was just as anxious as Canada that a deal be struck with Norway. On October 30, Peter Larkin, high commissioner of the United Kingdom, sent Skelton a telegram stating that his government would be willing to withdraw its claim to Jan Mayen Island were it to benefit the negotiations with Norway. He added that although the island had been discovered by Henry Hudson (1607–08), the "British claim is shadowy."[35] He closed with a request that if the Canadian prime minister and minister of the Department of the Interior approve, he would like to know what amount the Canadian government proposed to compensate Sverdrup, before also requesting that the matter be taken up by the Northern Advisory Committee. Meanwhile, Harry Batterbee, assistant secretary, Dominions Office, United Kingdom, cornered Skelton— who was still in London—and advised him that "the Foreign Office are very anxious to get forward with their negotiations with the Norwegians, and if you could do anything to hurry Ottawa up, we would be very grateful."[36]

One might ask why Britain was so eager for Canada to complete the negotiation with Norway over the Sverdrup Islands. The islands could not have meant much to Britain, other than its support for a member of the Commonwealth of Nations. But the fact that Norway had been fostering resentment over the protracted Bouvet issue had become somewhat of a sore point in that country, and it even had the suggestion of a potential threat for Britain. In addition, Norway was aggrieved over the sector principle, which had forestalled its economic activity around Franz Joseph Land compliments of the Soviet Union and which was putting pressure on its whaling activity in the Antarctic by Britain. Britain was rightfully concerned, especially given Vogt's veiled threat to Lindley over Bouvet Island, where he mentioned that he "was very averse to applying such heavy machinery as that provided by arbitration at the Hague or by an appeal to the League of Nations for settling a dispute of such insignificant practical importance as that involved in the question of Bouvet Island."[37] And furthermore, the question had aroused great public interest here, and, in his opinion, no Norwegian Government could give up their claim without an appeal either to arbitration or League of Nations. He would strongly deprecate such a development, more especially as he feared the dispute, if not amicably settled, might easily be extended to other areas both in the Antarctic and North Canada.[38]

The Hague referred to the Permanent Court of Arbitration, an esteemed body that had been established in 1899 to arbitrate disputes between member nations. As well, Vogt's advice that the permanent court might investigate other issues in both the Arctic and Antarctic where Britain's sovereignty was being challenged, was more than a simple concern to Britain, for it was endeavouring to establish complete domination[39] in the Antarctic and any official scrutiny of British activities there would put its plans at risk. Canada settling with Norway over the Sverdrup issue and Britain's earlier acquiescence to Norway over the Bouvet Island issue, and soon to be surrender of Jan Mayen Island, would go a long way toward taking the steam out of Norway's rancour. There was no time to lose as far as Britain was concerned.

Following Skelton's meeting with Harry Batterbee, he was asked to attend the Interdepartmental Committee on the Antarctic with Batterbee in chair. Batterbee relayed to Skelton that the government was ready and willing to recognize the Norwegian claim over Jan Mayen Island, although given the advice from Lindley in Oslo, that may not be enough to convince the Norwegians to relinquish their claim over the Sverdrup Islands. Skelton replied that, yes, the Sverdrup Islands had been discovered by Otto Sverdrup between 1898 and 1902, but since then Norway

had taken no steps, by occupation or otherwise, to consolidate any claim which discovery might have given them. On the other hand, there were strong Canadian claims on the ground both of contiguity and of administrative arrangements. The Canadian Government had organized a number of patrols of the North West Mounted Police [Royal Canadian Mounted Police] in the Arctic and these patrols had, in the last few years, been extended to the Otto Sverdrup Islands.... In fact, owing to Norway's failure to follow up her original discovery, the islands have now been definitely included in the Canadian sector.[40]

Skelton then mentioned Bordewick's involvement, which he called a "curious development,"[41] who, when he was in Canada in the spring had produced a letter from the Norwegian prime minister stating that the Norwegian government might give up its claim to the Sverdrup Islands were the Canadian government to compensate Sverdrup for the expenses he incurred during his four-year expedition.[42] The amount suggested was £50,000 to £60,000. Skelton considered that to be exorbitant and offered that a smaller grant to Sverdrup for the complete abandonment of Norway's claim would be more appropriate, and that the United Kingdom's recognition of Norway's sovereignty over Jan Mayen Island would be "very helpful"[43] in the negotiations.

A few days before Skelton's meeting with the Interdepartmental Committee on the Antarctic, Prime Minister Mowinckel had delivered a speech on "Norwegian Policy in Polar Region[s]"[44] in which he stated that he objected to the "doctrine of Polar Sector put forward by Canada, Australia, Soviet Union and other countries."[45] His opinion was later picked up in a Canadian Press dispatch from London:

> New despatches from London had intimated that Premier Mowinckel of Norway contested the right of this country (Canada) to mark out sectors of the Arctic as possessions in which Canada's interests were paramount. The Norwegian Premier asserted in a speech at Bergen that Norway adhered to the view that territory could be claimed only when it had actually been occupied, and that since Canada had not occupied all the Arctic this country's interest in unoccupied territory could not be admitted.[46]

In response to the Norwegian prime minister's comments, noted Canadian educator and McGill University professor Colonel Wilfred Bovey gave a talk in reference to the subject islands in which he stated:

> We can claim discovery of these Arctic islands by British and Canadian explorers. Canada has, in an extremely broad sense of the word, taken possession of the islands, but international law requires us to do more; it requires us to exercise control over them. If we do not do so and continue to exercise it, any other nation could take the archipelago over according to the strict letter of international law. Our Arctic expeditions, our police posts, our radio installations are therefore no extravagance, but are essential to our holding the Far North.[47]

The Canadian government also voiced its opinion, comments that were picked up by a Canadian Press reporter that same month:

That the opinions of Premier Mowinckel in this respect will not affect the right which Canada claims to the Arctic islands north of the Canadian mainland, between longitude 60 and longitude 141, was flatly asserted by Government officials here. Several attempts have been made in the past to disprove Canada's ownership of that archipelago, but recognition was now general, and Norway appears to be the only nation that was still contesting it.[48]

Given that the Norwegian government had already offered Sverdrup permission to make his own deal with the Canadian government upon satisfaction of which it indicated it would relinquish its claim to the Sverdrup Islands, Prime Minister Mowinckel's jab at Canada smacked of nothing more than sour grapes. As well, his mention of "occupation" being paramount to claiming sovereignty over remote Arctic islands according to international law, seemed somewhat disingenuous considering that Norway had never attempted to occupy or even administer the Sverdrup Islands.

Canada was also anxious to have the negotiations with Sverdrup behind it, and on November 26, the Northern Advisory Board met to discuss the latest developments and to devise a solution. Although Skelton was still in London, the meeting was convened with the secretary, Major D.L. McKeand, assistant director of the Northwest Territories and Yukon Branch, reading aloud segments of Sverdrup's *New Land*, specifically the passages referencing the financing of Sverdrup's expedition. The opinion expressed was that "Norway had no good claim to sovereignty over the so-called 'Sverdrup Islands,'"[49] but the information gathered by Sverdrup had been of value to the Canadian government: "In this connection it was pointed out that in his patrols, Inspector Joy of the Royal Canadian Mounted Police, had taken with him a copy of Sverdrup's narrative covering his exploration of the territory and found the account to be quite accurate and of considerable service."[50]

At the conclusion of the meeting, it was moved by Commissioner Starnes and seconded by Mr. Harkin that the minutes of the meeting as well as the minutes of the May 30 and May 31 meetings, plus exhibits, be copied and forwarded "to the Minister of the Interior for submission to the Governor in Council with a recommendation that Dr. Skelton be authorized to negotiate with Captain Sverdrup, or his representative, with a view to settling the matter of compensation; that the amount of compensation to not exceed $25,000 or, if in the form of an annuity during the lifetime of Captain Sverdrup, $2,400 (which is the amount of pension now granted to Captain Bernier)."[51] It was to be made clear to Sverdrup, however, that the award was only compensation for the work that he had conducted during his four years in the Canadian Arctic.

On November 30, Prime Minister W.L. Mackenzie King, acting in his capacity of secretary of state for external affairs, sent a telegram to Skelton through the high commissioner, advising him that he was authorized to negotiate with Bordewick compensation for Sverdrup in the amount agreed upon by the Northern Advisory Board. Skelton in turn sent a telegram to Bordewick to meet him in Paris. Attending that meeting on December 6 and 7 were Skelton, Ernest Lapointe, the Canadian minister of justice, Bordewick and Commander Sverdrup. At the meeting, Skelton informed Bordewick and Sverdrup the amount he was authorized to offer. Sverdrup was obviously disappointed, so Bordewick wrote a letter to Prime Minister Mackenzie King a week later, after having conferred with his own government, to advise him that the offer did not meet with the Norwegian government's expectations.

Skelton had also mentioned to the pair that, given the Norwegian minister's conversation with Lord Cushendun in London, where a *quid pro quo* arrangement involving Bouvet Island had been suggested by the Norwegian minister, Vogt, then the $25,000 offer only represented a "reward for personal services rendered."[52] Bordewick responded in his letter that after consulting with his government he had been advised that the Norwegian minister in London had neither been instructed nor authorized to offer a *quid pro quo* solution to the matter and that the abandonment of Britain's claim to Bouvet Island had been nothing but an act of grace. This, of course, had not been the recollection of Lord Cushendun, who recalled that "M. Vogt stuck to his point, however, with some tenacity."[53]

Bordewick's letter to the prime minister also laid out a detailed financial analysis of the cost of Sverdrup's expedition and why his reward should be greater than $25,000. The Norwegian minister in Paris, Wedel Jarlsberg, in a private meeting with Lapointe and Skelton, had suggested that $100,000 would be more appropriate and would somewhat mirror Captain Bernier's pension if one were to calculate his $2,400 annual pension retroactively from 1902 and then add ten years for the estimated balance of Sverdrup's life. Bordewick advised that Sverdrup would be happy to accept that amount as an adequate reward.

Settling the compensation matter was becoming even more urgent, given that the Norwegian general election was just around the corner and that the next government might not be so accommodating. Lord Passfield telegraphed the British high commissioner with a request to inform Skelton immediately that he was to advise whether the planned course of action to trade Jan Mayen Island for the Sverdrup Islands was tenable and how much compensation was to be granted to Sverdrup. Even Canadian Trade Commissioner Frederick Palmer, who was in Oslo and in touch with the Sverdrup "group," advised that the Norwegians were becoming impatient. It was obvious that Britain needed answers, and that Skelton had yet to pass along his report of the Paris meeting or update Britain on what the Canadian government was thinking, making it even more nervous.

On January 3, 1930, Robert Hadow, first secretary of the British High Commission, wrote to Skelton with the comment that: "For your private and confidential information the Norwegian Minister expressed his purely personal belief that the Norwegian claim to the Sverdrup Islands was not a very serious one and was being put forward mainly as a background for the claim for compensation on behalf of Sverdrup."[54] Hadow further advised Skelton that the whole affair hung on the compensation to Sverdrup and asked him to communicate that to the Dominion Office "for their own use or for such use as they can make of it."[55] It was becoming painfully obvious, though, that the $25,000 offered to Sverdrup was insultingly low, a fact that others agreed with, and that something had to be done about it, and quickly.

A month after the Paris meeting with Bordewick and Sverdrup, Skelton finally passed along a brief report in letter form to Hadow, outlining the offer made to Sverdrup. The letter also included a revised offer that Skelton requested be passed along to Lord Passfield. That offer would be a "pecuniary grant" to Sverdrup with no mention of Norway's claim to the Sverdrup Islands. As well, it would be incumbent upon Norway to recognize Canada's sovereignty over the subject islands. To facilitate the arrangement further, Norway's claim to Jan Mayen Island, and even Peter I Island if necessary, would be considered. As for the reward to Sverdrup, it would not exceed $25,000 cash, but would be sweetened with a life annuity of $2,400 to be retroactive to the previous April, but with a condition that all of Sverdrup's original maps, diaries and other material would be turned over to the Canadian government.

In essence, the Canadian government's goal was to negotiate as small a cash reward as possible while emphasizing that the reward was for Sverdrup's scientific and exploratory work and nothing more. The matter would be settled without any acknowledgment of Norwegian claims, because any such acknowledgement in territory already owned and administered by Canada could possibly place in doubt the 1880 transfer of the Arctic Archipelago to Canada from Britain, and might encourage other nations with historical interests in the Arctic to consider claims.

Meanwhile, another Norvegia Expedition had "discovered" an approximate sixty-mile (ninety-six kilometre) stretch of land between Enderby Land and Kemp Land in the Antarctic, which it had taken possession of in the name of the king of Norway. However, it was made very clear to the Norwegian prime minister by Charles Wingfield, minister of the United Kingdom in Norway (Wingfield had replaced Lindley), that the United Kingdom "claimed the whole of the sector between Enderby Land and the Ross Sea."[56] Despite the gnashing of teeth, it turned out to be a non-event anyway when the Norwegian prime minister distanced himself from the actions of the Norvegia Expedition by reiterating that it was a privately financed affair and therefore not eligible to annex foreign land in the name of the Norwegian government. Britain was obviously relieved, given that Norway's annexation of this land would have strained the agreement the two countries had struck in November 1928 regarding restricting foreign nations from annexing Antarctic territory claimed by Britain.[57] However, Prime Minister Mowinckel did use his media spotlight to once again decry the sector policy in the Antarctic. Although the affair had little to do with Sverdrup and his compensation, the members of the Interdepartmental Committee on the Antarctic made a point of notifying the Canadian government not to use Peter I Island in its negotiations, given the recent remarks of the Norwegian prime minister.

On January 24, 1930, Skelton sent a telegram to Bordewick outlining the new offer of $25,000 cash plus a life annuity of $2,400, this being the government's final offer. Following that, the minister of the United Kingdom in Norway met with Norway's prime minister, who appeared to be satisfied with the second offer presented to Sverdrup as long as Sverdrup agreed to it. Sverdrup, however, was still not happy, which prompted Bordewick to reach out to the premier of Ontario by telegram for advice, complaining that he was "absolutely unable make Sverdrup accept offer made firstly because he feels government unjustly underrating his great explorations which cost him personally sixty two thousand dollars secondly because he feels indebted partly split with surveying [surviving?] Members of expedition."[58] Premier Ferguson then contacted Prime Minister Mackenzie King, who informed him "that he was not aware of any grounds for an increase in the offer."[59]

On February 11, Bordewick sent a telegram directly to Skelton, stating: "Your telegram January twentyfourth. Feel offer far below Paris expectations. Settlement can now be arranged provided life annuity be calculated according special medical opinion of Sverdrup and his family's exceptional high vital power which suggests capitalization at fortytwothousand once for all making total grant sixtyseventhousand dollars cash."[60] Skelton forwarded the telegram to Oswald Finnie with the comment that Bordewick had made an "ingenious suggestion."[61]

The following day the Northern Advisory Board met to discuss Bordewick's suggestion, and it was determined that because "Commander Sverdrup was still a man of outstanding physique and might live for a number of years"[62] (the board was obviously unaware that Sverdrup was terminally ill), in reference to the potential increased cost of settling with a long-term annuity rather than an immediate cash payout, that Bordewick's latest offer should be accepted. The settlement motion was moved by Finnie and seconded by Skelton. The prime minister concurred as long as the minister of the interior agreed, which he did. Skelton then wrote to Robert Hadow in Britain to instruct him to contact his minister in Oslo regarding the settlement, but to emphasize to him that the offer must in no way mention Norwegian claims to the islands and that Norway must recognize them as Canadian territory. Skelton then sent a telegram to Bordewick approving his suggestion, but mentioned to him that it was contingent upon Sverdrup providing original unpublished maps, diaries and notes. Bordewick concurred by telegram, but some months later, after Sverdrup's compensation had been settled, advised that some of the material requested by the Canadian government was unavailable, although Sverdrup's original diaries and copies of his maps were eventually turned over to Canada.[63]

Despite a major hurdle being achieved, the deal was not yet concluded, much to the dismay of the Canadian government. In a final snag, Charles Wingfield reported that Prime Minister Mowinckel was content with the cash settlement to Sverdrup, but he had some conditions. The subject islands must be referred to specifically by name and there was to be no mention of the sector principle. As well, he reserved the right of Norwegians to fish in the surrounding waters and to hunt on the islands, stating that Norway had similar rights over the northern coast of Greenland.[64] The first two conditions were reasonable, but the final one was news to Canada and was considered to be unacceptable.

The Arctic Islands Preserve, established by order-in-council in 1926, pro-hibited hunting of any kind by anyone of European descent without the express permission of the commissioner of the Northwest Territories, although Inuit could hunt and trap at will (an exemption was made for prospectors to take game for food, but only by prior consent). So, for Canada to make an exception for the Norwegians was not going to happen. Even "most favoured nation status" was considered unacceptable and Herr Esmarch, the Norwegian secretary gen-eral of foreign affairs, who was representing the Norwegian government in Prime Minister Mowinckel's absence, recognized that offering that to Norway could potentially open the floodgates to petitions from other nations (most-favoured-nation status is a principle "that countries should treat all their trade partners equally—that no one country should be 'more favoured'").[65]

Given the explanation regarding the Arctic Islands Preserve, Canada expected that Norway would withdraw its insistence on fishing and hunting rights for Norwegians, so Canada and Britain began to discuss the logistics for the exchange with Norway. The Canadian high commissioner sent a tele-gram to the United Kingdom advising that were the Norwegian government to agree, then two notes would be prepared, one for the Sverdrup Islands to be prepared by Canada, and one for Jan Mayen Island to be prepared by Britain. A few days would separate the two to avoid the suggestion of an exchange. As well, Esmarch advised that "he did not wish our understanding to appear as a bargain, since other nations, who were ready to recognize Norwegian claims to Jan Mayen Island without compensation[,] might be encouraged to attach conditions to their consent."[66]

There was one stipulation from Canada, however, and that was that the trans-actions had to be completed by August 6, the date the defeated Mackenzie King government had to leave office. Esmarch replied that Prime Minister Mowinckel was laid up with a case of gout and would not be returning to work until August 8. On that day, Daniel Steen, chargé d'affaires, Legation of Norway in the United Kingdom, sent a note to Arthur Henderson, secretary of state for foreign affairs, United Kingdom, asking him to advise the Canadian government that

the Norwegian Government, who do not as far as they are concerned claim sovereignty over the Sverdrup Islands, formally recognize the sovereignty of His Britannic Majesty over these islands.

At the same time my Government is anxious to emphasize that their recognizance of the sovereignty of His Britannic Majesty over these islands is in no way based on any sanction whatever of what is named "the sector principle."[67]

That note was followed on the same day by another note from Steen, stating that the prior note had been based on the assumption that the Canadian government would not "interpose any obstacles to Norwegian fishing, hunting or industrial or trading services in the areas which the recognition comprises."[68] Peter Clutterbuck, principal, Dominion Office, was perplexed. Everyone thought that the fish/hunt matter was dead, and now the Norwegians were asking for that plus more, and that "more" was in the form of permission to conduct industrial and trading activities on the islands. Although he recognized that the request did not "imply the conditions of special rights, it might well be interpreted as a guarantee of national treatment"[69] (national treatment is a "principle that says countries should treat imported goods, services and *intellectual property* (trademarks, copyrights and patents) the same way as they treat their own").[70]

Skelton wrote to William Cory, deputy minister, Department of the Interior, a few days later to ask his advice over offering Norway most favoured nation treatment, and after consulting with Richard Bennett, the newly minted Progressive Conservative prime minister, he also sent a letter to Robert Hadow, United Kingdom, stating that "every possible consideration"[71] will be given to Norwegians over fishing and hunting rights. As soon as Oswald Finnie learned of Skelton's letter, he wrote to Cory to express his surprise: did Skelton not know about the Arctic Islands Preserve, he wondered? Included in his letter to Cory was a map outlining the boundaries of the preserve as well as a copy of the current game regulations, which Finnie suggested that Cory could forward to Skelton should he so desire.

Following a meeting of the Northwest Territories Council, where the issue was discussed, Skelton wrote a follow-up letter to Hadow, contributed to and edited by Finnie,[72] with an explanation of the terms of the Arctic Island Preserve, where he explained that Norway's condition of fish/hunt privileges for its citizens was not possible. He offered that once the Norwegian government understood that

unless further steps are taken to protect the areas reserved as hunting and trapping preserves for the sole use of the aboriginal population of the North-West Territories, there is grave danger that these natives will be reduced to want and starvation through the wild life being driven out of said preserves by the exploitation of the same by white traders and other white persons.[73]

Skelton again wrote to Hadow on September 4, outlining the latest developments, the content of which Hadow telegraphed to Charles Wingfield in Oslo, who on September 12 met with the secretary general of foreign affairs in Prime Minister Mowinckel's absence, to discuss Norway's second note with regard to the fish/hunt issue. Wingfield was thereby informed that the Norwegian government was not aware of the order-in-council protecting game in the Canadian Arctic for the Indigenous population, and although he was not at liberty to overturn the note, he suggested that the Canadian government should "indicate their inability to give the assurance asked for [because of] this Order-in-Council, and point out that Norwegians would be placed in the same position as British subjects and other persons with the exception of Eskimos and Indians."[74]

On October 11, Wingfield wrote to Howard Smith, head of the League of Nations, General and Western Department, Foreign Office, United Kingdom, that he had received a telephone call from Mr. Alex Nansen, a solicitor attached to the Norwegian legation, who also happened to be the brother of the explorer Fridtjof Nansen and a close personal friend of Otto Sverdrup's. He informed Smith that he had heard that Smith had Sverdrup's settlement cheque and wanted to know if it was made out to him personally. Smith offered that it was. Nansen advised Smith that Sverdrup was dying, but had not yet been told of that fact, and that Sverdrup was ready to provide him with a power of attorney to receive and cash the cheque.

On November 5, Nansen presented the power of attorney to the Chancery in Oslo and after receipt of the funds signed the following note for Sverdrup:

> I hereby acknowledge receipt of draft for £13,767.21d. from the Government of Canada in recognition of my contributions to the knowledge of the Arctic Archipelago in the Sverdrup Islands area, and in full payment for maps, notes and other material bearing on the said region, which I have delivered for transmission to the Government of Canada. I am prepared to offer my services to the Government of Canada for consultation in regard to this region at any time that may be desired."[75]

On the same day, in perhaps a face-saving gesture, the Norwegian government recognized that were it not for the order-in-council creating the Arctic

Islands Preserve, Canada would have accommodated the Norwegian fish/hunt request, and that should the regulations change, any application from a Norwegian citizen would be treated "in the most friendly manner."[76]

Twenty months after writing to Prime Minister Mackenzie King, Sverdrup had finally been rewarded for his scientific and exploratory work, and Canada had secured a vast area of its Arctic against any future Norwegian threat. Three weeks later Sverdrup succumbed to his cancer, oblivious to the seriousness of his condition almost to the end.

Dundas Harbour: The Second Year

A few days following the publication of a newspaper article announcing the satisfactory conclusion to the Sverdrup issue, retired Commander Joseph Bernier sent a letter to Sir George Perley, acting Canadian prime minister, to congratulate him on the settlement. But Bernier being Bernier, he could not resist the temptation to boast about his own achievements, his motive likely being to inform the prime minister that he had taken possession of the Sverdrup Islands decades earlier.[1]

He wrote that

> the Government decided to send me in 1904 to the Hudson Bay, and in 1906-7 to the Arctic Islands, and it was during these years and 1908-9 that I took possession, for the Dominion of Canada, [of] the whole of the Arctic Archipelago, from 60 Meridien West to 141 degrees West, up to 90 degrees North, which is reported in the "Cruise of the Arctic" for 1906-7-8-9, and I beg to enclose (1) Sir Wilfrid Laurier's approval† (2) Hon Mr. Meighen's letter (3) Hon Charles Stewart, Minister of the Interior (4) Mr. Rodolphe Lemieux (5) Sir James Lougheed, Minister of the Interior, approving of my work, which chart can be seen at the Department.[2]

Bernier's hubris elicited a sharp rebuke from Oswald Finnie, who wrote to William Cory, deputy minister, Department of the Interior, two weeks later with a draft letter for the minister's signature. His note stated that

> with regard to the material submitted by Captain Bernier for the Acting Prime Minister's information, there is no record showing that Captain Bernier was ever, at any time, formally commissioned by our Government to claim any areas in the Arctic for Canada. It is true that Sir Wilfrid Laurier, at a Canadian Club luncheon in Ottawa, said some flattering things about Captain Bernier which, in view of the circumstances under which they were said, cannot be taken too seriously. With regard to the letters from the

different Ministers, they were, as you see, nothing but polite acknowledgments of his communications.

It is, of course, nothing short of absurd to contend that a proclamation issued by Captain Bernier on the CGS "Arctic" when at James [Jones] Sound, claiming the whole archipelago, could have any possible bearing on our titles to islands which were hundreds of miles distant as were the Sverdrup Islands. In fact, the considered view of the Governmental authorities best qualified to speak on such matters is that Captain Bernier's claiming of these islands for Canada threw a cloud on our titles. The greater portion of the archipelago was discovered by British explorers, which fact is the root of our title as, by the Order in Council of 1880, everything that was owned and claimed by the Imperial authorities in that area was transferred to Canada.[3]

Bernier, of course, in 1906 and 1908 had been instructed by the government to take possession of former British discoveries as well as any new discoveries that he should make. However, when Finnie had asked him for the records of his expeditions, he had excluded those two instructions, which was probably because "he did not want Finnie to know his sweeping claims made in 1907 and 1909 were not authorized."[4] Finnie, therefore was unaware of Bernier's orders, and in an effort to sidestep any further discussion, his draft letter for the minister's signature was simply to thank Bernier for his communication.[5] It was Bernier, however, who had used his government authority during those early years to not only claim sovereignty over many new and previously discovered Arctic islands, but also to proclaim that Canada owned the whole of the Arctic Archipelago from "long 60° w. To 141° w up to latitude 90° n,"[6] in what would be one of the earliest references to the sector principle.

That same principle, which was anathema to Norway, was still a hot topic of conversation in the United Kingdom, and at the 1930 Imperial Conference in London, the consensus was that it was now generally accepted in the Arctic, but Britain was still anxious about its application in the Antarctic, where it was concerned that "public statements of support should be avoided, since the wide application of this principle in the Antarctic could give rise to unwelcome claims by nations such as Chile and Argentina."[7]

In Canada, Finnie was now downplaying the importance of the sector principle in the Arctic, and in a memo to Cory he wrote:

While Canada has stood for the sector principle the application of that principle, it is thought, is not now of paramount importance insofar as the Arctic archipelago is concerned, for, with the single exception of the Sverdrup Islands, all the other land area[s] in the sector north of Canada can reasonably be claimed to be ours by right of discovery, or by the terms of the Imperial Order in Council of 1880. The recognition by Norway of our sovereignty over the Sverdrup Islands removes the one cloud to our title. Continued occupation and reasonable development are, of course, essential to the maintenance of our sovereign rights in that area.[8]

While Skelton, Finnie and Cory had been wrestling with the Sverdrup issue, Constable Taggart had been dropped back to the Dundas Harbour detachment on Devon Island to continue his representation there, together with other members of the force, as an essential element in the RCMP's maintenance of Canada's sovereign rights in the Arctic. Joy, too, disembarked briefly for his annual inspection of the detachment before proceeding south. He later wrote that

the alterations in the surroundings of the quarters and other buildings; the widening and improving the paths; the hunting, painting, whitewashing, etc., would indicate that Corporal Timbury and Constable Hamilton have worked very hard since the spring thaw. The buildings inside and outside, including the Eskimo quarters, were exceptionally clean and all stores and equipment were in good order and neatly arranged.[9]

Taggart wrote upon his arrival:

Unloaded my outfit and took a load of supplies around the peninsula to the Detachment. The boys had the buildings painted and nicely fixed up. Mailed my letters. We all went aboard 10 p.m., had a few shots of whiskey, talked a little while to Anstead and said good-bye to everyone. They gave us a grand send-off from the ship which sailed at midnight, leaving Timbury, Hamilton and myself with two Eskimo families. We watched her leave the harbour and she gave us three blasts of her whistle as a last farewell.[10]

"Paddy" Hamilton wrote that the *Beothic* did not tarry too long after dropping Taggart off at the detachment because the ice was beginning to accumulate in the harbour, pushed south by a combination of wind and tide. He wrote that

> after the usual "Good-bye, Good luck, God bless you and take good care of yourselves. See you next year," the ship with one long blast of her whistle moved slowly out of the harbour on her way south to Ponds [sic] Inlet and Pangnirtung. Once again we were marooned on Devon Island for another year, with no hope of seeing a different face until the arrival of the ship twelve months hence.[11]

As ominous as Hamilton's lament was, the men were too busy to be concerned with their own feelings of isolation and loneliness. There were three officers, two Inuit families and seventy dogs to feed, which meant a constant vigilance for game. Taggart wrote on September 6: "We are beginning to worry about dog feed. Winter will soon be here and all we have is two walrus and a few seals for feed for over seventy dogs; but we can't do much till the ice pack comes in, which we hope won't be long."[12] The problem with hunting on the water by boat was that walrus and seal when killed tended to sink, although Taggart and Kipumii had devised a unique way of retrieving the carcasses with a hook and line dragged across the ocean floor. Otherwise, the animals would often resurface after ten hours or so, their buoyancy caused by post-mortem gases, at which point they could be retrieved.

The lack of dog feed spurred Taggart and Kipumii to quickly take up where they had left off prior to Taggart's long patrol, and within a few days of his arrival at the detachment, both of them had loaded the rowboat with a week's worth of supplies and rowed to Croker Bay to find game. En route they discovered a walrus washed up on the beach, which they cut up and cached, and while setting up their tent they spotted a bearded seal in the bay which they killed, but it sank before they could reach it. Bearded seals were especially valued because of their thick hides, which were used for dog harnesses and shoe leather. It was a disappointing loss. The following day the wind was so strong that they had to weight the tent down with rocks and any thought of using the rowboat in the ten-foot swells was abandoned. Both Taggart and Kipumii walked inland where Taggart discovered several ancient Inuit graves that had been constructed from rocks in the shape of igloos.

When the sea calmed a couple of days later, they returned to the detachment, although at that point all three of the officers were suffering from what Taggart suspected was a slight case of ptomaine poisoning. Hamilton believed it was from a tin of tomatoes or sardines that the three had consumed one night. Illness or injury were serious matters at the detachments since not all posts were equipped with two-way radios, and even then, there was no possibility of evacuation by ship or aircraft. The men had to tough out their various maladies, which fortunately were more often than not reasonably mild and of short duration, something that both Taggart and Timbury were soon to experience.

The first year that the three officers had spent together saw a haphazard arrangement of duties, which tended to cause friction, but for the second year, the three devised a more efficient and fair routine. Hamilton wrote that

one man took over the cooking for a week. His duties also included scrubbing out the detachment, cleaning the stove, looking after the fire, and keeping the water barrels full of ice. A second man took the meteorological readings, kept the diary and fed the dogs. Thus, the third man was left to his own devices and could do as he pleased. Actually, the only man who had to be at the detachment all the time during the week was the cook. In this way, no one of us could feel that he was doing more than his share of the work, and it led to better harmony amongst us all.[13]

It was not until October 22 that the sea ice had thickened sufficiently for Taggart to feel hopeful, yet cautious, in harnessing his dogs and taking his qamutiik out for a run—he had not harnessed his dogs since his last excursion at Bache Peninsula in July. Complicating matters, the land was still largely bare of snow. Taggart wrote a few days later that: "The ice was terrible; we went over stretches of dark (thin) ice one hundred feet wide, some wider, the ice would bend and roll under the dogs and kometic. I was scared stiff several times. I guess the only reason we didn't go through was because the dogs were racing."[14] Travelling at this time of year was necessary because it was the beginning of fox trapping season when Taggart, Hamilton, Kipumii and Qamaniq were busy laying their traps in areas where they had had success the previous year. And the fact that the traps had to be checked often was convenient for scouting game as well. Initially, however, travel had to be conducted in the four dwindling hours of daylight to avoid thin ice in the dark. A couple of months later, when the light was nothing but a reminder, Taggart wrote: "It is very unpleasant travelling in the dark all the time. A person has to be very careful or he will get lost."[15]

Christmas rolled around with as much fanfare as would be expected in the south. Taggart wrote of the day: "Hazy and dark, fairly mild. Got out of bed 6 a.m., fixed up the house, had a shave, straightened up my bed, turned the dogs loose for the day, then I made breakfast. Spent the morning baking bread and getting the dinner ready. Timbury and Hamilton were busy laying the table, getting seats and putting out presents for the Eskimos. Timbury cooked the ptarmigan while I made the sauce for the puddings. The Eskimos came over 12:30 p.m. and gave us each some presents of ivory. They had a good time eating everything in sight. I took two indoor snaps while they were at the table and hope that they turn out all right. Washed up 2:30 p.m. then everyone turned in for a few hours sleep. At 8 p.m. the Eskimos came over again and we gave them another feed of sweet stuff mostly. We played cards for an hour or so then listened to KDKA broadcasting messages. We got quite a number from different people, the Commissioner, McKenzie [sic], Finnie, etc. I received three from home, one from Mother and Father, one from Edith and one from Alex in Belfast. I was very much surprised to get the last one as this is the first news I have had that Alex has gone back to Ireland. Radio signed off at 3 a.m. Went to bed 4 a.m."[16]

The following day Taggart noted that it was one of the darkest days of the winter: "I couldn't see anything except the dogs in front and a dark blur of the shore line in places. More than once I thought I was lost but I always found a land mark."[17] Five days later he celebrated his twenty-fifth birthday, writing that this is "the last day of the year so I felt lucky this morning,"[18] which materialized in the form of two fox skins. Hamilton also ventured to note that this was the time of short days and storms: "Then the Arctic blizzards began. They seemed worse to me this second year than the year before. No one can imagine what it is like, who hasn't actually experienced it, to sit in the house with the temperature outside down to about 45 below zero and hear the wind howling at a steady sixty miles or so an hour and filling the air with snow as fine as sand which would blind and choke anyone venturing outside to brave the elements. Storms such as these might last four or five days without letting up, and then one morning, we would wake up and wonder what was wrong, until we realized the unusual quiet and stillness meant another storm was over."[19]

The cold, dark days of winter were largely spent close to the detachment except for trapline checks. On January 1, 1930, Taggart and Kipumii returned from Croker Bay and Cape Home with thirteen fox between the four men who had traps. Travelling in the dark, however, was not without its risks and both Taggart and Kipumii damaged their qamutiit in the rough ice. In Taggart's opinion, Lancaster Sound was the worst place in the Arctic for pressure ice. Taggart wrote the next day that "we are expecting the moon shortly. This is the last moon we will bother about as we weill [sic] have the sun in another month."[20] But, the temperature was still cold and in the detachment the men had to wear heavy clothing and fur stockings to keep warm. Even the Inuit complained of the cold and when the women came over to wash the floor, the water froze just feet from the roaring stove.

Gradually the light began to return. At first it was just an orange glow in the east about noon, increasing ever so incrementally until on February 6th Taggart wrote: "I saw the sun for about an hour today. The clouds were in the way the rest of the time it was above the horizon so that I couldn't see just when it came up and when it set, but I guess it was above the horizon for over two hours, at least this day last year it was shining that length of time."[21]

Buoyed by the return of the light and motivated by the lack of dog feed as well as a desire to vary their diet, Taggart and Kipumii left the detachment at 11:00 a.m. on February 7 headed for the igloo at Cape Home. Their goal was to check their traps, but also to hunt for a bear. Leaving the igloo at the cape at 10:00 a.m. on the 8th, they sledded west for about three hours when bad luck struck. Taggart, who was walking beside his qamutiik, heard Kipumii shout and instead of turning around he threw himself backward onto his sled so that he could see behind him and landed right on a walrus harpoon which punctured his thigh. When Kipumii arrived he informed Taggart that he had shouted because he had to put down one his dogs which had broken its leg. Looking at Taggart's injury, he remarked that he could see the fat beneath the skin. The wound was one inch long and of similar depth. Fortunately it bled little so the two continued their search for a bear, building an igloo five miles east of Cuming Inlet midway along Devon Island's south coast.

The next morning Taggart was of two minds. He wanted to secure a bear, but was now becoming worried that if he neglected his wound for too long it would become infected. Regardless, he and Kipumii left their gear at the igloo and travelled west five miles past Cuming Inlet, but still failed to find a bear. The following morning they decided to return to the post, stopping only at the Cape Home igloo for a stew before proceeding by moonlight to the detachment, arriving at 11:00 p.m. Taggart noted that they had travelled forty-five miles (seventy-two kilometres) that day and that it was the only time that he had returned to the detachment empty-handed. He cleaned and dressed his now gaping wound and remarked in his diary that "it sure looks bad, but I think it will be all right—I hope so anyway."[22]

On February 24, Hamilton and Timbury decided that they would make a test run to Cape Home in anticipation of completing a much longer patrol at the end of March. Running into a strong blizzard, they hunkered down for the night in an old igloo at Croker Bay. The following morning the blizzard was still raging, so Hamilton tried to convince Timbury that it would be best to wait it out. Timbury, however, advised that if they were ever going to make a long patrol then they would encounter worse days. They packed up and sledded toward Cape Home, but as soon as they left the lee of the island's cliffs and pushed out onto the ice in the bay, the blizzard came down on them with a vengeance. Visibility was almost zero and the two quickly became separated. Hamilton believed that Timbury was ahead of him and so he continued west, hoping to reach land on the other side of the bay where he would search for him. When he arrived there, and there was no sign of Timbury, Hamilton knew that it would be fruitless to try to locate the Cape Home igloo in the storm. He crafted a makeshift shelter, fed his dogs and made a cup of tea, hoping to find Timbury the next day.

The following morning, Hamilton pressed on to Cape Home and located the igloo a couple of hours later, but there was no sign of Timbury. The only other option was to return to the post to get help, but as he sledded east he came across Timbury heading in the opposite direction. Timbury informed him that he was on his way to the Croker Bay igloo to make something to eat. He explained that the previous evening his dogs had led him to the ice edge and when he stopped suddenly, one dog was already in the water. He had to cut it loose and then swing his qamutiik back into the wind, but his dogs refused to face it so he had to drift with the wind, eventually overturning his qamutiik for a rudimentary shelter while he waited out the storm. He froze his face in the process. Now, all he wanted was a meal, so he proceeded west to the igloo at Croker Bay while Hamilton continued on to the post. On arrival at the detachment, Taggart prepared Hamilton a meal and took care of his dogs. He then asked Kipumii to go to the Croker Bay igloo and bring Timbury back to the detachment. An hour shy of Croker Bay, Kipumii met Timbury, who was already on his way back, and accompanied him safely to the detachment.

When Timbury arrived he was met by Taggart who wrote:

Then I got a shock; his face was badly swollen, his eyes were nearly closed, his nose was twice the size it should be and was discoloured, all the skin was off the bridge and the flesh was showing black... Earlier in the evening though Timbury scared the life nearly out of one of the Eskimo kids, a girl of about fifteen. She did not know he had his face frozen and when she first saw him she screamed and ran to me. Timbury certainly looked "tough" and I don't wonder the kid was afraid of him. I'm afraid Timbury might lose part of his nose. This is the first time I have seen anyone so badly frozen so I can't tell very well how it will turn out. I bandaged Hamilton's chin after washing it in warm water, but Timbury said his would be all right. He would have to wear a mask if he was to have it all covered and I guess he wouldn't like that.[23]

The following day, Taggart, who was still recovering from his harpoon injury, completed a trifecta of fresh injuries at the post, thus adding to Timbury's and Hamilton's frostbite, when he twisted his knee while trying to extricate one of the rowboats from a snow drift. First the harpoon puncture, now this. He thought that he had dislocated one of the bones in his leg because he could not straighten it. He wrote that he spent the rest of the day trying to get his leg in shape, and further remarked that Timbury's face was looking "very bad" and Hamilton's face was "not so bad," although he had no skin left on his chin. Taggart's bad luck extended to Kipumii as well. Taggart wrote of Kipumii that

since last fall he has had a run of bad luck. First he had his best dog killed, then his boat was smashed; his kometic has been smashed three times, then he had another dog killed; had his ankle very badly sprained, now he has broken his harpoon and lost the lance. He said that he expects something to happen to his rifle soon.[24]

On March 10, the three officers learned via the KDKA Northern Messenger service that the *Beothic* would not be leaving North Sydney until July 31 on its annual patrol and would not return to port until September 20. Although all were excited to receive their estimated date of departure, Taggart was somewhat disappointed given that he had planned a long car trip with his sister, Edith, and his brother John. The Inuit were also excited because they would be returning to Pond Inlet to be reunited with their families and friends, but little did they know what was in store for them.

Three weeks later, on March 30, Timbury and Hamilton, accompanied by Kipumii, driving ten dogs each, left on their long patrol to Beechey Island and beyond. From Beechey Island the trio planned to proceed "across Wellington channel to Cornwallis island, northwards along the eastern coast of that island, across Maury channel to Baillie Hamilton island, thence back to Devon island to mount Franklin, then to Grinnell peninsula, and then back to Dundas Harbour by the same route."[25]

For the first day, no ice was found in the sound and there was scant snow on the land, which made travel difficult. They camped at an old igloo at Croker Bay and the next day proceeded west to Cape Home along the sea ice near the shore. The following day they travelled on the sea ice for about ten miles (sixteen kilometres) before coming across terrain that "was too rough and rugged to make any kind of headway, miles upon miles of new ice of about two feet in thickness extending from shore to horizon which had been continually broken and pressed up into high ridges anywhere from ten to fifty feet high."[26] Hamilton wrote: "We had handles on our sleds with which we were able to assist the dogs by guiding the sleds through between the boulders and ice hummocks."[27] Somewhat reminiscent of Timbury's journey to Beechey Island the previous year to check on the cached stores for Inspector Joy, they were again consigned to the deep snow between the land and the pressured sea ice, both men and dogs struggling to push the qamutiit around and through the ruptured landscape.

When the trio arrived at Cuming Inlet, Hamilton wrote that

by noon, we were confronted with new ice and numerous open leads. We thought that after passing a small glacier we might find the going better if we took to the land. However, much to our disappointment, we found the land ran almost vertically up from the sea, and the only possible way of continuing was through the rough ice. Keepomee climbed a way up the cliff to see if he could pick out some sort of trail through the ice, but he reported it all looked alike, and we would just have to work our way through. It took us nearly six hours to cover a distance of approximately eight miles as our sleds were constantly becoming wedged in the ice or overturned. Once Timbury's sled went into the sea water, but he did not get wet as he was not riding on it. Fortunately, his dogs had kept on the firm ice, and with the help off [sic] all three of us we were able to pull the sled out. Dog traces were continually caught up and sometimes cut by the new sharp ice. Quite often, it was necessary to relash our loads after a bad spill. We also had to take turns in helping each other to haul our loads over pressure ridges. It was a relief when, at last, we came into contact with smooth ice."[28]

The following day was worse than the last since the party was consigned to the shore ice, often travelling beneath a cliff face rife with boulders that threatened to crash down upon them. They reached Beechey Island on April 8, breaking camp just before noon the following day to travel back to the southwest corner of Devon Island.

At noon on the 11th, the conditions of the ice had improved somewhat so headway was made toward Cornwallis Island, where they stopped for the night. Five days later saw them camping near the eastern coast of Dundas Island, having travelled up the east coast of Cornwallis and Baillie-Hamilton Islands, both of which are located just off the west coast of Devon Island south of the Grinnell Peninsula. On the 18th they angled toward Mount Franklin, reaching Point Hogarth on Devon Island's west coast. There they discovered a bear den where they holed up for the next three days, having become storm-bound. At one point, Kipumii left the den to check on his dogs and discovered a large bear standing very near to him. He surmised that the dogs had been too cold to give warning. Kipumii released his dogs to attack the bear, giving him precious moments to grab his rifle and shoot it. It was a welcome addition to their larder. Timbury remarked: "It is a known fact that the polar bear wanders extensively during wind storms or blizzards."[29] A few days later, Timbury wrote that when they arrived back at Beechey Island it was so warm that they rolled their eiderdown sleeping bags out on the beach in front of Sir John Franklin's memorial plinth and had a comfortable sleep. Repeating their inbound journey, they arrived back at the detachment on May 2, having travelled 750 miles (1,207 kilometres).

When Taggart heard the commotion of the trio's return, despite his knee still troubling him, he got up to welcome them home. He had a small keg of beer waiting for them and half a dozen loaves of bread. They consumed one-and-a-half loaves plus a pound of butter. Two days later, Taggart remarked that the sun did not set, but despite this welcome sign, the next few weeks were beset with cold, wind and snowstorms. On June 6, however, he wrote: "I found six little red flowers today—the first this year."[30] By the middle of June, the men had released their dogs since they were no longer needed given that the ice was quickly disappearing from the harbour and there was no snow left on the land.

Taggart set up a tent in the yard, remarking that it was getting too warm to sleep in the house at night. There was palpable excitement from both the officers and the Inuit regarding the anticipated arrival of the *Beothic*, and Hamilton, with Taggart's help, began to build boxes for his fox skins, preparatory to loading them aboard the ship.

Taggart wrote on July 30 that "all the Eskimos are excited and eagerly looking forward to the arrival of the ship. They are going back to Ponds [*sic*] Inlet this year and are anxious to see their friends and relations."[31] Based on the departure date, the ship was not expected to arrive at Dundas Harbour until sometime during the second week of August. By August 9, the men as well as the Inuit were becoming anxious, walking the hills behind the detachment, staring out to sea and hoping for the first glimpse of smoke from the *Beothic*'s funnel. Taggart wrote: "Had a look to see if I could see the ship or its smoke. The boat is not due for another week, but everyone is watching in case she might come early."[32] Nine days later, Taggart noticed that the Inuit were feeling a little "blue" because of the delayed ship, but at 5:00 p.m. he heard Timbury shout that he could see smoke. The sighting motivated the men to quickly dress in their best clothes, pile into the motorboat and make their way out to meet the ship. Once the ship anchored in the harbour, the men scrambled up a rope ladder that had been thrown over its side and once onboard they met Inspector Joy who was on his annual inspection tour.

After a round of salutations and a catch-up, Taggart, Hamilton and Timbury returned to the detachment to fetch their gear, boarding the ship for good at 4:00 a.m. while Corporal Dersch and Constables Currie and Boleau assumed control of the detachment motorboat to begin their two-year stint. Just prior to boarding the ship, Taggart had participated in a round of good-byes with the Inuit who had served them so well. They had just been informed that they would not be evacuated to Pond Inlet that year because there were no positions available for them there. Taggart wrote that "the Eskimos were crying when we three fellows left them behind. I guess they were disappointed they have to stay at Dundas Harbour another year."[33]

That single incident introduced a small sample of one of the darkest chapters in Inuit relationships with the Canadian government, which used the weight of its authority to pressure the Inuit into accepting where they would live and for how long. Ten years earlier, James Harkin, commissioner of Dominion Parks, had made the government's position abundantly clear on that matter when he produced a report about British sovereignty in the northern islands in which he stated that "eventually if investigation shows that there are important natural resources in the Northern islands the Government should transfer Eskimos from other Canadian areas to establish small centres of population."[34]

Sovereignty was still very much at top of mind then and the government needed the Inuit to live on these remote Arctic islands as a demonstration of occupancy, to protect them against Greenlandic poachers, and later to protect them against an increased US presence during and following World War II. During the cold war, the US strengthened its military presence in the Canadian Arctic due to the threat of Soviet aggression.[35] Canada was rightfully concerned that the US military's occupation of its north threatened its sovereignty over the region. As a protective measure, Inuit were relocated to these remote locations in the early 1950s, the incentives being better living conditions, abundant game and a two-year time frame. Once relocated, however, some families were split up and sent to different communities, and the promises that were made quickly evaporated. It took some families three decades to make their way back to where they had been uprooted from. The effect on the Inuit of these relocations was so troublesome that a Royal Commission was struck in 1994 that identified the process as being "inherently coercive."[36]

Although the Inuit at Dundas Harbour were not relocated, that they were not given a choice whether they could leave or stay, bore the same sense of "coercion" that would haunt the 1950s relocations. The late Samuel Arnakallak, in a conversation with his late sister, Elisapee Ootoova, shed some light on why that occurred. He stated that "the police tended to boss Inuit around prior to the Second World War.... I think they were just like the RCMP today, but Inuit at that time would just say yes. I think they used to say 'yes' too easily. I don't think that they thought that there was anything wrong with saying 'yes'."[37] Philippa Ootoowak, Elisapee's daughter-in-law, added that "in general the older Inuit would just accept what the Qallunaat (non-Inuit) told them even though they did not agree with it. Arguing was not culturally acceptable."[38]

The author and anthropologist Hugh Brody examined that specific cultural behaviour in his book, *The Other Side of Eden*. There, he reviewed some aspects of the Inuit language, Inuktitut, with an Inuit tutor, the late Simon Anaviapik, a traditional Inuk who was well versed in the nuances of his language. Brody wrote that "during one of our lessons, Anaviapik talked about white people who came from the south and bossed Inuit around. He gave the example of a policeman who was especially domineering, who gave orders that resulted in men working intolerable hours, and had sexual liaisons with women who did not like him."[39] Anaviapik then introduced the term, *ilira*, to Brody, and explained

> what might make you feel *ilira*: ghosts, domineering and unkind fathers, people who are strong but unreasonable, whites from the south. What is it that these have in common? They are people or things that have power over you and can be neither controlled nor predicted. People or things that make you feel vulnerable, and to which you *are* vulnerable.[40]

He went on to tell Brody that the Qallunaat had items that the Inuit needed, such as guns, ammunition and various foodstuffs like tea and flour, and stated that they "had power and there was no equality."[41] With so much at stake, as well as the Inuit's cultural proclivity at that time to acquiesce in the face of government pressure, it was no wonder that the Inuit at Dundas Harbour felt that they had no choice but to comply.

The ship weighed anchor soon after the men boarded and began to steam to the west on the next leg of its Eastern Arctic patrol. Taggart found his bunk at 5:00 a.m., and when he awoke at noon, the ship was off Graham Harbour, located about two-thirds along Devon Island's south coast. About 10:00 p.m. the ship met the pack ice just southeast of Cornwallis Island. Taggart turned in at 2:00 a.m., but two hours later was awoken by the noise of the ship reversing its engines. The *Beothic* lay in thick ice just to the south of Griffin Island, but by 1:00 p.m. the ice had begun to loosen sufficiently for the ship to resume its westward push, its immediate goal being Bathurst Island. Captain Falk wanted to reach Winter Harbour on Melville Island's south coast that season, but Taggart expected that it would not make it that year because the ice was too thick. When just south of Bathurst Island, Joy asked Taggart if he remembered their camp there. It was hard to forget, being one of the coldest days of their long patrol.

On account of the heavy ice, during the morning of August 25, the captain decided to put the ship about and began to steam back toward Lancaster Sound, making headway toward Pond Inlet on Baffin Island's northeast coast. He spent fifteen hours in the crow's nest guiding the ship through narrow leads in the ice. Taggart was concerned that the ship would be frozen in for the winter. Two days later they passed Beechey Island, the captain, still aloft, guiding the ship through the fractured ice. By 6:00 p.m. on August 28, the ship was lying to at the entrance to Navy Board Inlet due to heavy fog and rough seas. The fog cleared at 5:00 p.m. the following day and the ship entered the inlet, later encountering heavy seas in Eclipse Sound just short of Pond Inlet. It anchored off the Pond Inlet detachment at 11:00 p.m. on August 29, with all the men going ashore to meet the officers at the detachment as well as the local missionaries and the two employees of the Hudson's Bay Company post. The men spent the night ashore and the next day were occupied with unloading and checking stores for the detachment. On the 31st, they re-boarded the ship, which sailed at 2:00 p.m.

At 6:00 p.m. on September 1, the ship anchored off the community of River Clyde, located to the south almost midway down Baffin Island's east coast. There the patrol's doctor went ashore to provide health checks to the local Inuit. Taggart accompanied him and spent the time speaking with the two Hudson's Bay Company employees stationed there. Three days later, at 1:30 p.m., the ship arrived at Pangnirtung, located on the north shore of Cumberland Sound. It was a good-sized community, comprised of an RCMP detachment, a Hudson's Bay Company post, and a mission as well as a doctor's office. Taggart and company spent the evening at the post, boarding the ship at midnight, and by September 9, the *Beothic* lay off the community of Lake Harbour on Baffin Island's south coast, waiting for the Inuit pilot to escort the ship into the harbour. Taggart wrote that "the buildings at this post are the best in the Eastern Arctic,"[42] although he learned that the area was largely devoid of game.

The next day was spent checking the RCMP stores, and by 10:00 p.m., the men were once again aboard. The ship sailed at 5:30 a.m. on September 11, headed for Chesterfield Inlet on the west coast of Hudson Bay where it anchored fifteen miles (twenty-four kilometres) offshore due to the shallow water early on the morning of September 14. Later that morning the ship cautiously moved into position 300 yards (274 metres) offshore of the RCMP detachment. Taggart wrote that "this is a large settlement. Besides the Police there is an R.C. Mission, a wireless station, a hospital, the Hudson Bay Co. and a detachment of the RCAF.... Bill and I walked all over the place and decided that it is the most desolate Post in the Eastern Arctic—and a poor game country."[43]

The following morning Taggart was offloading some dogs onto a trap-boat when he and Bill were severely bitten on their hands. The doctor patched them up and because of their wounds they were excused from the backbreaking toil of offloading two years' worth of stores as well as eighty tons (seventy-two tonnes) of coal for the Chesterfield Inlet detachment. Two days later the ship weighed anchor and made its way toward Port Burwell, arriving there on September 22 after a short stop at an abandoned RCMP detachment at the eastern end of Coates Island located at the mouth of Hudson Bay. The ship sailed from Port Burwell the following day after Inspector Joy had concluded his inspection. Taggart wrote that once underway the ship was rolling heavily with all manner of possessions crashing about in the dark. The ship's gunnels would disappear under water and the sea would slosh over to the other side of the deck when she righted herself. Cups and plates could be heard crashing about as they were ejected from their resting places onto the floor. Many men were sick.

On September 27, the ship docked at North Sydney and the first thing that Taggart noticed was the unpleasant smell of the harbour. After a day of merrymaking, the men were instructed to report to the train station; they were transported to Ottawa, arriving just after noon on September 30. There they were met by a police truck that took them to the police barracks.

This was by no means the end of Taggart's career with the RCMP or his time in the Arctic. Although he did leave the force on May 26, 1931, after his three-year enlistment period had expired, he re-engaged with the RCMP on December 8, 1932, the prior year having been spent in the employ of the Ontario Provincial Police. On January 1, 1934, he was once again assigned to "G" Division, Northwest Territories, this time to Baker Lake, which is located approximately 200 miles (321 kilometres) inland from the entrance to Chesterfield Inlet on Hudson Bay's west coast. He returned south to Depot Division on September 1, 1935, and subsequently was assigned to three other divisions before retiring on December 7, 1957, having achieved the rank of sergeant. He never forgot his extraordinary adventure at Dundas Harbour and his long patrol with Inspector Joy and Special Constable Nukappiannguaq, and he was forever regaling his family with stories from his time there, always reminding them that it was all about Canadian sovereignty.

Although Taggart was finished with the Arctic, the Arctic was not finished with him, and thirty years following his retirement, RCMP HQ reached out to him regarding a letter they had just received from Pond Inlet. A member of Anna Ataguttiaq's family was searching for him. Taggart must have known what the letter was about, but to be confronted with such a moral dilemma so late in his life was difficult, so he chose silence over facing what he must have known would be an awkward and embarrassing complication. Better to leave well enough alone. But some things will not be denied, and twenty-seven years following the receipt of that letter by RCMP HQ, and twenty years following

Taggart's death at the age of ninety on April 24, 1994, his children would receive the surprise of their lives.

The other two members of the long patrol would not be blessed with such a long life. Just before Taggart retired in 1957, Nukappiannguaq succumbed to illness at a hospital in Greenland at the age of sixty-three. That he had been an extraordinary RCMP Special Constable over his eight years with the force was evident through his actions on the many patrols he participated in, as well as the voluminous literature and expedition reports praising his guiding and dog-handling skills as well as his hunting prowess.

According to Peter Schledermann, a senior research associate with the Arctic Institute of North America, Nukappiannguaq served the RCMP loyally. He wrote that: "Few of the longer sled patrols took place without him, and he served practically throughout the entire first period of the RCMP presence in the High Arctic."[44] He was a guide on Inspector Joy and Constable Taggart's long patrol to the outer fringes of the Eastern Arctic in 1929 and two years later accompanied Stallworthy on the difficult search for the German geologist and explorer, Hans K.E. Krüger, who had finally assembled his expedition together, but had disappeared without a trace somewhere around Meighen Island, thereby adding another casualty to the long list of lost Arctic explorers. Stallworthy himself was almost lost during the search, falling into a crevasse on the eastern shore of Ellesmere Island, but fortunately for him his companion was Nukappiannguaq, who rescued him. Despite being such an indispensable member of the force, as well as a bridge between two cultures, when an inquiry was made to RCMP HQ to provide him with an RCMP pension, it was denied.

Meanwhile, Inspector Joy continued with his inspections of the Eastern Arctic. But following his long patrol, he was beset with illness. This was not the first time that an arduous patrol had compromised his health. At the conclusion of his 1,300-mile trek to Axel Heiberg Island from Bache Peninsula in 1926 to place a Canadian footprint there following Admiral Byrd's question to Commander Mackenzie at Etah whether a Canadian had ever set foot on the island, Joy was hospitalized briefly upon his return to Ottawa. Retired RCMP Arctic veteran, Corporal Robert Pilot, who has researched and written about Joy's life, wrote that "he returned to Bache Peninsula totally exhausted, suffering from congestion and chest pains and was looking forward to his transfer south in the summer. He left Bache Peninsula on ss Beothic and upon his arrival in Ottawa, was admitted to a hospital for a complete medical examination after which he took a vacation for several months."[45]

In fact, he was probably not a well man before his long patrol with Constable Taggart and Nukappiannguaq, despite comments from his superiors about his "robust" physique. Of course, the mind-numbing cold, interminable blizzards and the exhaustive labour sledging through, up and over formidable fields of pressure ice along the route of his patrol would compromise anyone's health, but for Joy it had been especially hard. All three men had lost considerable weight during the arduous trek, but the loss for Joy was perhaps verging on critical. Taggart's comment on May 4, 1929, that Joy was feeling "tough" was telling. Hospitalized upon his return to Ottawa, Joy spent a month resting and visiting with a woman he had met on one of his many speaking engagements, Carmel Murphy, to whom he soon proposed. Their wedding was planned for the following year.

Joy would once again head north on the *Beothic* at the end of July 1931 on his annual inspection tour, but upon his return in September, he was again seriously ill and was hospitalized, this time for several weeks. His wedding was therefore postponed until April 30, 1932. Adding to his stress, the Eastern Arctic Sub-District office had been relocated to Montreal from Ottawa, which meant a significant commute to see his fiancée, who was still living with her parents in Ottawa.

On the day before his wedding, April 29, 1932, Joy arrived in Ottawa about 1:30 a.m. by train from Montreal. He visited the headquarters of Superintendent J.W. Phillips to pick up a bottle of cough syrup he had left there previously. He was complaining of a cold which he had had for about a week. Following that he checked into his room at the Chateau Laurier and lay down on the bed. It had been arranged that he would meet Carmel for lunch, but when he failed to show, his room was entered and he was found to be unconscious on the bed. He was rushed to hospital where at 7:00 p.m. he was pronounced dead. He was only forty-three. His shattered fiancée would never marry and would herself die at the early age of forty-nine.[46]

Decades later, following Constable Taggart's death on April 24, 1994, his surviving spouse, Beth Taggart, told her son, Peter, that she had heard a rumour that Joy had taken his own life on the eve of his wedding. But a good friend of Joy's fiancée, Helen McKinae, in 1986 had confided in her Ottawa neighbour, who happened to be former RCMP Corporal Robert Pilot, that under no circumstances was that true. Joy's health was simply tragically compromised, evidence for which lay in his repeated hospitalizations in the few years prior to his death, as well as the thorough "Report of Illness, and Death" prepared by Dr. D.A. Whitton, the attending acting assistant surgeon, who reported Joy's death as "Acute Pulmonary Congestion with Myocardial Failure." That finding is consistent with Joy's previous bouts of illness and his actions on the day of his death.

That Joy had made an impression over his twenty-three years of service in the RCMP, most of which was spent in the Canadian Arctic, was an understatement. His funeral was accorded full military honours, a distinction normally reserved for state officials, complete with a gun carriage bearing his remains to his final rest, his horse trailing behind, saddle draped in black, boots reversed in the stirrups. Attending was Commissioner J.H. MacBrien, among the who's who of RCMP HQ, complete with a multitude of officers, Ottawa City police and firemen. Joy left a legacy that was neatly captured by a reporter with the *Ottawa Evening Journal*, who wrote: "The tribute paid to this gallant adventurer was something more than accorded even a great statesman or famous soldier. It had about it the glamour of high romance, of a tragically terminated love story, of the sudden and untimely termination of a brilliant career as a Knight errant of the Arctic."[47] Commissioner MacBrien wrote of Joy following his death: "He was a most efficient officer, and was considered as the country's leading expert on matters affecting the lands near the Arctic Circle."[48]

Joy's patrol, however, known as "The Longest Patrol," has understandably been elevated to mythic proportions, and it will live on as a testament to the fortitude and endurance exhibited by these three men, all in the service of strengthening Canada's sovereign claim to its Arctic. The importance of this patrol was revealed at a meeting of the Northern Advisory Board regarding Norway on May 30, 1929, just at the conclusion of Joy, Taggart and Nukappianguaq's journey, where "the consensus of opinion seemed to be that Canada by administration of the territory as evidenced by the supervision of trade, by the Arctic patrols, by the establishment of outposts and particularly by the patrols of Inspector Joy, had succeeded in perfecting its claim to these Arctic lands."[49] Although Canada's struggle to protect its north was not yet over, and indeed is still ongoing, the extraordinary RCMP patrols had at least served their purpose at a critical juncture in Canada's demonstration of its sovereign rights in the Arctic while also capturing the attention of the world.

CHAPTER TWELVE

Elisapee

This small chapter is a departure from the story that precedes it. As you have read, that story is about Canada's early efforts to establish and protect its sovereignty in the Arctic and Canada's national police force's pivotal role in that process. This chapter is a consequence of that in that it deals with the relationship between the RCMP and the Inuit: in this case an intimate relationship between a young RCMP officer stationed at Dundas Harbour in 1930 and a young Inuit woman who was employed there. The young RCMP officer in question was none other than Constable Reginald Andrew Taggart, and the young Inuit woman, Anna Ataguttiaq.*

A light-skinned girl with dark brown, curly hair was born to Anna at Dundas Harbour on January 6, 1931, her biological father having departed for the south approximately five months earlier. The child would be named Qiliqti at birth, but at her baptism in the Anglican church eleven years later she would be christened Elisapee (Elizabeth). Elisapee would grow up to be an amazingly accomplished woman, winning many awards for her advocacy work as well as for the preservation of her culture.

Philippa Ootoowak, Elisapee's daughter-in-law, commented about Taggart and Anna's relationship, writing that: "It was certainly not an unusual occurence and understandable in the circumstances."[1] In fact, these occurrences were all too common despite the RCMP brass forbidding such relationships. So common, in fact, that light was made of it by way of a satirical cartoon by S.D. Callis in the RCMP *Quarterly Supplement* for 1950, which depicted a sheepish officer behind whom was standing his Inuit wife and three small children. The caption read, "… YES SIR, 5 YEARS MORE OF NORTHERN DUTY…."

As for the nature of Anna's and Reginald's relationship, I have not pursued that beyond the obvious conclusion. So with that in mind I am going to lead

---

* "Anna" is a baptismal name provided by missionaries.

you down a different path, one that follows Elisapee's family members as they search for and finally discover the family of her late biological father eighty-three years following her birth.

On September 23, 2013, Peter Taggart, the youngest child of Reginald and Beth Taggart, responded to a message that he had received on his online Ancestry account. The message was from Philippa Ootoowak, a community archivist at Pond Inlet, who, without revealing the true nature of her query, wrote that she was "... very interested in the RCMP members stationed at the Dundas Harbour Detachment in the past."[2] She went on to explain that some Pond Inlet elders were either born there or had spent time there, and concluded her letter with a request: "If you have any records/photos of Reginald Taggart's time in the area or photographs of your family we would be very interested to see them. I have found a couple in RCMP books but would like to see more of the family as he appears to have been a member that learned to adapt well to his time in the north."[3] Puzzled but intrigued, Peter asked her in return: "What pictures would you be interested in?"[4] Philippa believed that she had finally found the subject of her quest, but Peter was still in the dark. The light would not be switched on for several months.

Born in England, Philippa trained as a nurse before travelling to Canada in 1970 where she worked in that capacity at a number of locations throughout the Canadian eastern north. In March 1973, she arrived at Pond Inlet, where she worked for two years before leaving to work in Yellowknife, NWT. Following a ten-month stint there, she returned to Pond Inlet where she met and subsequently married Elisapee's eldest child, Jayko. Philippa was very close to her mother-in-law, and both were curious about the identity of her biological father. He had been a mystery to Elisapee all her life, but she had a vague recollection of him through a photo that she had seen when she was much younger. Philippa wrote that: "She had an idea of his Inuktitut name from others and a few things such as he was well liked by her (half) brother (Sam Arnakallak), he was a good hunter and he had a bible that he had been given by his family before coming north."[5]

In the mid-1980s, Philippa, then retired from nursing, and her husband, who was also interested in finding his mother's biological father and therefore his paternal grandfather, had the good fortune to meet a retired Mountie, Robert Christy, who had served at the Pond Inlet detachment in the early 1930s and who had returned to Pond Inlet for a visit. Over tea with Philippa and Jayko at their home, Philippa told him about her quest to discover her mother-in-law's birth father. Christy provided Philippa with a list of the Dundas Harbour members serving there at the same time that he was at the Pond Inlet detachment and then suggested that she write to the RCMP Archives at Regina, Saskatchewan, for further information. Her letter of October 4, 1987, to the RCMP at Regina listed the four members who were at Dundas Harbour, which included Inspector Joy, Corporal

Peter Taggart meets his sister, Elisapee, for the first time, eighty-three years after her birth.

Photo courtesy Peter Taggart

Timbury, and Constables Taggart and Hamilton, before explaining that she was conducting research into the history of the RCMP at Dundas Harbour, specifically for the years 1928 through 1930 inclusive. She then asked four questions: "1) Were there any other members stationed at DH during these years?; 2) Are there any photos available?; 3) Were any from Britain or all Canadian?; 4) Are any still alive today?"[6]

Philippa's letter went on to inform the reader that the specific nature of her inquiry was "to find the name of my mother-in-law's father,"[7] but that she did not intend to "cause any family upsets"[8] in the process. She merely wanted the name for the family's records, and perhaps a photograph for Elisapee. As Elisapee's now late mother, Anna, had been confused about names due to her age, Philippa wrote that perhaps too many years had passed.

Stan W. Horrall, RCMP historian, replied to Philippa from Ottawa the following January with apologies for the delay. His letter suggested that he had both good and bad news. The good news was that he had located Mr. Taggart and asked for his permission to release his address, but the bad news was that he had refused and did not wish to be contacted. In her February reply, Philippa wrote that: "I do understand, however, that you were not able to release Mr. Taggart's present address to us without his permission and perhaps he himself would not wish to bring back memories of many years past into his life today. I have spoken to my mother-in-law about this and she felt the same way except that we had hoped to obtain a photograph either old or more recent. Also to learn his date of birth and whether he is Canadian or British by birth, in order that we might be more certain as to whether Mr. Taggart was indeed her father."[9] Philippa concluded her letter with the promise that they would not "pursue the matter further unless it is his wish for us to do so."[10]

Horrall responded a month later with the comment that: "At the time Mr. Taggart joined the RCMP the men were not asked precise questions about the date and place of their birth. Certificates of birth were not commonplace then as they are now. I do believe, however, that Mr. Taggart came from Ireland. He joined the RCMP in 1927. To do that he had to be at least eighteen years of age, or look as if he was eighteen. This means that he was born by 1909 at the latest."[11]

Despite her comment that she would not "pursue the matter further," Philippa was not content to let the matter rest, so she again reached out to Horrall on January 7, 1989, this time to advise him that based on information gathered earlier, they were pretty sure that Taggart was Elisapee's birth father. The day before Elisapee's fifty-eighth birthday (January 6, 1989), the family had presented her with a photo of Taggart that Philippa had found in a book,[12] which showed a picture of Taggart when he was at Baker Lake (1934–1935). Jayko asked his uncle, Samuel Arnakallak (Elisapee's half-brother), who was about six years old when he left Dundas Harbour in 1932 and who knew Taggart and liked him, whether the constable in the picture was the same man who had been at Dundas Harbour when he was there. Based on the curly reddish hair and prominent nose, he was sure that it was the same man. Elisapee was delighted.

The following month, another RCMP historian, William Beaten, responded to Philippa's latest letter, advising her that as far as he knew Taggart was still alive, but that he had not changed his mind about being contacted. This time, Philippa abided by her comment to not "pursue the matter further," and let it drop. But fourteen years later, in September 2013, she stumbled upon the Taggart family tree on her online Ancestry account. This renewed her interest and it is at that point that she reached out to Peter.

Meanwhile, Philippa's sister-in-law, Jedidah (Jeeteetah) Merkosak, Elisapee's eldest daughter, was busy with her own inquiries into the identity of her mother's biological father. Jedidah is a photographer; in fact she has been interested in photography most of her life and has won some awards for her artful photos. Little did she know that her interest in photography would one day lead her to a pivotal family connection. Jedidah was born in an outpost camp ten miles (sixteen kilometres) from Pond Inlet, and it was not until

Sisters-in-law, Jedidah Merkosak and Philippa Ootoowak. Courtesy Philippa Ootoowak

she was seven years old that her family moved into a government-sponsored, prefabricated house closer to Pond Inlet. At the age of nine, her father, Bethuel Ootova, was sent to Hamilton, Ontario, to be treated for tuberculosis, and eight months later her mother, Elisapee, joined him to be treated for the same disease. The couple's five children were taken in by a children's hostel in Pond Inlet and for the first time, Jedidah was sent to school.

It was at the Federal Day School, where a few of the teachers were photographers, that Jedidah was introduced to the art and craft of photography. She would often borrow her paternal uncle's camera to further her interest, but from clicking the shutter to looking at her photos was an exercise in patience. She would drop her undeveloped film off at the Hudson's Bay Company store, but would wait months before her photos were returned to her. She later purchased a small camera of her own which she used until later in life when her now late husband, Simon, bought a 35 mm camera that opened up a whole new world of opportunity for her. Jedidah wrote in her biography for a Nunavut calendar published by Baffin Photography in 2020, that "I especially like to take photos of nature, landscapes, seascapes and I love to take hikes out from the town. Nature calms me and rejuvenates me. Photography and nature feed my soul."[13]

One of her photos, which she had posted online, attracted the attention of an interested viewer in Northumberland, England, and although Jedidah was usually hesitant to talk to strangers, somehow the contact acted as a catalyst for her to open up about her life and her quest to locate her mother's biological father: "... chatting with her and somehow I felt comfortable talking about that, my mother's half, her Inuit half. That was the end of the conversation and I went to sleep that night, and apparently she was a member for what is it, Ancestry.ca?"[14] The name, Taggart, had been mentioned in the conversation, so Jedidah's English contact made a connection through her Ancestry account and then searched for and discovered a likely Facebook account.

Peter remembered that "... it was about January of 2014 and my wife, Marion, was on Facebook. She had a Facebook account that she had forgotten about from many years earlier and she got a message that came through and somebody was interested in Reginald Taggart."[15] Peter responded to the inquirer who happened to be Jedidah: "Jeeteeta, yes, my father was Reginald A. Taggart. I would like to know what your interest is in my Dad?"[16] Jedidah replied: "I understand that your father was with the RCMP and was stationed briefly in Pond Inlet, Nunavut, on the northern tip of Baffin Island, and Dundas Harbour in Lancaster Sound. My grandparents were with him and I have been looking for him for quite some time."[17] Peter replied: "Jeeteeta, your search appears to be over. I recall several stories Dad told me about his time in the north with the RCMP. Tell me about your grandparents."[18]

Now came the shocker. Jedidah continued: "The reason I have been searching for your father, is that we, mother and I, have been so curious as to where he might be. A few years ago I learned that he was from Ireland and that he moved to Canada. My mother's mother, Anna Ataguttiaq, was married to Joanasie Kippomie, but he was not my mother's biological father, but Reginald was. My mother is half white and half Inuk. She just turned 83 years old, and was born in Dundas Harbour, Lancaster Sound in 1931. I think it was shortly after Reginald left or wasn't stationed there anymore...."[19]

Peter, momentarily stunned, replied: "Wow! So it would appear that your mother is my half sister, and I am your uncle. A real mind blower. Wow."[20] Jedidah replied: "Wow! Is the correct word after so many years to find you, the missing piece in our lives! That would be that my mother is your half sister and you are my uncle."[21] Peter wanted to ask so many questions but was at a loss to know where to start. Jedidah replied: "I know and I understand if I shocked you, forgive me if I do. Your father left around September and my mother was born on January 6, 1931. My grandmother was probably 4 or 5 months pregnant, so I would assume he knew about the pregnancy. According to my mother, my grandmother used to have some pictures a long time ago but they have long lost them. My mother, as child, would carry around a picture of your father, but then lost it."[22]

Following Peter's brief description of his family, Jedidah replied that:

We are so excited to learn about your life! Thank you so much for your responses. I will print off the photos you sent and give them to my mother whose name is Elizabeth K. Ootova. Since we don't have "th" in our language, we write her name as Elisapee. She has received numerous awards from the Department of Education, a Jubilee Year Award which she received in Ottawa when the Queen was celebrating her 50th year reign, a Governor General's Award, an Order of Canada, and last year another Diamond Jubilee Award for her outstanding contribution to her fellow Inuit. She also wrote and participated in the making of a dictionary in our dialect for our region, and an encyclopedia in Inuktitut.[23]

Peter replied that he had spent several hours online discovering his new found half-sister, and that not only was he very impressed, but it was very evident from the colour of her hair and prominent nose that they were related.

Following her conversation with Peter, Jedidah excitedly phoned her sister-in-law, Philippa, to tell her the good news. Philippa was thrilled, writing to Peter three days later:

I wanted to write to you in a less formal capacity as I had a surprise telephone call from my sister-in-law Jeeteeta Merkosak late last Tuesday evening telling me she had made contact with you. She was very happy with your quick and welcoming response which is wonderful. I am pleased that this introduction came from her as a direct descendent rather than myself or others as in-laws.

I feel you deserve a little more explanation as Jeeteeta's and my recent quests to locate you were not connected! As you know I was working as the archivist with a general interest in RCMP members stationed in the North Baffin area over the years, their lives and families etc. so that their contribution and connection to many families in what is Nunavut is not forgotten. Over the years several families travelled with members of the RCMP or worked with them as special constables whilst wives sewed, mended clothes and cooked. Children grew up connected to different detachments. Today whenever the PI Archives receives a new set of photographs from those early days there is always much interest and many stories.[24]

Philippa went on to describe how she came to determine that Constable Reginald Taggart was likely Elisapee's birth father:

1) He was one of or the youngest member stationed there at the time 2) He had curly reddish hair 3) He enjoyed being out "on the land" ie learning about hunting, travelling by dogsled and boat etc. from the Inuit, and became skilled in many areas. 4) RCMP records also detail his bravery fending off a polar bear attack during a long patrol. 5) He left the Dundas Harbour Detachment in the Fall (likely September) before Elisapie was born (Jan 6 1931) so never knew her in person. Elisapie's birth is recorded in the 1931 RCMP report for the detachment. 6) Elisapie's older brother the late Samuel Arnakallak recalled liking this member as a young child as he was always kind to him. He also remembered his mother watching the ship leave that year and being very upset.

From all this information I could only conclude that Reginald Taggart was the most likely person to have fathered Elisapie and I told her this for which she seemed thankful….In reality I have no proof that Reginald Taggart is the biological father of Elisapie but everything seems to point towards this.[25]

Approximately a week later, following Jedidah's and Peter's sharing of their respective family photos, Jedidah informed him that:

I did share them with my mother and some of my siblings, and my children, and of course my husband, Simon (whose grandmother was half white too; of Scottish descent) as they are very much interested. When I first gave the photos to my mother, she said that she wished to tell her mother in heaven about them, and when she saw the picture of Reginald she noticed his nose right away and she feels that she resembles him in that area….[26]

Philippa concluded her email on the 29th with: "I am so excited by all this and I hope the idea of the possible extra family member is not too overwhelming for your siblings to absorb."[27] It was exactly the opposite, but in order to confirm beyond a shadow of a doubt the familial line, John, Reginald's and Beth's eldest surviving son, asked Elisapee to submit to a DNA test that was then compared to his own. The test came back positive. The Taggart family had just added 143 plus members to their family, and Elisapee had discovered five half-siblings she never knew existed: Bill (deceased), John, James, Alice and Peter.

Peter could not wait to meet his new-found relations, so in early July 2014 he began to make arrangements to fly to Pond Inlet. Departing Vancouver, British Columbia, on July 13, he flew directly to Ottawa where he overnighted with relatives. The following morning, he boarded a Boeing 737 for the approximate three-hour direct flight to Iqaluit, the capital of Nunavut. There, he was surprised to be greeted by one of Elisapee's daughters, Mekai, her husband, Gary, and her daughter, Catriona. Jedidah's daughter, Constance, was also there with her daughter, Martha, and son, James, and Christine Ootoova, who is Elisapee's son Caleb's daughter, also showed up with her daughter, Alana. With an hour layover at Iqaluit, Mekai suggested that there was enough time to squire him around town in her car before he boarded the Bombardier Dash 8 for the final three-hour leg to Pond Inlet.

As the plane began its flight, Peter began to get nervous. He was about to meet his half-sister, thus breaking a secret his father had kept for decades. The flight "... gave me a lot of time to think about the days events so far, and what was to come. I was a bit anxious for sure, but also very much looking forward to seeing Elisapee and the rest of the family. Meanwhile as I looked out the plane window, overlooking Baffin Island, the landscape was predominantly white with snow and ice."[28] When he landed at Pond Inlet "... I was a bit taken aback when I entered the reception area to find the room full of smiling people. Then I realized, *I was related to all of them!* The anxiety was gone. Elisapee was at the centre of the crowd. We hugged each other and then she spoke to me in Inuktitut. An interpretation was unnecessary. What a heartwarming experience."[29]

Two years later, Alice, Reginald and Beth's only daughter, made her own journey north to meet her sister. Growing up with four brothers, she had always wished that she could have had a sister. For Alice, it was love at first sight when she met Elisapee; she finally had the sister she had always dreamed about. She later wrote that: "We not only had a new sister but were related through her to a sizeable extended family. In the beginning we communicated by email. The first picture I saw of Elisapee was a contemporary one which was put side by side with a picture of our father taken about the same age. When I saw it I thought: 'She looks more like Dad than I do.'"[30]

Since it was difficult for the rest of the Taggart clan to travel to Pond Inlet, a family gathering was held in Victoria in June 2017. The guests of honour were Elisapee and her daughter, Jedidah, both of whom stayed with Alice. Alice wrote that: "We spent one afternoon at a campsite where we built a fire and had a picnic. I noticed tears in her eyes. There, all felt a real connection."

This was John and his wife Angela's first contact with his northern relations, and his first impression of Elisapee was that "… she was so petite…. But she exuded confidence."[31] John then invited Elisapee and Jedidah to his and Angela's place in Surrey where they were put up in a suite in their complex. John toured them around town, but the highlight of their visit was when Elisapee graced them with a selection of *ayayaa* songs.* John recalled that "… she was an accomplished singer who performed in Europe during a tour which included the Queen."[32]

The meetings in Pond Inlet and Victoria only strengthened the familial ties, and perhaps Elisapee's biological father, Reginald Taggart, would be smiling today if he could only see the two parts of his once disparate family united. His love for the Arctic had come full circle. When Peter had a one-on-one with Elisapee at Pond Inlet, he told her that "… her Dad spoke very fondly about his time in the North. The Arctic gave him life. He became a man in the North."[33] Alice also reflected on her Dad's time there: "The North had always been part of him. The RCMP went there to lay claim to the North for Canada. The North also laid claim to all who lived there, however briefly."[34]

---

*   Traditional Inuit songs used to convey stories at gatherings.

Epilogue

Although the preceding pages deal with an Arctic still very much encased in ice, a medium that defined how people lived, worked, accessed food, socialized and generally behaved, today's reality presents a very different climate, both literally and figuratively. Then, the ice offered a form of protection, a security that is now fast disappearing under the searing heat of climate change which is seeing the Arctic warm at four times the average global rate. Fortunately, interlopers are no longer searching for land in the Canadian Arctic, but a rapidly warming climate is not only erasing the traditional way of life for many Inuit, but it is also exposing it to new and dangerous threats—such as potential trespasses by foreign nations through our waterways, pollution, and resource extraction.

The Northwest Passages are now becoming navigable with greater frequency, in many cases however, only with the assistance of Canadian icebreakers. That was first proven in the late summer/early fall of 2013 with the Canadian-encouraged west-to-east transit of the *Nordic Orion*, a Danish bulk coal and ore carrier. This passage highlighted the incredible value of these waterways. Leaving Vancouver, British Columbia, on September 6, the ship was able to bulk up her load by 25 per cent because the alternative route, the Panama Canal, has load/depth restrictions due to its shallow water. The transit also cut 1,000 kilometres from the voyage, saving four days' passage and considerable operating expense—albeit with the aid of free Canadian icebreakers, whose assistance then would have cost about $50,000 per day.

As is evidenced by this experience, the advantages of accessing these northern trade routes are significant, and soon the assistance of Canadian icebreakers may be unnecessary given the current rate of climate change. The global environment was definitely the winner here, given that fewer greenhouse gases were emitted during the abbreviated voyage, but potential accidents in this delicate environment still make these northern commercial transits risky.

What does all of this mean for Canadian sovereignty in the Arctic? The danger is that some view these passages as international waters and would use them at their will. Canada, however, views the Northwest Passages as its sovereign territory and insists that any ships weighing over 300 tonnes register with the Canadian Coast Guard prior to proceeding through them. As well, ice-free areas are now the subject of greater interest for those searching for oil and gas beneath the sea floor. Never has this been so apparent than in the Beaufort Sea, a body of water shared by both the US and Canada, and whose long-standing dispute over the delineation of the international maritime boundary has yet to be resolved.

Approximately ten decades following Inspector Joy, Constable Taggart and Nukappiannguaq's strategic journey, people in the Arctic now live largely modern lives complete with televisions, automobiles, snow machines, cellphones, and air transport, although many still rely on traditional uses of the land. But the long RCMP dogsled patrols are no longer required, having been replaced by mechanization, permanent detachments in most communities and an increased presence by the Canadian Armed Forces as well as NORAD surveillance. What all this means is that there are many more eyes watching the Canadian Arctic than there were in the 1920s.

As well, a significant intergovernmental forum known as the Arctic Council was established in Ottawa in 1996 to explore issues of sustainable development, the environment and those of the Indigenous peoples of the Arctic. Council members consist of the eight Arctic nations that fall within the Arctic Circle: Canada, Denmark (Greenland), Finland, Iceland (through its island, Grimsey), Norway, Russia, Sweden and the United States. Other states have been admitted as "observer states" and Indigenous peoples as "indigenous permanent participants." Each member nation takes its turn to chair the organization. Unfortunately, Russia's horrific invasion of Ukraine in 2022 while in the chair prompted the other members to cease co-operation with it. Now that the chair has rotated to Norway (every two years the chair changes), council business has resumed—to a limited degree, though, given that Russia's criminal action has become a major impediment to one of the stated goals of the forum which is to seek "peace, stability, and constructive cooperation in the Arctic."

This level of observation and administration in the Arctic was unthinkable when our trio was making its slow progress across the ruptured ice, employing in part technology developed by North America's most northern residents thousands of years ago. But were it not for the assistance and teaching skills of the Inuit and the actions of the young RCMP officers, Canada might have looked very different today. I, for one, am very grateful for their service.

Endnotes

CHAPTER ONE

Vague Inheritance

1 Text from the Royal Charter granted to the Hudson's Bay Company, May 2, 1670.

2 Janice Cavell, ed., introduction to *Documents on Canadian External Relations: The Arctic, 1874–1949* (Ottawa: Global Affairs Canada, 2016), xiii.

3 Regan Shrumm, "Hudson's Bay Point Blanket," *The Canadian Encyclopedia*, Historica Canada, December 18, 2018.

4 David J. Hall, "North-West Territories (1870–1905)," *The Canadian Encyclopedia*, Historica Canada, February 7, 2006; last edited August 18, 2022.

5 *Canada Gazette*, October 9, 1880, 389, canada.ca.

6 James White, Technical Advisor, Department of Justice, to O.D. Skelton, Under-Secretary of State for External Affairs, May 25, 1925; Enclosure: Memorandum from James White, Technical Advisor, Department of Justice, Cavell, *Documents on Canadian External Relations*, Document #365, 563–71.

7 Robert Hall, Naval Secretary to the Admiralty, to R.G.W. Herbert, Under-Secretary of State for the Colonies, January 28, 1879; Enclosure: Minute from Ernest Blake, Clerk in the North American and Australian Department, Colonial Office, United Kingdom, to Mr. Bramston, January 29, 1879, Cavell, *Documents on Canadian External Relations*, Document #31, 38–39.

8 Cavell, introduction to *Documents on Canadian External Relations*, xiv.

9 Robert Bourke, Parliamentary Under-Secretary of State for Foreign Affairs, to R.G.W. Herbert, Under-Secretary of State for the Colonies, March 28, 1874; Enclosure 2: William A. Mintzer to George Crump, Acting Consul of United Kingdom at Philadelphia, February 10, 1874, Cavell, *Documents on Canadian External Relations*, Document #3, 5–6.

10 A.W. Harvey to R.G.W. Herbert, Under-Secretary of State for the Colonies, January 3, 1874, Cavell, *Documents on Canadian External Relations*, Document #1, 1.

11 Robert Hall, Naval Secretary to the Admiralty, to R.G.W. Herbert, Under-Secretary of State for the Colonies, April 21, 1874; Enclosures: Report by Frederick Evans, Hydrographer, Royal Navy, April 20, 1874; Minutes, Sir H. Holland, Notes from Assistant Under-Secretary of State for the Colonies, United Kingdom, to J. Lowther, Parliamentary Under-Secretary of State for the Colonies, United Kingdom, April 25, 1874, Cavell, *Documents on Canadian External Relations*, Document #4, 6–7.

12 Dispatch from Lord Carnarvon, Secretary of State for the Colonies, to Governor General Dufferin, April 30, 1874, Cavell, *Documents on Canadian External Relations*, Document #5, 8.

13 Memorandum by Frederick John Evans, Hydrographer, Royal Navy, December 2, 1874, Cavell, *Documents on Canadian External Relations*, Document #8, 10–11.

14 Robert Hall, Naval Secretary to the Admiralty, to R.G.W. Herbert, Under-Secretary of State for the Colonies, December 4, 1874; Enclosure: Minutes/Notes prepared by Ernest Blake and William

Dealtry, Clerk and Principal Clerk of the North American and Australian Department, Colonial Office, United Kingdom, December 19, 1874, Cavell, *Documents on Canadian External Relations*, Document #10, 12–17.

15   Dispatch from Lord Carnarvon, Secretary of State for the Colonies, to Lord Dufferin, Governor General, January 6, 1875, Cavell, *Documents on Canadian External Relations*, Document #11, 16–17.

16   Memorandum from L.S. Huntington, President of the Privy Council, to Lord Dufferin, Governor General, April 30, 1875, Cavell, *Documents on Canadian External Relations*, Document #13, 18–19.

17   Cavell, *Documents on Canadian External Relations*, footnote 170, 117; see also "The Boundaries of the Dominion," Canada, Debates of the Senate, May 3, 1878, 903.

18   Gordon W. Smith, *A Historical and Legal Study of Sovereignty in the Canadian North: Terrestrial Sovereignty, 1870–1939*. Edited by P. Whitney Lackenbauer (Calgary, AB: University of Calgary Press, 2014), 30–31.

19   Cavell, introduction to *Documents on Canadian External Relations*, xv. Cavell's introduction refers to a memorandum from Sir John A. MacDonald, Acting President of the Privy Council, to Governor General W.J. Ritchie, September 23, 1882, Document #39, 48.

20   Memorandum from Mackenzie Powell, President of the Privy Council, to Governor General Henry Strong (Acting Governor), approved on October 2, 1895, Cavell, *Documents on Canadian External Relations*, Document #64, 82–84.

21   Memorandum from R.J. Cartwright, Acting President of the Privy Council, to the Governor General, December 18, 1897, Cavell, *Documents on Canadian External Relations*, Document #87, 114–17.

22   Memorandum from E. Deville, Surveyor General, to A.M. Burgess, Deputy Minister of the Interior, February 13, 1896, Cavell, *Documents on Canadian External Relations*, Document #68, 89–90.

23   Memorandum from Clifford Sifton, Minister of the Interior, to W.F. King, Chief Astronomer, December 11, 1903, Cavell, *Documents on Canadian External Relations*, Document #128, 164.

24   Cavell, introduction to *Documents on Canadian External Relations*, xix.

25   Cavell, introduction to *Documents on Canadian External Relations*, xxvii.

26   William Edward Hall, *International Law* (Oxford: Clarendon Press, 1880), 85–86.

27   L. Oppenheim, *International Law: A Treatise*. Vol. 1, *Peace*. 2nd ed. (London: Longmans, Green and Co., 1912), 293; digitized by Project Gutenberg, gutenberg.org.

28   Instructions from Louis H. Davies or François Gourdeau, Minister or Deputy Minister of Marine and Fisheries, to W. Wakeham, Commander, Canadian Government Expedition, April 23, 1897, Cavell, *Documents on Canadian External Relations*, Document #77, 98–101.

29   Davies or Gourdeau to Wakeham, April 23, 1897; Cavell, *Documents on Canadian External Relations*, footnote 144, 100.

30   Davies or Gourdeau to Wakeham, April 23, 1897.

31   W. Wakeham, Commander, Canadian Government Expedition, to François Gourdeau, Deputy Minister of Marine and Fisheries, September 28, 1897, Cavell, *Documents on Canadian External Relations*, Document #83, 110; Cavell, *Documents on Canadian External Relations*, footnote 159, 110.

32   Wakeham to Gourdeau, September 28, 1897.

33   Memorandum from O.S. Finnie, Director, Northwest Territories and Yukon branch, to R.A. Gibson, Acting Deputy Minister of the Interior, April 24, 1928, Cavell, *Documents on Canadian External Relations*, Document #429, 665.

34 Dispatch from the Earl of Minto, Governor General, to Alfred Lyttelton, Secretary of State for the Colonies, November 17, 1903, Cavell, *Documents on Canadian External Relations*, Document #122, 154.

35 Clifford Sifton, Minister of the Interior, to Deputy Minister James Smart, March 31, 1903, Cavell, *Documents on Canadian External Relations*, Document #108, 137–38.

36 Instructions from Frederick White, Comptroller, North-West Mounted Police, to J.D. Moodie, Officer Commanding "M" Division, Hudson Bay, August 5, 1903, Cavell, *Documents on Canadian External Relations*, Document #114, 145–46.

37 White to Moodie, August 5, 1903.

38 Frederick White, Comptroller, Royal North-West Mounted Police, to Sir Wilfrid Laurier, President of Privy Council, February 19, 1907, Cavell, *Documents on Canadian External Relations*, Document #170, 221–23.

39 Dominion of Canada Sessional Paper No. 28, 1906, Part IV, Report of Superintendent J.D. Moodie on Service in Hudson Bay (per ss *Neptune* 1903–04), 12.

40 Moodie on Service in Hudson Bay.

41 Instructions from François Gourdeau, Deputy Minister of Marine and Fisheries, to Albert P. Low, Commander, Canadian Government Expedition, August 8, 1903, Cavell, *Documents on Canadian External Relations*, Document #116, 147–48.

42 Report from J.D. Moodie, Officer Commanding "M" Division, Hudson Bay, to Frederick White, Comptroller North-West Mounted Police, December 8, 1903, Cavell, *Documents on Canadian External Relations*, Document #125, 158–60.

43 J.D. Moodie, Officer Commanding "M" Division, Hudson Bay, to Frederick White, Comptroller, North-West Mounted Police, December 9, 1903, Cavell, *Documents on Canadian External Relations*, Document #126, 160–62.

44 Decoded telegram (paraphrased) from Alfred Lyttleton, Secretary of State for the Colonies, to Lord Minto, Governor General, March 18, 1904, Cavell, *Documents on Canadian External Relations*, Document #134, 170.

45 Lyttleton to Lord Minto, March 18, 1904.

46 Lyttleton to Lord Minto, March 18, 1904.

47 James White, Geographer, Department of the Interior, to Arthur Whitcher, Secretary, Geographic Board, May 5, 1904, Cavell, *Documents on Canadian External Relations*, Document #137, 171–72.

48 White to Whitcher, May 5, 1904; Cavell, *Documents on Canadian External Relations*, footnote 66, 171.

49 Report from J.D. Moodie, Officer Commanding "M" Division, Hudson Bay, to Frederick White, Comptroller, Royal North-West Mounted Police, September 3, 1904, Cavell, *Documents on Canadian External Relations*, Document #145, 185–187; Cavell, footnote 104, 185.

50 Moodie to White, September 3, 1904; Cavell, *Documents on Canadian External Relations*, footnote 105, 187.

51 W.G. Ross, *The Journal of Captain Comer* (Toronto: University of Toronto Press, 1984), 104.

52 C.P. Lucas, Assistant Under-Secretary of State for the Colonies, to Sir Charles Hardinge, Under-Secretary of State for Foreign Affairs, Foreign Office, July 19, 1906, Cavell, *Documents on Canadian External Relations*, Document #161, 206–12.

53 Cavell, introduction to *Documents on Canadian External Relations*, xxi.

54   Memorandum from Frederick White, Comptroller, North-West Mounted Police, to Sir Wilfrid Laurier, President, Privy Council, January 2, 1904. Cavell, *Documents on Canadian External Relations*, Document #130, 166–67.

55   White to Laurier, January 2, 1904.

56   White to Laurier, January 2, 1904.

CHAPTER TWO

Sovereign Expeditions

1   Pierre Berton, *Klondike: The Last Great Gold Rush, 1896–1899*, rev. ed. (Toronto: McClelland and Stewart Limited, 1977), 158.

2   Sam Steele, *Forty Years in Canada: Reminiscences of the Great North-West with Some Account of His Service in South Africa* (Toronto: Prospero Books, 2000), 296.

3   Steele, *Forty Years*.

4   Steele, *Forty Years*.

5   Steele, *Forty Years*, 298.

6   Berton, *Klondike*, 215.

7   Steele, *Forty Years*, 299.

8   House of Commons Debates, October 23, 1903, vol. 6, 14817.

9   W.C. Bompas, DD, Bishop of Selkirk, to the Minister of the Interior, Cavell, *Documents on Canadian External Relations*, Document #72, 94.

10   T.C. Fairley and Charles E. Israel, *The True North—The Story of Captain Bernier* (Toronto: MacMillan, 1957), 65. Captain Joseph Bernier had gone to Germany to purchase the ss *Gauss* at a cost of $75,000.

11   William R. Morrison, *Showing the Flag: The Mounted Police and Canadian Sovereignty in the North, 1894–1925* (Vancouver: UBC Press, 1985), 96.

12   W.G. Ross, ed., *The Journal of Captain George Comer* (Toronto: University of Toronto Press, 1984), 106.

13   The letter "R" refers to the word "Royal," which was awarded by King Edward VII to the force on June 24, 1904, to recognize the North-West Mounted Police's excellent service during the Boer War. Nora and William Kelly, *The Royal Canadian Mounted Police: A Century of History* (Edmonton: Hurtig, 1973), 119.

14   Draft instructions from Frederick White, Comptroller, Royal North-West Mounted Police, to Supt. J.D. Moodie, Commander, Canadian Government Expedition, September 9, 1904, Cavell, *Documents on Canadian External Relations*, Document #146, 187–88.

15   Instructions from François Gourdeau, Deputy Minister of Marine and Fisheries, to Captain J.E. Bernier, Sailing Master, DGS *Arctic*, September 12, 1904, Cavell, *Documents on Canadian External Relations*, Document #148, 191.

16   Report from Supt. J.D. Moodie, Officer Commanding "M" Division, Hudson Bay, to Frederick White, Comptroller, North-West Mounted Police, December 8, 1903, Cavell, *Documents on Canadian External Relations*, Document #125, 158–60.

17   Supt. J.D. Moodie, Officer Commanding "M" Division, Hudson Bay, to Frederick White, Comptroller, Royal North-West Mounted Police, January 25, 1905, Cavell, *Documents on Canadian External Relations*, Document #150, 193–94.

18 C. Fitzpatrick, Minister of Justice, to Sir Wilfrid Laurier, Prime Minister, March 11, 1905; Enclosure 1, Dr. Henri-Marc Ami, Assistant Paleontologist, Geological Survey, to C. Fitzpatrick, Justice Minister, March 1, 1905; Enclosure 2, draft memorandum to the Privy Council, Cavell, *Documents on Canadian External Relations*, Document #152, 195–97.

19 Fitzpatrick to Laurier, March 11, 1905.

20 H.-M. Ami, Assistant Paleontologist, Geological Survey, to Sir Wilfrid Laurier, Prime Minister, October 26, 1903, Cavell, *Documents on Canadian External Relations*, Document #119, 151.

21 Prime Minister Wilfrid Laurier to Senator William C. Edwards, October 29, 1903, Cavell, *Documents on Canadian External Relations*, Document #121, 153–54.

22 Instructions from François Gourdeau, Deputy Minister Marine and Fisheries, to Captain J.E. Bernier, Commander, Canadian Government Expedition, July 24, 1906, Cavell, *Documents on Canadian External Relations*, Document #165, 215; Cavell, *Documents on Canadian External Relations*, footnote 142, 215.

23 Cavell, *Documents on Canadian External Relations*, footnote 142, 215.

24 Gourdeau to Bernier, July 24, 1906.

25 Captain J.E. Bernier, Commander, Canadian Government Expedition, to François Gourdeau, Deputy Minister of Marine and Fisheries, September 29, 1906, Cavell, *Documents on Canadian External Relations*, Document #169, 220–21.

26 Frederick White, Comptroller, Royal North-West Mounted Police, to Sir Wilfrid Laurier, President of Privy Council, February 19, 1907, Cavell, *Documents on Canadian External Relations*, Document #170, 221–23.

27 White to Laurier, February 19, 1907.

28 Cavell, *Documents on Canadian External Relations*, footnote 147, 222.

29 Fairley and Israel, *The True North*, 97.

30 Fairley and Israel, *The True North*.

31 Memorandum from Captain J.E. Bernier, Commander, Canadian Government Expedition, to G.J. Desbarats, Acting Deputy Minister, Marine and Fisheries, July 20, 1908, Cavell, *Documents on Canadian External Relations*, Document #190, 293–94.

32 Fairley and Israel, *The True North*, 105.

33 Captain J.E. Bernier, Commander, Canadian Government Expedition, to G.J. Desbarats, Deputy Minister of Marine and Fisheries, September 2, 1909, Cavell, *Documents on Canadian External Relations*, Document #191, footnote 265, 294–95.

34 Cavell, introduction to *Documents on Canadian External Relations*, xxii.

35 Cavell, introduction to *Documents on Canadian External Relations*, footnote 25, xxii; also see "American Thanksgiving Day," *London Times*, November 26, 1909, 14.

36 Alan MacEachern, "J.E. Bernier's Claim to Fame," *Scientia Canadensis: Canadian Journal of the History of Science, Technology and Medicine* 33, no. 2 (2010): 43–73.

37 Dispatch from Earl Albert Grey, Governor General, to Lewis V. Harcourt, MP, Secretary of State for the Colonies, August 26, 1911. Attachment from Arthur Keith, Clerk, Colonial Office, UK. Cavell, *Documents on Canadian External Relations*, Document #197, 301–02.

38 Cavell, introduction to *Documents on Canadian External Relations*, xxii.

39 Alexander Johnston, Deputy Minister of Marine and Fisheries, Instructions to Captain J.E. Bernier, July 5, 1910, *Report on the Dominion Government Expedition to the Northern Waters and Arctic*

Archipelago of the DGS [Dominion Government Ship] "Arctic" in 1910 (Ottawa: Department of Marine and Fisheries, 1911), www.canadiana.ca.

40   Vilhjalmur Stefansson to Prime Minister R.L. Borden, February 4, 1913; Enclosure: Memorandum by Vilhjalmur Stefansson, Plan of Proposed Arctic Expedition, Cavell, *Documents on Canadian External Relations*, Document #198, 302–04.

41   Fred L. Boalt, " 'I'm Going North to Find the Lost Continent and Its People,' Says Stefansson to Star Man," *Seattle Star*, June 12, 1913.

42   Stefansson to Borden, February 4, 1913, 302–04.

43   Richard J. Diubaldo, *Stefansson and the Canadian Arctic* (Montreal: McGill-Queen's University Press, 1978), 64.

44   Memorandum from R.L. Borden, President of Privy Council, to Governor General, February 22, 1913, Cavell, *Documents on Canadian External Relations*, Document #200, 306–08.

45   Borden to Governor General, February 22, 1913.

46   Instructions from G.J. Desbarats, Deputy Minister of Naval Service, to V. Stefansson, Commander, Canadian Arctic Expedition, May 29, 1913, Cavell, *Documents on Canadian External Relations*, Document #205, 313–17; Cavell, *Documents on Canadian External Relations*, footnote 296, 314.

47   Vilhjalmur Stefansson, "The Region of Maximum Inaccessibility in the Arctic," *Geographical Review* 10, no. 3 (September 1920): 167–72, https://www.jstor.org/stable/207749.

48   Fergus Fleming, *Barrow's Boys* (New York: Grove Press, 1998), 239.

49   Memorandum from R.L. Borden, President of the Privy Council, to the Governor General, February 22, 1913, Cavell, *Documents on Canadian External Relations*, Document #200, 306–08.

50   Borden to Governor General, February 22, 1913, Cavell, *Documents on Canadian External Relations*, footnote 283, 308.

51   Borden to Governor General, February 22, 1913; Cavell, *Documents on Canadian External Relations*, footnote 282, 307.

52   Sergeant F.J. Fitzgerald diary, December 4, 1908, quoted in Diubaldo, *Stefansson and the Canadian Arctic*, 44.

53   Diubaldo, *Stefansson and the Canadian Arctic*, 78.

54   Chipman diary, April 4, 1914, quoted in Diubaldo, *Stefansson and the Canadian Arctic*, 88.

55   John R. Cox to Mrs. Anderson, July 7, 1914, quoted in Diubaldo, *Stefansson and the Canadian Arctic*, 89.

56   Cavell, *Documents on Canadian External Relations*, footnote 298, 319. Stefansson discovered Lougheed and Meighen Islands in 1916; however, it is believed that Lougheed Island had originally been discovered by the explorer Sherard Osbord, who named it Findlay Island.

57   Cavell, *Documents on Canadian External Relations*, footnote 298, 319. Borden Island was later found to be two islands, the smaller of which was named after Prime Minister Mackenzie King in 1949.

CHAPTER THREE

Administering the Eastern Arctic

1   Note from H. Grevenkop Castenskiod, Minister of Denmark in the United Kingdom, to Earl Cursor of Kedleston, Secretary of State for Foreign Affairs, April 12, 1920; Enclosure: Knud

Rasmussen to Greenland Administration, March 8, 1920, Cavell, *Documents on Canadian External Relations*, Document #215, 326–29.

2   Knud Rasmussen, introduction to *Across Arctic America: Narrative of the Fifth Thule Expedition* (Fairbanks: University of Alaska Press, 1999).

3   Memorandum from Oswald S. Finnie, Director, Northwest Territories and Yukon Branch, to Department of the Interior, April 24, 1925, Cavell, *Documents on Canadian External Relations*, Document #352, 542–44.

4   Canada. *House of Commons Debates*, May 12, 1922, MP Joseph Shaw, 1751.

5   Vilhjalmur Stefansson to Prime Minister W.L. Mackenzie King, March 11, 1922, Cavell, *Documents on Canadian External Relations*, Document #271, 417–22.

6   Canada. *House of Commons Debates*, June 10, 1925, vol. 4, 4084.

7   Memorandum from W.L. Mackenzie King, President of the Privy Council, to Governor General Byng of Vimy, June 5, 1925, Cavell, *Documents on Canadian External Relations*, Document #371, 576; Cavell, *Documents on Canadian External Relations*, footnote 94, 576.

8   Senate Debates, 10th Parliament, 3rd Session, vol. 1, 266–74.

9   Captain J.E. Bernier, Commander, Canadian Government Expedition, to Louis-Philippe Border, Minister of Marine and Fisheries, October 3, 1907, Cavell, *Documents on Canadian External Relations*, Document #179, 259–61.

10 David Hunter Miller, "Political Rights in the Arctic," *Foreign Affairs* 4, no. 1 (October 1925): 59–60; memorandum from L.B. Pearson, First Secretary of External Affairs, September 23, 1929, Cavell, *Documents on Canadian External Relations*, Document #459, 703–12; Cavell, *Documents on Canadian External Relations*, footnote 45, 709.

11 G.J. Desbarats, Deputy Minister of Naval Services, to V. Stefansson, Commander, Canadian Arctic Expedition, April 3, 1918, Cavell, *Documents on Canadian External Relations*, Document #209, 320–21.

12 Stefansson to L.C. Christie, Legal Advisor, Department of External Affairs, September 25, 1920, Cavell, *Documents on Canadian External Relations*, Document #221, 344–48; Cavell, *Documents on Canadian External Relations*, footnotes 32–35, 345.

13 Cavell, *Documents on Canadian External Relations*, footnote 33, 345.

14 Stefansson to Christie, September 25, 1920.

15 Memorandum by J. Pope, Under-Secretary of State for External Affairs, for Prime Minister W.L. Mackenzie King, November 20, 1920, Cavell, *Documents on Canadian External Relations*, Document #231, 372.

16 Diubaldo, *Stefansson and the Canadian Arctic*, 164.

17 Minutes of Meeting of Advisory Technical Board, October 1, 1920, Cavell, *Documents on Canadian External Relations*, Document #222, 348–57.

18 William Barr, *Back from the Brink: The Road to Muskox Conservation in the Northwest Territories*. Komatik Series 3 (Calgary, AB: Arctic Institute of North America, University of Calgary, 1991), 86.

19 *Canada Gazette*, no. 46, vol. LI, Ottawa, May 18, 1918, 4030.

20 Minutes of Meeting of Advisory Technical Board, October 1, 1920, Cavell, *Documents on Canadian External Relations*, Document #222, 348–57.

21 Secret memorandum for Prime Minister Arthur Meighen by L.C. Christie, Legal Advisor, Department of External Affairs, October 28, 1920, Cavell, *Documents on Canadian External Relations*, Document #225, 359–62.

22   Memorandum from W.W. Cory, Deputy Minister of the Interior, to J.B. Harkin, Commissioner of Dominion Parks, November 24, 1920. Enclosure: Strictly confidential memorandum by Commissioner of Dominion Parks, Cavell, *Documents on Canadian External Relations*, Document #230, 367–71.

23   Cory to Harkin, November 24, 1920.

24   Email correspondence from the late Brian Sawyer to Tom Smith, July 23, 2000.

25   Prime Minister Arthur Meighen to Vilhjalmur Stefansson, February 19, 1921, Cavell, *Documents on Canadian External Relations*, Document #239, 383.

26   Secret memorandum for Prime Minister Arthur Meighen by L.C. Christie, Legal Adviser, Department of External Affairs, February 28, 1921: "Exploration and Occupation of the Arctic Islands. Wrangel Island," Cavell, *Documents on Canadian External Relations*, Document #240, 383–84.

27   Decoded telegram (paraphrased) from Winston Churchill, Secretary of State for the Colonies, to Governor General on June 8, 1921, Cavell, *Documents on Canadian External Relations*, Document #255, 403.

28   Memorandum for Prime Minister Arthur Meighen by L.C. Christie, Legal Advisor, Department of External Affairs, October 28, 1920, Cavell, *Documents on Canadian External Relations*, Document #225, 359–62; Cavell, *Documents on Canadian External Relations*, footnote 64, 359.

29   Memorandum from Surveyor General E. Deville to W.W. Cory, Deputy Minister of the Interior, October 29, 1920, Cavell, *Documents on Canadian External Relations*, Document #226, 362.

30   Charles Armstrong, the prime minister's private secretary, to Vilhjalmur Stefansson, March 1, 1921, Cavell, *Documents on Canadian External Relations*, Document #241, 384.

31   Memorandum from J.B. Harkin, Commissioner of Dominion Parks, to W.W. Cory, Deputy Minister of the Interior, March 15, 1921, Cavell, *Documents on Canadian External Relations*, Document #243, 385–87.

32   Vilhjalmur Stefansson to Robert Falconer, president of the University of Toronto, March 13, 1921, reproduced in Jennifer Niven, *Ada Blackjack, a True Story of Survival in the Arctic* (New York: Hyperion, 2003), 29.

33   Diubaldo, *Stefansson and the Canadian Arctic*, 171.

34   Canada. *House of Commons Debates*, May 12, 1922, 1751.

35   Canada. *House of Commons Debates*, May 12, 1922, 1751.

36   Canada. *House of Commons Debates*, May 12, 1922, 1751.

37   Canada. *House of Commons Debates*, May 12, 1922, 1751.

38   Decoded telegram from Governor General Byng of Vimy to the Secretary of State for the Colonies, July 18, 1924, Cavell, *Documents on Canadian External Relation*, Document #325, 503.

39   Byng, July 18, 1924; Cavell, *Documents on Canadian External Relations*, footnote 268, 503.

40   Memorandum from J.B. Harkin, Commissioner of National Parks, to W.W. Cory, Deputy Minister of the Interior, May 13, 1921, Cavell, *Documents on Canadian External Relations*, Document #250, 396–98.

CHAPTER FOUR

Justice in the Arctic

1   Instructions from A. Bowen Perry, Commissioner, Royal Canadian Mounted Police, to Staff Sergeant Joy, Commanding Pond Inlet Detachment, July 6, 1921, Cavell, *Documents on Canadian External Relations*, Document #263, 408–09.

2   Dominion of Canada Sessional Papers 1922, Sessional Paper No. 28, 21.

3   C.R. Harington, "A.H. Joy (1887–1932)," *Arctic* 35, no. 4 (December 1982): 558–559.

4   Dominion of Canada Sessional Papers 1921, vol. 8, Sessional Paper No. 28, Report of the Royal Canadian Mounted Police for the Year Ended September 30, 1920, 20.

5   Dominion of Canada Sessional Papers 1923, Sessional Paper No. 21, Report of the Royal Canadian Mounted Police, 33.

6   T.H. Cory, *Factual Record Supporting Canadian Sovereignty in the Arctic* (Ottawa: Department of Mines and Resources, 1985), 125.

7   Peter Freuchen, *Vagrant Viking, My Life and Adventures*, trans. Johan Hambro (New York: Julian Messner, 1953), 188–90.

8   Information on the Janes killing has been gleaned from Shelagh D. Grant, *Arctic Justice: On Trial for Murder, Pond Inlet, 1923* (Montreal: McGill-Queens University Press, 2002).

9   See http://www.internationalboundarycommission.org.

10 T.C. Fairley, *Sverdrup's Arctic Adventures*, adapted from Otto Sverdrup, *New Land: Four Years in the Arctic Regions*, with added chapters by T.C. Fairley (London: Longmans, Green and Co., 1959), 70.

11 Herbert Patrick Lee, *Policing at the Top of the World* (Toronto: McClelland & Stewart, 1928), 26.

12 Lee, *Policing*, 99.

13 Dominion of Canada Sessional Papers 1924, vol. 5, Sessional Paper No. 21, Commissioner's Report, 35.

14 Dominion of Canada Sessional Papers 1923, Commissioner's Report, 118.

15 Dominion of Canada Sessional Papers 1924, vol. 4, Sessional Paper No. 21, 34.

16 Cory, *Factual Record Supporting Canadian Sovereignty*, ch. 7, "Pangnirtung," 142.

17 Dominion of Canada Sessional Papers 1924, vol. 4, Sessional Paper No. 21, 34.

18 Dominion of Canada Sessional Papers 1914, vol. 24, Sessional Paper No. 28, 40.

19 Sessional Paper No. 28.

20 Dominion of Canada Sessional Papers 1915, vol. 23, Sessional Paper No. 28, 23.

21 K.S. Coates and W.R. Morrison, "'To Make These Tribes Understand': The Trial of Alikomiak and Tatamigana," *Arctic* 51, no. 3 (September 1996): 220–30.

22 Coates and Morrison, "To Make These Tribes Understand."

23 Coates and Morrison, "To Make These Tribes Understand."

24 Dominion of Canada Sessional Papers 1918, vol. 12, Sessional Paper No. 28, 356.

25 Dominion of Canada Sessional Papers 1923, vol. 5, Sessional Paper 21, 136.

26 Ken Coates and William R. Morrison, introduction to *Arctic Show Trial: The Trial of Alikomiak and Tatamigana, 1923*, compiled by P. Whitney Lackenbauer and Kristopher Kinsinger, (Calgary: Arctic Institute of North America, University of Calgary, 2017), v.

27 Dominion of Canada Sessional Papers 1923, vol. 5, Sessional Paper No. 21, 136.

28   Information on the execution was found in a personal letter from Inspector Stuart T. Wood to James Ritchie, Officer Commanding, RCMP, Edmonton, March 8, 1924 (copy of letter provided by Ritchie's granddaughter, retired Judge Jane Auxier).

29   Morrison, *Showing the Flag*, 160. Footnote 63 identifies the quote's origin from communication between T.L. Cory and O.S. Finnie, Director, Northwest Territories Branch of the Department of the Interior, September 12, 1922. Department of the Interior, Northern Administration Branch Papers, RG 85, vol. 607, file 2580, Public Archives of Canada.

CHAPTER FIVE

Securing the Arctic

1   Herbert Patrick Lee, *Policing the Top of the World* (Toronto: McClelland and Stewart, 1928), 192–94.

2   Dominion of Canada Sessional Papers 1925, vol. 61, no. 4, Sessional Paper no. 21, Commissioner's Report, 39.

3   Cory, *Factual Record Supporting Canadian Sovereignty*, 131.

4   Otto Sverdrup, *New Land: Four Years in the Arctic Regions*, trans. Ethel Harriet Hearn, vol. 1 (London: Longmans, Green, and Co., 1904), 94.

5   Dominion of Canada Sessional Papers 1925, vol. 61, no. 4, Sessional Paper no. 21, Commissioner's Report, 60.

6   Dominion of Canada Sessional Papers 1925, vol. 61, no. 4, Sessional Paper no. 21, Commissioner's Report, 60.

7   Dominion of Canada Sessional Papers 1925, vol. 61, no. 4, Sessional Paper no. 21, Commissioner's Report, 62.

8   Dominion of Canada Sessional Papers 1925, vol. 61, no. 4, Sessional Paper no. 21, Commissioner's Report, 35.

9   Dominion of Canada Sessional Papers 1925, vol. 61, no. 4, Sessional Paper no. 21, Commissioner's Report, 35.

10   Cavell, introduction to *Documents on Canadian External Relations*, xxvi.

11   Memorandum from Oswald Finnie, Director, Northwest Territories Branch, Department of the Interior, to J.B. Harkin, Commissioner of National Parks, January 18, 1922, Cavell, *Documents on Canadian External Relations*, Document #267, 412–13.

12   See Haughton Mars Project, https://www.nasa.gov.

13   Dominion of Canada Sessional Papers 1926, Royal Canadian Mounted Police Report for the Year Ended September 30, 1926, 57.

14   Note from Acting Consul General of Norway S. Steckmest, to Secretary or Under-Secretary of State for External Affairs, March 12, 1925, Cavell, *Documents on Canadian External Relations*, Document #339, 519–20.

15   Steckmest to External Affairs, March 12, 1925.

16   Cavell, introduction to *Documents on Canadian External Relations*, xxvi.

17   James White, Technical Advisor, Department of Justice, to Oswald Finnie, Director, Northwest Territories and Yukon Branch, Department of the Interior, April 4, 1925; Enclosure: Memorandum by James White, Technical Advisor, Department of Justice, Cavell, *Documents on Canadian External Relations*, Document #343, 524–33.

18 Enclosure: White, Department of Justice, Cavell, *Documents on Canadian External Relations*; also see Sverdrup, *Four Years in the Arctic*, vol. 2, 449–50.

19 Captain J.E. Bernier, CGS *Arctic*, to Oswald Finnie, Director, Northwest Territories and Yukon Branch, Department of the Interior, March 26, 1925, Cavell, *Documents on Canadian External Relations*, Document #342, 522–23.

20 Bernier to Finnie, March 26, 1925; also see Cavell, *Documents on Canadian External Relations*, footnote 11, 523.

21 White to Finnie, April 4, 1925; Enclosure: Memorandum by White.

22 White, Memorandum, 529.

23 White, Memorandum, 528.

24 White, Memorandum.

25 Quoted in a dispatch from H.G. Chilton, Chargé d'affaires, Embassy of United Kingdom in United States, to Austen Chamberlain, MP, Secretary of State for Foreign Affairs, June 25, 1925, Cavell, *Documents on Canadian External Relations*, Document #384, 598–99.

26 Memorandum from Oswald Finnie, Director, Northwest Territories and Yukon Branch, Department of the Interior, to R.A. Gibson, Acting Commissioner of Northwest Territories, April 17, 1925, Cavell, *Documents on Canadian External Relations*, Document #347, 535–36.

27 Finnie to Gibson, April 17, 1925.

28 Cavell, introduction to *Documents on Canadian External Relations*, xxvii.

29 Memorandum from J.A. Wilson, Assistant Director, Royal Canadian Air Force, May 12, 1925, Cavell, *Documents on Canadian External Relations*, Document #362, 557–60.

30 Minutes of Meeting of Northern Advisory Board on May 13, 1925, Cavell, *Documents on Canadian External Relations*, Document #363, 560–61.

31 Memorandum from Oswald Finnie, Director, Northwest Territories and Yukon Branch, Department of the Interior, to R.A. Gibson, Deputy Commissioner of the Northwest Territories, April 20, 1925, Cavell, *Documents on Canadian External Relations*, Document #349, 537–38.

32 Cavell, introduction to *Documents on Canadian External Relations*, xxvii.

33 Minutes of Northern Advisory Board on April 23, 1925, Cavell, *Documents on Canadian External Relations*, Document #353, 544–47.

34 James White, Technical Advisor, Department of Justice, to Dr. O.D. Skelton, Under-Secretary of State for External Affairs, May 25, 1925; Enclosure: Memorandum by James White, Technical Advisor, Department of Justice, Cavell, *Documents on Canadian External Relations*, Document #365, 563–71.

35 Cavell, introduction to *Documents on Canadian External Relations*, xxvii.

36 Cavell, *Documents on Canadian External Relations*, footnote 78, 563.

37 White to Skelton, May 25, 1925; Enclosure: Memorandum by James White, Cavell, *Documents on Canadian External Relations*, Document #365, 563–71.

38 White to Skelton, May 25, 1925; Enclosure: Memorandum by James White; Cavell, *Documents on Canadian External Relations*, footnote 87, 591.

39 Note from Frank B. Kellogg, Secretary of State, United States, to H.G. Chilton, Chargé d'affaires, Embassy of United Kingdom in United States, June 19, 1925, Cavell, *Documents on Canadian External Relations*, Document #380, 594.

40 Papers Relating to the Foreign Relations of the United States, 1925, vol. 1, 800.014Arctic/10, Secretary of State Kellogg to British Chargé d'affaires Chilton, https://history.state.gov/historicaldocuments/frus1925v01/d401.

41 Note from H.G. Chilton, Chargé d'affaires, Embassy of United Kingdom in United States, to Frank B. Kellogg, Secretary of State, United States, July 2, 1925, Cavell, *Documents on Canadian External Relations*, Document #387, 604–05; Cavell, *Documents on Canadian External Relations*, footnote 136, 605.

42 Cavell, footnote 136, 605.

43 House of Commons Debates, June 10, 1925, 4069.

44 House of Commons Debates, June 10, 1925, 4069.

45 House of Commons Debates, June 10, 1925, 4069.

46 Cavell, introduction to *Documents on Canadian External Relations*, xxvii–xxviii.

47 Dr. O.D. Skelton, Undersecretary of State for External Affairs, to James White, Technical Advisor, Department of Justice, July 13, 1925, Cavell, *Documents on Canadian External Relations*, Document #389, 606–07.

48 David Hunter Miller, "Political Rights in the Arctic," *Foreign Affairs* 4, no. 1 (October 1925): 47–60.

49 Miller, "Political Rights."

50 Miller, "Political Rights," 51.

51 Miller, 60.

52 Memorandum from W.L. Mackenzie King, President of Privy Council, to Governor General Lord Julian Byng, June 5, 1925, Cavell, *Documents on Canadian External Relations*, Document #371, 576–85.

53 W.L. Mackenzie King to Lord Byng, June 5, 1925; Cavell, *Documents on Canadian External Relations*, footnote 94, 576.

54 Dr. O.D. Skelton, Under-Secretary of State for External Affairs, to A.F. Sladen, Governor General's Secretary, June 13, 1925, Cavell, *Documents on Canadian External Relations*, Document #375, 588–89.

55 Note from H.G. Chilton, Chargé d'affaires, United Kingdom Embassy in the United States, to Frank B. Kellogg, Secretary of State, United States, June 15, 1925, Cavell, *Documents on Canadian External Relations*, Document #377, 590–91.

56 Chilton to Kellogg.

57 Chilton to Kellogg; Cavell, *Documents on Canadian External Relations*, footnote 114, 591.

58 W.W. Cory, Deputy Minister of the Interior, to Commissioner Cortlandt Starnes, Royal Canadian Mounted Police, June 29, 1925, Cavell, *Documents on Canadian External Relations*, Document #385, 601–02.

59 Richard E. Byrd to W.W. Cory, Deputy Minister of the Interior, May 8, 1925, Cavell, *Documents on Canadian External Relations*, Document #359, 554–55; Cavell, footnote 67, 554.

60 Dr. O.D. Skelton, Under-Secretary of State for External Affairs, to A.F. Sladen, Governor General's Secretary, December 7, 1925, Document #401, Cavell, *Documents on Canadian External Relations*, 629–631; Cavell, footnote 166, 629.

61 Cavell, footnote 166, 629.

62 Cavell, footnote 166, 629.

63 Wilfrid Bovey to Major-General J.H. MacBrien, Chief of General Staff, Department of National Defence, January 25, 1927, Cavell, *Documents on Canadian External Relations*, Document #424, 658–60.

64   Bovey to MacBrien, January 25, 1927.

65   Bovey to MacBrien, January 25, 1927.

66   Memorandum from Oswald S. Finnie, Director, Northwest Territories and Yukon Branch, to
     W.W. Cory, Deputy Minister of the Interior, February 8, 1927, Cavell, *Documents on Canadian
     External Relations*, Document #425, 660–61.

67   Memorandum from R.M. Anderson, Chief of Biology, National Museum of Canada, to W.W.
     Cory, Deputy Minister of the Interior, October 1928, Cavell, *Documents on Canadian External
     Relations*, Document #434, 671–73.

68   Anderson to Cory, October 1928; Cavell, *Documents on Canadian External Relations*, footnote
     225, 673.

CHAPTER SIX
Axel Heiberg Island

1   Memorandum from Commissioner Cortlandt Starnes, Royal Canadian Mounted Police, to
    Minister of Justice, May 8, 1925, Cavell, *Documents on Canadian External Relations*, Document
    #360, 555–56.

2   Commissioner Cortlandt Starnes, Royal Canadian Mounted Police, to Director Oswald Finnie,
    Northwest Territories and Yukon Branch, Department of the Interior, May 19, 1925, Cavell,
    Documents on Canadian External Relations, Document #364, 562.

3   C.R. Harington, Paleobiology Division, National Museum of Natural Sciences, "Nookapingwa
    (1893–1956)," *Arctic Profiles* (Ottawa: National Museum of Natural Resources), 163–65.

4   Sverdrup, *New Land*, vol. 1, 224.

5   Dominion of Canada Sessional Papers 1926, Royal Canadian Mounted Police Report for the Year
    Ended September 30, 1926, 60.

6   Royal Canadian Mounted Police Report, 1926.

7   Sverdrup, *New Land*, vol. 2, 171–72.

8   Royal Canadian Mounted Police Report, 1926, 61.

9   Sverdrup, *New Land*, vol. 2, 355.

10   Royal Canadian Mounted Police Report, 1926, 62.

11   Commissioner Cortlandt Starnes, Royal Canadian Mounted Police, to Oswald Finnie, Director,
     Northwest Territories and Yukon Branch, Department of the Interior, May 22, 1926, Cavell,
     Documents on Canadian External Relations, Document #413, 645–46.

12   Starnes to Finnie, May 22, 1926.

13   Memorandum from Oswald Finnie, Director, Northwest Territories and Yukon Branch, to
     Deputy Minister of the Interior W.W. Cory, June 23, 1926, Cavell, *Documents on Canadian External
     Relations*, Document #415, 647–49.

14   Note from Ludvig Aubert, Consul General of Norway, to W.L. Mackenzie King, Secretary of State
     for External Affairs, February 6, 1926, Cavell, *Documents on Canadian External Relations*, Document
     #404, 634.

15   Aubert to King, February 6, 1926; Cavell, *Documents on Canadian External Relations*, footnote
     171, 634.

16 Note from Consul General of Norway, Ludvig Aubert, to Secretary of State for External Affairs, W.L. Mackenzie King, September 27, 1926, Cavell, *Documents on Canadian External Relations*, Document #421, 654.

17 Minutes of Northern Advisory Board meeting, held January 13, 1927, Cavell, *Documents on Canadian External Relations*, Document #422, 654–56; Cavell, footnote 200, 655.

18 John Swettenham, *McNaughton*, vol. 1, 1887–1939 (Toronto: Ryerson Press, 1968), 216.

19 Note from Ludvig Aubert, Consul General of Norway, to W.L. Mackenzie King, Secretary of State for External Affairs, March 26, 1928, Cavell, *Documents on Canadian External Relations*, Document #428, 663–64.

20 Aubert to King, March 26, 1928; Cavell, *Documents on Canadian External Relations*, footnote 214, 664.

21 Prince Feisal speaking to T.E. Lawrence in the film *Lawrence of Arabia*.

22 Cavell, *Documents on Canadian External Relations*, footnote 213, 664.

23 Memorandum from Oswald S. Finnie, Director, Northwest Territories and Yukon Branch, to R.A. Gibson, Acting Deputy Minister of the Interior, April 24, 1928, Cavell, *Documents on Canadian External Relations*, Document #429, 665.

24 Finnie to Gibson, April 24, 1928.

25 Finnie to Gibson, April 24, 1928.

26 Dispatch from L.S. Emery, Secretary of State for Dominion Affairs, to W.L. Mackenzie King, Secretary of State for External Affairs, April 30, 1928; Enclosure: Dispatch from F.O. Lindley, Minister of United Kingdom in Norway, to Sir Austen Chamberlain, Secretary of State for Foreign Affairs, March 12, 1928, Cavell, *Documents on Canadian External Relations*, Document #430, 666–68.

27 Lindley to Chamberlain, March 12, 1928.

28 Lindley to Chamberlain, March 12, 1928.

29 Lindley to Chamberlain, March 12, 1928.

30 Dispatch from Lord Cushendun, Acting Secretary of State for Foreign Affairs, to Mr. Gasgoigne, Chargé d'affaires, Legation of United Kingdom in Norway, October 23, 1928, Cavell, *Documents on Canadian External Relations*, Document #435, 673–75.

31 Cushendun to Gasgoigne, October 23, 1928.

32 Cushendun to Gasgoigne, October 23, 1928.

33 Memorandum by L.B. Pearson, First Secretary, Department of External Affairs, on September 23, 1929, Cavell, *Documents on Canadian External Relations*, Document #459, 703–12.

34 Memorandum from J.A. Wilson, Comptroller of Civil Aviation, to G.J. Desbarats, Deputy Minister of National Defence, January 2, 1930, Cavell, *Documents on Canadian External Relations*, Document #473, 725–27.

35 Cavell, *Documents on Canadian External Relations*, footnote 227, 675.

36 R.A. Gibson, Acting Deputy Minister of the Interior, to Dr. O.D. Skelton, Under-Secretary of State for External Affairs, December 17, 1928. Cavell, *Documents on Canadian External Relations*, Document #437, 677.

37 *Norges Kommunistblad* communiqué, November 16, 1928, Australian National Archives.

CHAPTER SEVEN
Dundas Harbour

1   Royal Canadian Mounted Police, Application for Northern Service, February 14, 1928.

2   RCMP application, 1928.

3   Dominion of Canada Sessional Papers 1928, Report of the Royal Canadian Mounted Police for the Year Ended September 30, 1928, Commissioner's Report, 71.

4   Reg Taggart to his mother, Florence Taggart, July 19, 1928.

5   Robert Warren Hamilton, "The Journey North" (unpublished manuscript provided by Hamilton's daughter, Sally), 1–2.

6   Taggart to his mother, July 19, 1928.

7   Taggart diary, July 24, 1928.

8   Taggart diary, July 25, 1928.

9   Hamilton, "The Journey North," 2–3; also see Taggart's letter to his mother, July 28, 1928.

10 National Film Board, *In the Shadow of the Pole*, 1928.

11 Hamilton, "The Journey North," 3.

12 Hamilton, "The Journey North," 3.

13 Taggart to Florence Taggart, July 26, 1928.

14 Taggart diary, July 26, 1928.

15 Hamilton, "The Journey North," 4.

16 Dominion of Canada Sessional Papers 1928, Royal Canadian Mounted Police Report for the Year Ended September 30, 1928, RCMP Commissioner's Report including Inspector Joy's notes, 71.

17 Information about Sam Arnakallak provided by Philippa Ootoowak, Pond Inlet Archivist, by email, April 21, 2022.

18 Dr. Shelagh D. Grant, interview with Sam Arnakallak, September 27, 1994.

19 Grant, *Arctic Justice*, 229.

20 Hamilton, "The Journey North," 4–5.

21 Pond Inlet Archives, interview with Samuel Arnakallak, 2012.

22 Interview with Arnakallak, 2012.

23 Hamilton, "The Journey North," 6.

24 Taggart to Florence Taggart, July 19, 1928.

25 Taggart to Florence Taggart, July 3, 1929.

26 Taggart diary, August 24, 1928.

27 Taggart diary, August 25, 1928.

28 Taggart diary, October 17, 1928.

29 Robert Warren Hamilton, *Dundas Harbour: The First Year*, 6, unpublished manuscript provided by Hamilton's daughter, Sally.

30 William R. Morrison, *Showing the Flag, The Mounted Police and Canadian Sovereignty in the North, 1894–1925* (Vancouver: UBC Press, 1985), 174.

31 Dominion of Canada Sessional Papers, vol. 3, Report of the Royal Canadian Mounted Police for the Year Ended September 30, 1929, 58.

32   RCMP Annual Report, 1929.

33   Dominion of Canada Sessional Papers, Report of the Royal Canadian Mounted Police for the Year Ended September 30, 1930, 54.

34   RCMP Annual Report, 1930.

35   William Barr, *Red Serge and Polar Bear Pants: The Biography of Harry Stallworthy*, RCMP (Edmonton: University of Alberta Press, 2004), 122.

36   Taggart to his brother John, August 3, 1929.

37   Hamilton, *Dundas Harbour: The First Year*, 12.

38   Hamilton, *Dundas Harbour: The First Year*, 11.

39   Report of the Royal Canadian Mounted Police 1929, 114.

40   Published KDKA broadcast schedule for the years 1931–32.

41   "Westinghouse Announces the Annual Arctic Broadcasting Schedule," *Canadian Jewish Review*, October 11, 1929, 16.

42   "Westinghouse Announces Schedule."

43   John Gilbert and Jerry Proc, "Wireless and the St. Roch: 1928–1950," *AWA Review* 33 (2020): 1.

44   Information on Barnsley and the service he provided to the *Bowdoin* was taken from *Vintage Radio*, April 2009, Jack Barnsley, "Canadian Station 9BP Reaches Arctic," December 1923, http://ww.k2tqn.net/oldradio/arrl/2009-04/Barnsley-9BP.htm.

45   Taggart diary, December 21, 1928.

46   Taggart to his mother, Florence, July 3, 1929; Taggart diary, December 21, 1928 entry.

47   Taggart diary, December 25, 1928.

48   Taggart diary, January 24–26, 1929.

49   Taggart diary, January 27, 1929.

50   Hamilton, *Dundas Harbour: The First Year*, 12–14.

CHAPTER EIGHT

Beechey Island

1   Inspector Joy to Florence Taggart, September 2, 1929.

2   Robert Warren Hamilton, "Dundas Harbour: The First Year" (unpublished manuscript provided by Hamilton's daughter, Sally), 15.

3   Taggart diary, February 12, 1929.

4   Dominion of Canada Sessional Papers, Report of the Royal Canadian Mounted Police for the Year Ended September 30, 1929, Corporal Timbury's Patrol Report, 74–76.

5   Corporal Timbury's Patrol Report, 1929.

6   Corporal Timbury's Patrol Report, 1929.

7   Taggart diary, February 4, 1929.

8   Hamilton, "Dundas Harbour: The First Year," 14.

9   Taggart diary, March 6, 1929.

10   Taggart diary, March 11, 1929.

11   Taggart diary.

12 Taggart to his mother, Florence, July 3, 1929.

13 Taggart diary, March 12, 1929.

14 Dominion of Canada Sessional Papers, Report of the Royal Canadian Mounted Police for the Year Ended September 30, 1929, Inspector Joy's Patrol Report, 63.

15 Taggart diary, March 13, 1929.

16 Joy's Patrol Report 1929, 63.

17 Joy's Patrol Report 1929, 63.

18 Taggart diary, March 15, 1929.

19 Joy's Patrol Report 1929, 63.

20 Taggart diary, March 18, 1929.

21 Taggart diary, March 21, 1929.

22 Taggart diary.

23 Elisha Kent Kane, *The United States Grinnell Expedition in Search of Sir John Franklin: A Personal Narrative* (Philadelphia: Childs and Peterson, 1856), 495–96.

24 Taggart diary, March 22, 1929.

25 Taggart diary, March 22, 1929.

26 Joy's Patrol Report 1929, 64.

27 Taggart diary, March 27, 1929.

28 Joy's Patrol Report 1929, 64.

29 Taggart diary, March 28, 1929.

30 Joy's Patrol Report 1929, 65.

31 Taggart diary, March 29, 1929.

32 Taggart diary, April 1, 1929.

33 Taggart diary, April 2, 1929.

34 Taggart diary, April 3, 1929.

35 Taggart diary, April 4, 1929.

36 Taggart diary, April 5, 1929.

37 Joy's Patrol Report 1929, 65.

38 Taggart diary, April 6, 1929.

39 Joy's Patrol Report 1929, 66.

40 Reginald Andrew Taggart, "North of the Arctic Circle," *Scarlet & Gold* 71 (1989): 12.

41 Joy's Patrol Report 1929, 66.

42 Taggart diary, April 11, 1929.

43 Taggart diary, April 12, 1929.

44 Taggart diary, April 13, 1929.

45 Taggart diary.

46 Inspector Joy's Patrol Report 1929, 66.

47 Joy's Patrol Report 1929, 67.

48 Taggart diary, April 18, 1929.

49 Taggart diary, April 19, 1929.

50 Taggart diary, April 20, 1929.

CHAPTER NINE
Bache Peninsula

1 Sir William Edward Parry, *Journal of a Voyage for the Discovery of a North-West Passage from the Atlantic to the Pacific*, Performed in the Years 1819-20 in His Majesty's Ships *Hecla* and *Griper* under the Orders of William Edward Parry, RN, FRS (London: John Murray, 1821) 92.

2 T.C. Fairley and Charles E. Israel, *The True North, The Story of Captain Joseph Bernier* (Toronto: Macmillan, 1957), 123.

3 Parry, *Journal of a Voyage for the Discovery of a North-West Passage*, 94.

4 Historic Sites and Monuments Board of Canada, Submission Report and Minutes, October 2006.

5 Joy's Patrol Report, 1929, 67.

6 Harold Griffin, "Daring Last North—Canadian Mounties Mush 1800 Miles In Unbroken Patrol Across the Roof of the World," *Vancouver Sunday Province*, December 18, 1932, front page.

7 Dominion of Canada, Report of the Royal Canadian Mounted Police for the Year Ended September 30th, 1929, Inspector Joy's Patrol Report, 67.

8 Joy's Patrol Report.

9 Taggart to Owen Beatty, July 23, 1988.

10 Taggart diary, April 25, 1929.

11 "Daring Last North," *Vancouver Sunday Province*.

12 Email from Dr. Andrea Tanner, Fortnum & Mason Company Archivist, July 21, 2022.

13 Inspector Joy's Patrol Report, 1929, 68.

14 Taggart diary, April 26, 1929.

15 Taggart diary, April 26, 1929.

16 Joy's Patrol Report, 1929, 68. Fortnum & Mason was established in 1707.

17 Joy's Patrol Report, 1929, 69.

18 Taggart diary, May 1, 1929.

19 Joy's Patrol Report, 1929, 69.

20 Joy's Patrol Report, 1929. In a letter to his mother, Florence, on July 3, 1929, Taggart wrote that he and Nukappiannguaq killed twenty-five caribou, not ten as Joy reported.

21 Taggart diary, May 5, 1929.

22 Taggart to his brother John, August 3, 1929.

23 Griffin, "Canadian Mounties Mush 1800 Miles."

24 Taggart diary, May 10, 1929.

25 Joy's Patrol Report, 1929, 70.

26 Joy's Patrol Report, 1929.

27 Taggart diary, May 18, 1929.

28 Joy's Patrol Report, 1929, 70.

29 Joy's Patrol Report, 1929, 70.

30 Taggart diary, May 26, 1929.

31   Taggart diary, May 27, 1929.

32   Taggart diary, May 28, 1929.

33   Taggart diary, May 29, 1929.

34   Taggart diary, May 31, 1929.

35   Joy's Patrol Report, 1929, 71.

36   Joy's Patrol Report, 1929, 62.

37   William Barr, *Red Serge and Polar Bear Pants: The Biography of Harry Stallworthy*, RCMP (Edmonton: University of Alberta Press, 2004), 118.

38   Harwood Steele, *Policing the Arctic, The Story of the Conquest of the Arctic by the Royal Canadian (formerly North-West) Mounted Police* (Toronto: Ryerson Press, 1936), 301. The excerpt is from a personal letter from Vilhjalmur Stefansson to Harwood Steele.

CHAPTER TEN

Sverdrup: The Final Chapter

1   Memorandum by Eivind Bordewick, May 7, 1929; Enclosure 1: Otto Sverdrup to Prime Minister W.L. Mackenzie King, April 22, 1929, Cavell, *Documents on Canadian External Relations*, Document #438, 678–80.

2   Cavell, *Documents on Canadian External Relations*, footnote 8, 682.

3   Memorandum by Eivind Bordewick; Enclosure 1: Otto Sverdrup to Prime Minister, the Right Honourable W.L. Mackenzie King, Cavell, *Documents on Canadian External Relations*, Document #438, 678–80; Cavell, footnote 3, 679.

4   Minutes of Meeting of Interdepartmental Committee on the Antarctic, May 13, 1929, Cavell, *Documents on Canadian External Relations*, Document #440, 682–83.

5   Coded telegram (paraphrased) from Leo Amery, Secretary of State for Dominion Affairs, to High Commissioner of the United Kingdom, May 29, 1929, Cavell, *Documents on Canadian External Relations*, Document #442, 684.

6   Memorandum by Charles Stewart, Minister of the Interior, May 30, 1929, Cavell, *Documents on Canadian External Relations*, Document #445, 691.

7   Otto Sverdrup, *New Land: Four Years in the Arctic Regions*, vol. 1, trans. Ethel Harriet Hearn (London, New York, and Bombay: Longmans, Green, and Co., 1904), 404.

8   Cavell, *Documents on Canadian External Relations*, footnote 279, 510.

9   Memorandum by Charles Stewart, Minister of the Interior, May 30, 1929, Cavell, *Documents on Canadian External Relations*, Document #445, 691.

10   Dispatch from L.S. Amery, Secretary of State for Dominion Affairs, to W.L. Mackenzie King, Secretary of State for External Affairs, May 30, 1929; Enclosure 2: Memorandum by Foreign Office, Cavell, *Documents on Canadian External Relations*, Document #443, 685–88.

11   Enclosure 2: Memorandum by Foreign Office, Cavell, *Documents on Canadian External Relations*, Document #443, 685–88.

12   Enclosure 2: Memorandum by Foreign Office, Cavell, *Documents on Canadian External Relations*, Document #443, 685–88.

13   Minutes of Meeting of Northern Advisory Board Subcommittee, Cavell, *Documents on Canadian External Relations*, Document #447, 693–94.

14   Memorandum for W.L. Mackenzie King, Prime Minister, from O.D. Skelton, Under-Secretary of State for External Affairs, June 3, 1929. Cavell, *Documents on Canadian External Relations*, Document #448, 694–95.

15   Skelton to Mackenzie King, June 3, 1929.

16   O.D. Skelton, Under-Secretary of State for External Affairs, to Eivind Bordewick, June 5, 1929, Cavell, *Documents on Canadian External Relations*, Document #450, 696–97.

17   W.L. Mackenzie King, Prime Minister, to Eivind Bordewick, June 6, 1929, Cavell, *Documents on Canadian External Relations*, Document #451, 697.

18   Decoded telegram (paraphrased) from William Clark, High Commissioner of United Kingdom, to Secretary of State for Dominion Affairs, June 7, 1929, Cavell, *Documents on Canadian External Relations*, Document #452, 698.

19   Clark, June 7, 1929.

20   Clark, June 7, 1929; Cavell, *Documents on Canadian External Relations*, footnote 27, 698.

21   Memorandum from O.S. Finnie, Director, Northwest Territories and Yukon Branch, to R.A. Gibson, Acting Deputy Minister of the Interior, June 22, 1929, Cavell, *Documents on Canadian External Relations*, Document #453, 699.

22   Taggart diary, August 3, 1929.

23   Taggart to John Taggart, August 3, 1929.

24   W.W. Cory, Deputy Minister of the Interior, to O.D. Skelton, Under-Secretary of State for External Affairs, August 12, 1929, Cavell, *Documents on Canadian External Relations*, Document #456, 700–01.

25   *Natural Resources Canada* 8, no. 10 (October 1929).

26   Inspector Joy to Florence Taggart, October 11, 1929.

27   Wikipedia, Peter I Island.

28   H.J. Seymour, Head of Northern Department, Foreign Office, to Sir Charles Davis, Under-Secretary of State for Dominion Affairs, September 7, 1929, Cavell, *Documents on Canadian External Relations*, Document #457, 701–02.

29   Cavell, *Documents on Canadian External Relations*, footnote 33, 703.

30   Memorandum by L.B. Pearson, First Secretary, Department of External Affairs, September 23, 1929. Cavell, *Documents on Canadian External Relations*, Document #459, 703–12.

31   Memorandum for Prime Minister W.L. Mackenzie King from O.D. Skelton, Under-Secretary of State for External Affairs, June 3, 1929, Cavell, *Documents on Canadian External Relations*, Document #448, 694–95.

32   Cavell, quotation taken from Pitt Corbett, *Leading Cases on International Law*, vol. 1, 4th ed., ed. Hugh H.L. Bellot (London: Sweet and Maxwell, 1922), 110. *Documents on Canadian External Relations*, Document #459, footnote 37 to L.B. Pearson Memorandum, 705.

33   Memorandum by L.B. Pearson, First Secretary, Department of External Affairs, September 23, 1929. Cavell, *Documents on Canadian External Relations*, Document #459, 703–12.

34   Pearson memo, September 23, 1929.

35   Decoded telegram from Peter Larkin, High Commissioner in United Kingdom, to Acting Under-Secretary of State for External Affairs, October 30, 1929, Cavell, *Documents on Canadian External Relations*, Document #462, 713.

36   H.F. Batterbee, Assistant Secretary, Dominion Office, to O.D. Skelton, Under-Secretary of State for External Affairs, November 13, 1929, Cavell, *Documents on Canadian External Relations*, Document #463, 713.

37   Dispatch from L.S. Amery, Secretary of State for Dominion Affairs, to W.L. Mackenzie King, Secretary of State for External Affairs, April 30, 1928; Enclosure: Dispatch from F.O. Lindley, Minister of United Kingdom in Norway, to Sir Austen Chamberlain, Secretary of State for Foreign Affairs, March 12, 1928, Cavell, *Documents on Canadian External Relations*, Document #430, 666–68.

38   Telegram from Sir F. Lindley to Sir Austen Chamberlain, February 17, 1928, National Archives Australia, A981, ANT 51, Part 1, Norwegian Claims.

39   Committee on British Policy in the Antarctic and Department of External Affairs, Report to the Imperial Conference, 1926, 2–3, National Archives of Australia.

40   H.F. Batterbee, Assistant Secretary, Dominion Office, to O.D. Skelton, Under-Secretary of State for External Affairs, November 13, 1929. Enclosure: Extract from minutes of meeting of Interdepartmental Committee on the Antarctic. Cavell, *Documents on Canadian External Relations*, Document #463, 713–15.

41   Enclosure: Extract from minutes of meeting of Interdepartmental Committee on the Antarctic.

42   Cavell, footnote 54, "This was presumably the letter in which Sverdrup was told that he was free to make an approach to the Canadian Government…. There is no copy in the Canadian files, and it seems unlikely that Bordewick provided an English translation, considering the stipulation in the letter that Norwegian commercial rights must be guaranteed." *Documents on Canadian External Relations*, 715.

43   Enclosure: Extract from minutes of meeting of Interdepartmental Committee on the Antarctic, Cavell, *Documents on Canadian External Relations*, Document #463, 713–15.

44   Decoded telegram from Peter Larkin, High Commissioner in United Kingdom, to Acting Under-Secretary of State for External Affairs, November 23, 1929, Cavell, *Documents on Canadian External Relations*, Document #465, 717.

45   Larkin telegram, November 23, 1929.

46   Canadian Press Dispatch, *Globe and Mail*, November 21, 1929, 5.

47   *Montreal Gazette*, November 23, 1929, 1.

48   Canadian Press Dispatch, *Globe and Mail*, Toronto, November 21, 1929, 5.

49   Minutes of Meeting of Northern Advisory Board, November 26, 1929, Cavell, *Documents on Canadian External Relations*, Document #466, 717–18.

50   Northern Advisory Board minutes, November 26, 1929.

51   Northern Advisory Board minutes, November 26, 1929.

52   Eivind Bordewick to Prime Minister Mackenzie King, December 13, 1929, Cavell, *Documents on Canadian External Relations*, Document #469, 720–22.

53   Dispatch from Lord Cushendun, Acting Secretary of State for Foreign Affairs, to Mr. Gascoigne (Oslo), Chargé d'affaires, Legation of United Kingdom in Norway, October 23, 1928, Cavell, *Documents on Canadian External Relations*, Document #435, 673–75.

54   R.H. Hadow, First Secretary, High Commission of United Kingdom, to O.D. Skelton, Under-Secretary of State for External Affairs, January 3, 1930, Cavell, *Documents on Canadian External Relations*, Document #474, 727.

55   Hadow to Skelton, January 3, 1930.

56   Minutes of meeting of Interdepartmental Committee on the Antarctic, Cavell, *Documents on Canadian External Relations*, Document #478, 730–32.

57   Code telegram from S.J.W. Passfield, Secretary of State for Dominion Affairs, to High Commissioner of United Kingdom, January 6, 1930. Cavell, *Documents on Canadian External Relations*, Document #475, footnote 74, 728.

58   Telegram from Eivind Bordewick to Premier G.H. Ferguson of Ontario, January 29, 1930, Cavell, *Documents on Canadian External Relations*, Document #481, 734–35.

59   Cavell, *Documents on Canadian External Relations*, footnote 81, 735.

60   Telegram from Eivind Bordewick to Under-Secretary of State for External Affairs. Cavell, *Documents on Canadian External Relations*, Document #484, 744.

61   Bordewick to Under-Secretary of State for External Affairs; Cavell, *Documents on Canadian External Relations*, footnote 97, 744.

62   Minutes of Meeting of Northern Advisory Board, Cavell, *Documents on Canadian External Relations*, Document #485, 745–46.

63   Telegram from Eivind Bordewick to Under-Secretary of State for External Affairs, February 28, 1930. Cavell, *Documents on Canadian External Relations*, Document #489, footnote 105, 748.

64   Dispatch from Charles Wingfield, Minister of the United Kingdom in Norway, to Arthur Henderson, MP, Secretary of State for Foreign Affairs, March 12, 1930, Cavell, *Documents on Canadian External Relations*, Document #490, 749–50.

65   Business Development Bank of Canada definition of most favoured nation status, bdc.ca.

66   Dispatch from Charles Wingfield, Minister of United Kingdom in Norway, to Arthur Henderson, MP, Secretary of State for Foreign Affairs, June 11, 1930, Cavell, *Documents on Canadian External Relations*, Document #498, 756–57.

67   Note from Daniel Steen, Chargé d'affaires, Legation of Norway in United Kingdom, to Arthur Henderson, MP, Secretary of State for Foreign Affairs, August 8, 1930, Cavell, *Documents on Canadian External Relations*, Document #504, 764.

68   Note from Daniel Steen, Chargé d'affaires, Legation of Norway in United Kingdom, to Arthur Henderson, MP, Secretary of State for Foreign Affairs, August 8, 1930, Cavell, *Documents on Canadian External Relations*, Document #505, 765.

69   Memorandum by P.A. Clutterbuck, Principal, Dominion Office, August 11, 1930, Cavell, *Documents on Canadian External Relations*, Document #506, 765–66.

70   Business Development Bank of Canada definition of National Treatment, bdc.ca.

71   O.D. Skelton, Under-Secretary of State for External Affairs, to R.H. Hadow, First Secretary, High Commission of United Kingdom, August 14, 1930, Cavell, *Documents on Canadian External Relations*, Document #509, 767–68.

72   O.D. Skelton, Under-Secretary of State for External Affairs, to R.H. Hadow, First Secretary, High Commissioner of United Kingdom, August 21, 1930. Cavell, *Documents on Canadian External Relations*, Document #514, 772–73.

73   Skelton to Hadow, August 21, 1930, Cavell, 772–73.

74   R.H. Hadow, First Secretary, High Commission of United Kingdom, to O.D. Skelton, Under-Secretary of State for External Affairs, September 15, 1930. Cavell, *Documents on Canadian External Relations*, Document #518, footnote 128, 775.

75   R.H. Hadow, First Secretary, High Commission of United Kingdom, to Legation of United Kingdom in Norway, plus Enclosure: Draft Receipt from Otto Sverdrup. Cavell, *Documents on Canadian External Relations*, Document #521, 778.

76   Note from Johan Mowinckel, Minister of Foreign Affairs, Norway, to Kenneth Johnstone, Chargé d'affaires, Legation of United Kingdom in Norway, November 5, 1930. Translation provided by Foreign Office, Cavell, *Documents on Canadian External Relations*, Document #524, 786–87.

CHAPTER ELEVEN
Dundas Harbour: The Second Year

1   J.E. Bernier to Acting Prime Minister Sir George Perley, November 13, 1930. Cavell, *Documents on Canadian External Relations*, Document #525, footnote 153, 788–89.

2   Bernier to Perley, November 13, 1930.

3   Memorandum from O.S. Finnie, Director, Northwest Territories and Yukon Branch, to W.W. Cory, Deputy Minister of the Interior, November 28, 1930, Cavell, *Documents on Canadian External Relations*, Document #526, 789–90.

4   Finnie to Cory, November 28, 1930; Cavell, *Documents on Canadian External Relations*, footnote 155, 790.

5   Cavell, footnote 154, 789.

6   Recorded on Bernier's plaque at Parry's Rock at Winter Harbour, Melville Island.

7   Memorandum from O.S. Finnie, Director, Northwest Territories and Yukon Branch, to W.W. Cory, Deputy Minister of the Interior, November 28, 1930; Cavell, *Documents on Canadian External Relations*, Document #527, footnote 156, 791.

8   Finnie to Cory, November 28, 1930.

9   Dominion of Canada Annual Report for September 30, 1929, vol. 3, 75.

10   Taggart diary, August 6, 1929.

11   Hamilton, "Dundas Harbour: The First Year," 18.

12   Taggart diary, September 6, 1929.

13   Robert Warren Hamilton, "Dundas Harbour, 1929–1930" (unpublished manuscript provided by Hamilton's daughter, Sally), 22.

14   Taggart diary, October 27, 1929.

15   Taggart diary, December 20, 1929.

16   Taggart diary, December 25, 1929.

17   Taggart diary, December 26, 1929.

18   Taggart diary, December 31, 1929.

19   Hamilton, "Dundas Harbour, 1929–1930," 22.

20   Taggart diary, January 2, 1930.

21   Taggart diary, February 6, 1930.

22   Taggart diary, February 10, 1930.

23   Taggart diary, February 27, 1930.

24   Taggart diary, March 13, 1930.

25 Dominion of Canada Report of the Royal Canadian Mounted Police for the year ended September 30, 1930, 58 (Timbury's report).

26 Timbury's report, 1930, 58–59.

27 Hamilton, "Dundas Harbour, 1929–1930," 25-26.

28 Hamilton, "Dundas Harbour, 1929–1930."

29 Timbury's Report, 1930, 60.

30 Taggart diary, June 6, 1930.

31 Taggart diary, July 30, 1930.

32 Taggart diary, August 9, 1930.

33 Taggart diary, August 20, 1930.

34 Memorandum from W.W. Cory, Deputy Minister of the Interior, to J.B. Harkin, Commissioner of Dominion Parks, November 24, 1920. Enclosure: From J.B. Harkin, Commissioner of Dominion Parks. Cavell, *Documents on Canadian External Relations*, Document #230, 367–71.

35 Madwar Sarnia, "Inuit High Arctic Relocations in Canada," *The Canadian Encyclopedia*, July 25, 2018.

36 René Dussault and Erasmus, *The High Arctic Relocations: A Report on the 1953–55 Relocation*. Report of the Royal Commission on Aboriginal Peoples (Ottawa: Canada Communication Group Publishing, 1994), ch. 5, "The Coercive Nature of the Project," 74.

37 Interview with Sam Arnakallak and his sister, Elisapee Ootoova, September 27, 1994.

38 Email from Philippa Ootoowak dated December 5, 2022.

39 Hugh Brody, *The Other Side of Eden* (Vancouver: Douglas and McIntyre, 2000), 42.

40 Brody, *Other Side of Eden*, 43.

41 Brody, *Other Side of Eden*.

42 Taggart diary, September 9, 1930.

43 Taggart diary, September 14, 1930.

44 Peter Schledermann, "The Muskox Patrol: High Arctic Sovereignty Revisited," *Arctic* 56, no. 1 (March 2003): 104.

45 Robert Sheffield Pilot, *To the Arctic*, ch. 1, unpublished manuscript, 8.

46 Much of the material presented here on Inspector Joy is compliments of Robert Sheffield Pilot, RCMP Arctic veteran, researcher and writer.

47 *Ottawa Evening Journal*, May 2, 1932.

48 *Geographical Journal of the Royal Geographical Society* 80, no. 6 (December 1932): 557–58, 559.

49 Minutes of the Meeting of the Northern Advisory Board, May 30, 1929, Cavell, *Documents on Canadian External Relations*, Document #446, 691–93.

CHAPTER TWELVE

Elisapee

1 Philippa Ootoowak, email to Peter Taggart, January 23, 2014.

2 A message board string on ancestry.com, September 23, 2013; provided by Peter Taggart.

3 Ancestry.com, September 23, 2013.

4 Ancestry.com, September 23, 2013.

5   Philippa Ootoowak, email to the author, December 6, 2022.

6   Philippa Ootoowak, email to the author, December 6, 2022; Enclosure: Philippa Ootoowak to RCMP Regina, October 4, 1987.

7   Ootoowak to RCMP Regina.

8   Ootoowak to RCMP Regina.

9   Philippa Ootoowak to S.W. Horrall, February 1, 1988.

10 Ootoowak to Horrall, February 1, 1988.

11 S.W. Horrall to Philippa Ootoowak, March 2, 1988.

12 Shirley Milligan, and Walter Oscar Kupsch, *Living Explorers of the Canadian Arctic* (Yellowknife, NT: Outcrop, the Northern Publishers, 1986), 74.

13 2020 Nunavut calendar, published by Baffin Photography.

14 Zoom interview with the author, October 13, 2022.

15 Interview with the author, October 13, 2022.

16 Peter Taggart, email to Jedidah Merkosak, January 20, 2014.

17 Jedidah Merkosak, email to Peter Taggart, January 20, 2014.

18 Peter Taggart, email to Jedidah Merkosak, January 20, 2014.

19 Jedidah Merkosak, email to Peter Taggart, January 20, 2014.

20 Peter Taggart, email to Jedidah Merkosak, January 21, 2014.

21 Jedidah Merkosak, email to Peter Taggart, January 21, 2014.

22 Merkosak to Taggert, January 21, 2014.

23 Jedidah Merkosak, email to Peter Taggart, January 22, 2014.

24 Philippa Ootoowak, email to Peter Taggart, January 23, 2014.

25 Ootoowak to Taggart.

26 Jedidah Merkosak, email to Peter Taggart, January 29, 2014.

27 Philippa Ootoowak, email to Peter Taggart, January 29, 2014.

28 Peter Taggart, email to the author, February 20, 2023.

29 Taggert to author, February 20, 2023.

30 Alice Casson's recollections of Elisapee, email message to the author, March 15, 2023.

31 John Taggart, email to the author, February 26, 2023.

32 John Taggart, email to the author, February 26, 2023.

33 Peter Taggart, email to the author, February 20, 2023.

34 Alice Casson's recollections of Elisapee, email message to author, March 15, 2023.

Bibliography

Barr, William. *Back from the Brink: The Road to Muskox Conservation in the Northwest Territories.* Komatic Series 3. Calgary: Arctic Institute of North America, University of Calgary, 1991.

Barr, William. *Red Serge and Polar Bear Pants: The Biography of Harry Stallworthy,* RCMP. Edmonton: University of Alberta Press, 2004.

Berton, Pierre. *Klondike: The Last Great Gold Rush, 1896–1899,* rev.ed. Toronto: McClelland & Stewart, 1977.

Boalt, Fred L. " 'I'm Going North to Find the Lost Continent and Its People,' Says Stefansson to Star Man." *Seattle Star,* June 12, 1913.

Brody, Hugh. *The Other Side of Eden.* Vancouver and Toronto: Douglas and McIntyre, 2000.

Bryce, Robert M. *Cook and Peary: The Polar Controversy, Resolved.* Mechanicsburg, PA: Stackpole Books, 1997.

Cavell, Janice, ed. *Documents on Canadian External Relations: The Arctic, 1874–1949.* Ottawa: Global Affairs Canada, 2016, https://epe.lac-bac.gc.ca/100/201/301/weekly_acquisitions_list-ef/2017/17-10/publications.gc.ca/collections/collection_2017/amc-gac/E2-39-Ar-2016.pdf.

Coates, K.S. and W.R. Morrison. " 'To Make These Tribes Understand': The Trial of Alikomiak and Tatamigana." *Arctic* 51, no. 3 (September 1998): 220–30.

Coates, Ken, and William R. Morrison. Introduction to *Arctic Show Trial: The Trial of Alikomiak and Tatamigana, 1923,* compiled by P. Whitney Lackenbauer and Kristopher Kinsinger. Calgary: Arctic Institute of North America, University of Calgary, 2017.

Cory, T.H. *Factual Record Supporting Canadian Sovereignty in the Arctic.* Ottawa: Department of Mines and Resources, 1985.

Diubaldo, Richard. *Stefansson and the Canadian Arctic.* Montreal: McGill-Queen's University Press, 1978.

Dussault, René and Erasmus. The High Arctic Relocations: A Report on the 1953–55 Relocation. Ch. 5, "The Coercive Nature of the Project." *Report of the Royal Commission on Aboriginal Peoples.* Ottawa: Canada Communication Group Publishing, 1994.

Fairley, T.C. and Charles E. Israel. *The True North—The Story of Captain Bernier.* Toronto: MacMillan, 1957.

Fairley, T.C. *Sverdrup's Arctic Adventures.* Adapted from Otto Sverdrup, *New Land: Four Years in the Arctic Regions,* with added chapters by T.C. Fairley. London: Longmans, Green and Co., 1959.

Finnie, Richard S., dir. *In the Shadow of the Pole.* 1928. North West Territories and Yukon Branch, Department of the Interior. Producers: Canadian Government Motion Picture Bureau.

Fleming, Fergus. *Barrow's Boys.* New York: Grove Press, 1998.

Freuchen, Peter. *Vagrant Viking, My Life and Adventures,* trans. Johan Hambro. New York: Julian Messier, 1953.

Gilbert, John and Jerry Proc. "Wireless and the St. Roch: 1928-1950." *AWA Review* 33, 2020.

Grant, Shelagh D. *Arctic Justice: On Trial for Murder, Pond Inlet, 1923.* Montreal: McGill-Queen's University Press, 2002.

Griffin, Harold. "Daring Last North—Canadian Mounties Mush 1800 Miles in Unbroken Patrol Across the Roof of the World." *Vancouver Sunday Province*, December 18, 1932.

Hall, David J. "North-West Territories." *The Canadian Encyclopedia*, Historica Canada, August 18, 2022, thecanadianencyclopedia.ca.

Hall, William Edward. *International Law*. Oxford: Clarendon Press, 1880.

Harington, C.R. "A.H. Joy (1887-1932)." *Arctic* 35, no. 4 (December 1982): 558–559, doi: https://doi.org/10.14430/arctic2370.

Harington, C.R. "Nookapingwa (1893–1956)." *Arctic Profiles*. Ottawa: National Museum of Natural Resources.

Harper, Kenn. *Thou Shalt Do No Murder: Inuit, Injustice and the Canadian Arctic*. Iqaluit: Nunavut Arctic College Media, 2017.

Johnston, Alexander. "Instructions to Captain J.E. Bernier, July 5, 1910." *Report on the Dominion Government Expedition to the Northern Waters and Arctic Archipelago of the DGS "Arctic" in 1910* (Ottawa: Department of Marine and Fisheries, 1911), www.canadiana.ca.

Kane, Elisha Kent. *The United States Grinnell Expedition in Search of Sir John Franklin: A Personal Narrative*. Philadelphia: Childs and Peterson, 1856.

Kelly, Nora and William Kelly. *The Royal Canadian Mounted Police: A Century of History*. Edmonton: Hurtig, 1973.

Lee, Herbert Patrick. *Policing the Top of the World*. Toronto: McClelland & Stewart, 1928.

MacEachern, Alan. "J.E. Bernier's Claim to Fame." *Scientia Canadensis: Canadian Journal of the History of Science, Technology and Medicine* 33, no. 2 (2010): 43–73.

Miller, David Hunter. "Political Rights in the Arctic." *Foreign Affairs* 4, no. 1 (October 1925): 47–60.

Morrison, William. *Showing The Flag—The Mounted Police and Canadian Sovereignty in the North, 1894–1925*. Vancouver: UBC Press, 1985.

National Aeronautics and Space Administration (NASA). "Haughton Crater Mars Project on Devon Island." NASA, https://www.nasa.gov/mission/haughton-mars-project-hmp/.

Niven, Jennifer. *Ada Blackjack, a True Story of Survival in the Arctic*. New York: Hyperion, 2003.

Oppenheim, L. *International Law: A Treatise*. Vol. 1, *Peace*. 2nd ed. (London: Longmans, Green and Co., 1912), 293; digitized by Project Gutenberg, gutenberg.org.

Osborne, Season L. *In the Shadow of the Pole*. Toronto: Dundurn, 2013.

Parry, William. *Journal of a Voyage for the Discovery of a North-West Passage from the Atlantic to the Pacific*. London: John Murray, 1821.

Rasmussen, Knud. *Across Arctic America: Narrative of the Fifth Thule Expedition*. Fairbanks, AK: University of Alaska Press, 1999. First published 1927 by G.P. Putnam's and Sons (New York).

Ross, W.G., ed. *The Journal of Captain Comer*. Toronto: University of Toronto Press, 1984.

Royal Commission on Aboriginal Peoples. *High Arctic Relocations: A Report on the 1953-1955 Relocation*. Toronto: Canadian Government Publishing, 1994.

Sarnia, Madwar. "High Arctic Relocations in Canada." *The Canadian Encyclopedia*, Historica Canada, July 25, 2018, thecanadianencyclopedia.ca.

Schledermann, Peter. "The Muskox Patrol: High Arctic Sovereignty Revisited." *Arctic* 56, no. 1 (March 2003): 1–109, doi: https://doi.org/10.14430/arctic606.

Shrum, Regan. "Hudson's Bay Point Blanket." *The Canadian Encyclopedia*, Historica Canada, December 18, 2018, thecanadianencyclopedia.ca.

Smith, Gordon W. *A Historical and Legal Study of Sovereignty in the Canadian North: Terrestrial Sovereignty, 1870–1939*. Edited by P. Whitney Lackenbauer. Calgary: University of Calgary Press, 2014.

Steele, Harwood. *Policing the Arctic: The Story of the Conquest of the Arctic by the Royal Canadian (formerly North-West) Mounted Police*. Toronto: Ryerson Press, 1936.

Steele, Sam. *Forty Years in Canada: Reminiscences of the Great North-West with Some Account of His Service in South Africa*. Toronto: Prospero Books, 2000. First published 1915 by Dodd, Mead & Co. (Toronto).

Stefansson, Vilhjalmur. "The Region of Maximum Inaccessibility in the Arctic." *Geographical Review* 10, no. 3 (September, 1920): 167–72, https://www.jstor.org/stable/207749.

Sverdrup, Otto. *New Land: Four Years in the Arctic Regions*, 2 vols. London: Longmans, Green and Co., 1904.

Swettenham, John. *McNaughton*, vol. 1, 1887–1939. Toronto: Ryerson Press, 1968.

Taggart, Reginald Andrew. "North of the Arctic Circle." *Scarlet and Gold* 71 (1989).

"Westinghouse Announces the Annual Broadcasting Schedule." *Canadian Jewish Review*, October 11, 1929.

Government Publications

Canada Gazette, October 1880, canada.ca.

Canadian Census of Aboriginal Peoples, Statistics Canada, www.150statcan.gc-ca.

Debates of the Senate of the Dominion of Canada, Fifth Session, Third Parliament, 1878, https://www.canadiana.ca/view/oocihm.9_08065_8/925.

Department of Marine and Fisheries. *Report on the Dominion Government Expedition to the Northern Waters and Arctic Archipelago of the DGS "Arctic" in 1910*. Ottawa: Department of Marine and Fisheries, 1911, www.canadiana.ca.

Dominion of Canada Sessional Papers, various years, https://parl.canadiana.ca/view/oop.debates _SOC1003_01/269.

House of Commons Debates, various years, https://parl.canadiana.ca.

Papers Relating to the Foreign Relations of the United States, 1925, Vol. 1, 800.014Arctic/10, https://history.state.gov/historicaldocuments/frus1925v01/d401.

Senate Debates, 10th Parliament, 3rd Session, Vol. 1, https://parl.canadiana.ca/view/oop.debates _SOC1003_01/269.

Newspapers

Globe and Mail

London Times

Montreal Gazette

Ottawa Evening Journal

Vancouver Sun

Vancouver Sunday Province

Seattle Star

Unpublished Materials

Correspondence between A.H. Joy and Florence Taggart, provided by Peter Taggart.

Correspondence between Constable Taggart and Florence Taggart, provided by Peter Taggart.

Diary of Constable Taggart, provided by John Taggart.

Diary of Robert Warren Hamilton, provided by Sally Hamilton.

Hamilton, Robert Warren. "The Journey North." Unpublished manuscript supplied by Sally Hamilton.

Hamilton, Robert Warren. "Dundas Harbour: The First Year." Unpublished manuscript supplied by Sally Hamilton.

Hamilton, Robert Warren. "Dundas Harbour: 1929–30." Unpublished manuscript supplied by Sally Hamilton.

Pilot, Robert S. "To The Arctic." Unpublished manuscript, 2023.

Archives

Library and Archives Canada

Pond Inlet Archives

Acknowledgements

Writing books is rarely ever a solo endeavour. A score of others is involved in the research, editing and publishing process, and although it would be difficult to mention everyone here, a few essential names stand out.

The first must go to the late John Taggart, who continued to share little tidbits of his father's Arctic adventures with me over the years until I eventually became curious enough to begin the research for this story. I applaud his perseverance. Next, I would like to acknowledge Janice Cavell, adjunct research professor at Carleton University in Ottawa. She is an Arctic scholar who forwarded me a link to a comprehensive collection of Arctic correspondence wrapped up in one large government publication that she had a lead hand in assembling, and which became the core of my project. Kudos also to her assistant editor, Joel Kropf, and to Marilyn Croot for preparation of the maps, among many others. Reading this historical correspondence was as fascinating and dramatic as living the actual events. There would have been no book without this valuable resource.

Sally Hamilton, daughter of Constable "Paddy" Hamilton, who served in the Arctic with Constable Reginald Taggart, was generous in her provision of her dad's diary and an unpublished manuscript he wrote about his time there, which offered a perfect counterpoint to Taggart's diaristic musings.

Philippa Ootoowak, a retired Pond Inlet archivist, was absolutely essential for verifying spellings of Inuit names, providing transcripts of various interviews with Inuit Elders, as well as offering advice on the many questions that I posed to her about the RCMP's early activities in the Arctic. Her reading of the text was also a great help. And her sister-in-law, Jedidah Merkosak, was equally valuable in the writing of the final chapter about her mother, Elisapee.

John Taggart's siblings, Alice and Peter, were interviewed. Were it not for Peter providing me with a collection of his father's Arctic maps and correspondence, and both of them providing me with a heartfelt description of their first meeting with their new-found Inuit relations, the book would not be as rich. Notable was the assistance rendered by Thomas Smith, who served with the RCMP in the Arctic as a young man and who retired as a provincial court judge in British Columbia, but who has maintained an intense interest in the Arctic throughout his life. Smith's knowledge and his library of Arctic documents was of invaluable help. Another RCMP Arctic veteran, Robert Pilot, was vital for sharing his knowledge and his writings about Inspector Alfred Herbert Joy.

I must also thank another Arctic scholar, Peter Kikkert, for directing me to a plethora of historical documents on the negotiations with the Norwegian government over the Sverdrup Islands.

There were many others, of course, but absolutely essential was Caitlin publisher, Vici Johnstone, as well as her staff: Sarah Corsie, editorial and production; Catherine Edwards, copyeditor; and Malaika Aleba, marketing and promotion, all of whom made the process easy.

Last but not least, I must thank my dear wife, Joan, for being by my side all these years and for being an honest critic of my work.

Any spelling or mistakes of fact are mine alone.

Index

About the Author

Photo by Joan Jamieson

Eric Jamieson is a retired career banker who took up writing outdoor and history articles for newspapers and magazines in his late 20s. He has authored three books: *South Pole: 900 Miles on Foot* (Horsdal and Schubart, 1996), co-authored with Gareth Wood; *Tragedy At Second Narrows: The Story of the Ironworkers Memorial Bridge* (Harbour Publishing, 2008); and *The Native Voice* (Caitlin Press, 2016). He was awarded the Lieutenant Governor's Medal for History Writing in 2009. He currently resides in North Vancouver with his wife, Joan.